D1297398

AMONG THE IBOS OF NIGERIA

HAIR-DRESSING AS A WORK OF ART

Charcoal dust and palm oil are freely used, but should necessity arise the structure must be cut away entirely, as it cannot be "undone."

AMONG THE IBOS OF NIGERIA

An account of the Curious & Interesting Habits, Customs & Beliefs of a little known African People by one who has for many years lived amongst them on close & intimate terms

G. T. BASDEN

FRANK CASS & CO. LTD.
1966

Published by Frank Cass & Co. Ltd.,
10 Woburn Walk, London W.C.1
by arrangement with Seeley, Service & Co. Ltd.

First edition 1921
New Impression 1966

Printed in Great Britain by
Thomas Nelson (Printers) Ltd., London and Edinburgh.

DEDICATION

TO MY BELOVED WIFE,
WHO HAS BRAVELY AND PATIENTLY BORNE
THE RESPONSIBILITIES OF HOME AND CHILDREN
WHILST I HAVE BEEN ABSENT IN NIGERIA,
THIS BOOK IS AFFECTIONATELY
DEDICATED.

PREFACE

THE responsibility for the appearance of this book does not altogether fall upon my shoulders. The suggestion to issue a more detailed account of the Ibo people sprang from a magazine article. What is hereinafter written is the result.

There is no necessity to inform the author that he is sadly lacking in style and diction and all the other marks of literary excellence. He is fully alive to his short-comings, and in the following pages will be found faulty sentences, loose constructions, and words and phrases that will grate harshly on the cultivated ear.

Literature is not my profession. I have simply striven to set forth in a plain way some of the things which the plain man may see and hear in Nigeria. The book has one recommendation: it is based on actual experience. There are probably errors which will need rectification. It would be sheer presumption to expect otherwise, for the longer one lives amongst West African natives, the more one is convinced that it is a practical impossibility for the European to comprehend fully the subtleties of the native character. Some white men claim to have done this, but my experience leads me to think that the claim can rarely, if ever, be substantiated with definite assurance. The depths may be sounded at times, but only by accident, and on most of such occasions the inquirer does not recognise that he has actually tapped the inner consciousness of the native. Let not this be thought strange, for the black man himself does not know his own mind. He does the most extraordinary things, and cannot explain why he does them. He is not controlled by logic: he is the victim of circumstance, and his policy is very largely one of drift. The will of the tribe or family, expressed or implied, permeates his whole being, and is the deciding factor in every detail of his life. It is a sort of intangible freemasonry; the essence of the primary instincts of the people. Men constantly act contrary to their better judgment, and, at times, even wrongly, because they firmly believe they have no alternative: they dare not oppose the wishes of their people. Consequently though there may be independent thought, there is seldom independent action, probably never where other members of the tribe or family are involved, however remotely. A further result, and one which must always be borne in mind by the foreign inquirer into primitive customs, is that the ideas of the native are indefinite. He has no fixed thoughts. He is under the influence of an atmosphere which emanates from the whole tribe. This subliminal consciousness, by which all his movements are controlled, becomes practically a sixth sense. It is inexpressible in words but, nevertheless, extremely powerful in action.

Knowing, therefore, from experience the great difficulty of fathoming the depths of the native mind, and having endeavoured to traverse some of the intricacies of native thought, I am bound to confess that I feel, after seventeen years, more puzzled over many things than I did after the same number of weeks in the country. I believe my experience is not unique. Old coasters have often expressed themselves to the same effect. Hence in putting into print the following pages I do so with no little diffidence. Though I have sifted the information as thoroughly as possible, yet I should still consider it highly presumptuous to think that no statement stands in need of revision. What is herein offered may, at least, form the basis for further and more complete investigation in the future.

There is one important problem with which I have not dealt specifically, namely, the Liquor Traffic, though the evils connected with it are mentioned incidentally in more than one chapter. The omission of the subject generally is deliberate. In some quarters it is a matter of controversy. We are, however, convinced that it is solely on economic grounds that this blot upon our national escutcheon is allowed to remain. Since the Commission appointed to inquire into the traffic issued its report, the attention of medical and other officials has been more particularly drawn to the question, and signs are not wanting which indicate a growing feeling in favour of total prohibition.

At the moment of writing the trade was more or less at a standstill owing to the European War. The German firms were arbitrarily prevented from shipping supplies to the coast. Revenue from the importation of Hamburg spirits, consequently, automatically ceased for the time being. May we not hope that the trade thus temporarily restricted may be abandoned ? Never in the history of West Africa has there been such a favourable opportunity for suppressing a form of trade which, though defended for purposes of revenue and commerce, cannot be morally justified.

The result of my observations is offered for what it is worth. It is the outcome of an honest attempt to ascertain some of the salient features of the life and customs of the Ibos. On essential things I have, for the most part, sought simply to put into readable English what I have learned from the natives themselves, as originally written or related by them. If its publication serves to arouse a sense of interest towards the Ibo speaking people, the labour spent will not have been in vain.

To any contemplating residence in the Ibo country, particularly those likely to be associated with native affairs, I would recommend a careful study of Levitical Law. In many ways the affinity between Native Law and the Mosaic System is remarkable. For comparative work the student will do well to peruse Joh. Warneck's *The Living Forces of the Gospel*,[1] especially Part I of the book. I have been greatly struck with the resemblances of Ibo to the Battak [2] customs described in this work. For general purposes I have found *British Nigeria*,[3] by Lieut.-Col. A. F. Lockyer-Ferryman, and *Fetishism in West Africa*,[4] by the Rev. Dr. R. H. Nassau, very profitable books.

[1] Translation from the German by the Rev. Neil Buchanan, published by Oliphant, Anderson and Ferrier.

[2] *The Battaks of Sumatra. Indian Archipelago.*

[3] Cassell and Co. [4] Duckworth and Co

In addition to many native friends, too numerous to mention by name, my thanks are due to the following: Captain R. M. Heron, for the use of his monograph on *Native Titles* (Chap. XXIV), in the preliminary investigation of which we were associated; to the intensely interesting journals compiled by the late Rev. Dr. James F. Schön, the Rev. Samuel Adjai Crowther (afterwards first Bishop of the Niger), and the Rev. J. C. Taylor during the expeditions of 1841, 1854 and 1857. Also to Dr. Eugene Stock for permitting me to make copious extracts from his monumental work, the *History of the Church Missionary Society* (Chap. XXIX).

I further record my sincere gratitude to the late Mrs. Herbert Crosfield and Mrs. C. H. Williams, for their practical assistance and counsel. I count myself fortunate to have had the benefit of their generous help in reading the MS., and for their many useful suggestions.

What is offered is not to be accepted necessarily as the views of the Society of which I have the privilege of being a member, nor those of my fellow-missionaries. The former sent me to the Niger; with some of the latter I have enjoyed many profitable discussions on Nigerian problems—missionary and otherwise—but I am alone responsible for every word and opinion expressed, except in those instances where direct quotations have been made from other writers.

GEORGE T. BASDEN.

AWKA,
SOUTHERN NIGERIA.
1920.

CONTENTS

CONTENTS

LIST OF ILLUSTRATIONS

AMONG THE IBOS OF NIGERIA

CHAPTER I

FROM LIVERPOOL TO ONITSHA

Probably there is no part of the world which has been more anathematised than the West Coast of Africa, and yet it has never ceased to cast its spell over men and to attract them to its surf-washed shores. Perhaps also no other country has been shrouded in so much mystery, or held in thrall by such powers of darkness.

More particularly the Niger has dominated the minds of men with a fascination well-nigh incomprehensible, except to those who have felt its influence. From the days of Pliny downwards no river has given rise to so many and varied speculations as to its course and ultimate discharge. Not until 1830 was the problem solved, when the brothers Lander passed down the river and, after many adventures, found themselves gazing after the sea at Brass. For thirty-five years intrepid explorers had been baffled in the task of tracing the course of the great river. Mungo Park and many of his successors in the quest had indeed fallen in the fight.

The discovery of the embouchure of the Niger by the Landers settled for ever all speculative theories as to its course, and cleared up a mystery which had been for years a subject of discussion amongst interested enthusiasts. Their success, however, had come too late. The toll of lives already exacted, and the disastrous endings of previous expeditions, had bred such hopeless despair that few were the seers whose vision could penetrate the dark clouds and foresee the possibilities of the Niger.

Government was not inclined to move any further in this matter of exploration, and probably those who advocated the decision felt that their action had been justified when the disasters of the ill-fated expedition of 1832–4 became known. Lander dead, together with thirty-eight others of the forty-eight who had set sail from Liverpool. Misfortune and death had pressed heavily upon them, yet those brave hearts, who went forth chiefly at the instigation of Macgregor Laird, laid the foundation of that prosperity which eventually, in the Providence of God, resulted in Nigeria being added to the British Empire.

The expedition of 1841 was practically due to the persistent efforts of Sir Thomas Fowell Buxton, whose name will ever be held in honoured remembrance in West Africa. Equipped with every necessary that thought could suggest and money supply, the expedition started on the great adventure, cheered by the good wishes of all, from Prince Albert (who had presided at the inauguration meeting at Exeter Hall, June 1, 1840) downwards. No expedition had ever gone forth under brighter auspices or with greater éclat. But alas! all too quickly enthusiasm changed to despair. The narrative of that ill-fated voyage up the Niger depicts an almost unparalleled series of disasters. "Its failure killed Fowell Buxton,"[1] and caused such profound depression that for years all further effort to open up the river was abandoned.

Thirteen years later the indefatigable Macgregor Laird, with dauntless energy and perseverence, succeeded in despatching the *Pleiad* under the command of Dr. Baikie. This venture was unique, and inaugurated a new era of Niger exploration, inasmuch as Dr. Baikie and his companions navigated hundreds of miles of the Niger, and they traced the course of the River Benue to within a short distance of Yola and, most wonderful to relate, returned without the loss of a single life.

[1] *History of C. M. S.*, Vol. I, p. 455.

This unprecedented success stirred up Laird to yet greater exertions, and after many struggles and rebuffs he succeeded in launching the expedition of 1857.

The two ships engaged, the *Dayspring* and the *George*, arrived at Aboh on the Niger on July 20 of that year, and five days later they reached Onitsha. The latter place was destined to become an important centre for the development of the country. The expedition laid the foundation of commercial and missionary enterprise amongst the Ibo people, and in the following pages an attempt is made to set forth some of the main facts concerning their lives and customs.

It was characteristic of the times, and of the English, that so much had been left to the persevering exertions of a private individual. In the enthusiastic days, just prior to the departure of the expedition of 1841, the Committee of the Church Missionary Society had expressed the hope that the Niger would be "a highway for the Gospel," but the honour of making such a prospect possible falls to Macgregor Laird. It was the humblest of beginnings, alike from a mercantile and a missionary point of view, and yet of such importance that within six years, Burton writes: "We shall never drop the Niger; the main artery of Western Africa north of the line must not be neglected."[1] Only those acquainted with the history of Nigeria since those adventurous days can adequately comprehend the marvellous strides taken in the opening up of the country. Writing with reference to the trading affairs of the Niger, Lieut.-Col. Mockler-Ferryman says:

"As an instance of the rapid development of a new land there is, perhaps, nothing more interesting in the commercial history of England than the opening up of the River Niger to trade. Fifty years ago there was not a single store-shed north of the Delta; to-day the banks of the main river and its branches, to a distance of nine hundred miles from the sea, are lined with British trading stations."[2]

[1] *Wanderings in West Africa* (R. F. Burton) Vol. II, p. 259.

[2] *British Nigeria* (Mockler-Ferryman), p. 55.

The progress to be recorded since the above words were penned is astounding, and it undoubtedly surpasses every expectation of the pioneers of British interests in Nigeria. Since the assumption of the administration of the country by our Government (Jan. 1, 1900) even greater progress can be recorded. The result is a complete upheaval of the political, economical and social affairs of the country. Every native institution has been shaken in its foundations and, at the present rate of progress, a great many of the most interesting facts concerning the primitive customs of the people will soon be matters of history and tradition only, hence this attempt to record some of these facts ere the period of transition be passed, when the old shall have been overwhelmed by the new.

The days of the "Palm-oil Ruffians" are over. For years the men who laid the foundations of the great commercial houses were dubbed with this sobriquet, and yet it is to their endurance, and often dare-devil pluck, that we owe much of our present prosperity. In them we see repeated the instinct for adventure, the blood and bone and the initiative of the Elizabethan mariners who started the Empire movement. Seldom now is the epithet applied to the coasters. On the other hand the West African steamer, as she rests alongside Prince's Landing Stage, Liverpool, is still occasionally irreverently addressed as the "monkey ship" by that indescribable product, the quayside labourer, who earns a more or less precarious livelihood by handling passengers' baggage.

From England to Sierra Leone the voyage is similar to any ordinary journey by sea. From that point there is a little more variation, chiefly arising from the fact that the transhipment of passengers and baggage is accomplished whilst the ship lies at anchor in the open roadsteads. The heavy rolling seas, as a rule, prohibit the use of companion-ladders, and recourse must be had to derricks and mammy-chairs. Native crews bring surf-boats alongside, and into these the traveller and his goods are dumped. The operation is very unpleasant at any time, and when the sea is rough it is decidedly uncomfortable. The native paddlers are very expert in handling their craft, and they need to be to avoid catastrophe. In the earlier days European passengers climbed down the vessel's side by the rope ladder, or were hoisted over in a barrel adapted for the purpose by the removal of a quarter section to allow for easy entrance and exit. Nowadays baskets or mammy-chairs are used.

Highly entertaining—to the onlookers—is the method of transhipping native passengers, of whom considerable crowds are carried between the coast ports. It had at least the merit of being very expeditious. A piece of stout canvas, some twelve feet square, was spread on the fore-deck, and upon this were huddled six or eight men. At once the four corners of the sail were gathered up and hitched to the derrick hook, and the bag of humanity was slung overboard without further ceremony. For a time it dangled at the end of the swaying rope, the poor imprisoned wretches being enveloped in darkness and, helpless to protect themselves as they were, bumped against the vessel's side. They remained suspended thus until the word was given to "let go," when the bundle was dropped with a run into the bottom of the surf-boat alongside. By that time arms and legs had become almost inextricably mixed up, but the unravelling was a marvel of speedy ingenuity. Three corners of the canvas were slipped off the hook, and then it was hauled up by the fourth corner, and the long-suffering beings shaken out and left to sort themselves at leisure.

It was astonishing how quickly a number of natives could be transferred by this rough-and-ready method, and, except for an occasional ducking, accidents appear to have been rare events.

Immense quantities of kola nuts, in charge of Mohammedan traders, are carried between the coast ports. They are bound up in huge round bundles containing some 3000 to 4000 nuts apiece, most carefully packed between fresh leaves and salt to prevent contact with the air; if exposed they soon harden and lose their value. The bundles are very heavy, and are carefully protected with stout coverings, the whole being enclosed in a network of strong cordage. Sometimes the foredeck is piled up with hundreds of bales of nuts, and they form one of the most valuable items of cargo.[1]

Passengers for the Niger proceed to the Forcados River and are there transferred to a launch or stern-wheel steamer, the latter being far preferable to the former. My first acquaintance with the Niger was whilst making the up-river passage in the old *Rattler*, a launch, most appropriately named, some thirty feet in length by about eight feet beam, driven by a small and noisy engine. In 1900 the number of passengers was so insignificant that the business of transport had scarcely been considered. The few who did travel up river were granted passages more or less as acts of courtesy, upon payment of a sum rather substantial in proportion to the facilities conferred. In the case of the *Rattler*, judging by appearances, most of the woodwork originally supplied for cabin fittings and other purposes had been appropriated by the enterprising engineer for firewood. The native has no compunction whatever in using the first thing that serves his end, and one has seen a neighbour's roof stripped of all the thatch within reach of the hand, it having been commandeered in order to start the kitchen fire.

On the occasion of my first passage the Niger was in full flood. At such a time it becomes an immense and imposing volume of water, or, more correctly, a saturated solution of mud. Navigation during the time of full river, i.e. whilst heavy rains are falling, still has its discomforts, but that season is more expeditious than the dry for travelling, inasmuch that when the water is low it frequently becomes a wearisome task to proceed either up or down stream. When nine days are occupied by a good steamer in traversing eighty miles, travelling is apt to become tedious ; it may be restful but is not very entertaining, although unexpected adventures occasionally enliven the proceedings. To the new-comer there is much that is novel and he, moreover, early discovers his own shortcomings and suffers from his lack of experience in the management of affairs. We had not proceeded many miles in the *Rattler* when we became aware of the fact

[1] See p. 267 (Chap. XXV) for note on kola nuts.

that no cooking utensils were on board, and we were forced to accept the loan of a small begrimed pot, the property of one of the native crew. This had to serve as teapot and to cook—in turn—every course comprising our menu. There was no special hardship in this until the other purposes for which it was used became known to us. It was not appetising to discover that the same little pot was used for stewing palm-oil chop—some of the ingredients of which were questionable—and later that it served as the wash-up basin for plates and dishes, and finally for some of the boys themselves !

In order to avoid the powerful current, small launches, when proceeding up stream, keep well in under the banks for the sake of the shelter afforded, but as the river is studded with islands, and deviates in its course, this entails frequent crossings from one side to the other. There is a certain amount of compensation in this, inasmuch as it permits close observation of the country through which one is travelling.

In the Delta districts the route is through a seemingly interminable mangrove swamp.[1] In every direction nothing meets the eye but water and dense banks of vegetation. In the dry season hundreds of high-and-dry sandbanks add another colour to the picture. On the sky-line there is one dead level of tree-tops, a prospect which is extremely monotonous.

Much credit is due to those Englishmen who endure life in these watery wastes, some in the interests of commerce, others in the administration of political affairs.

[1] Mangrove, Rizophera mangle of Linnæus. This tree, like the banian of the East Indies, is propagated by shoots thrown out from the upper branches ; these descend, take root, and become parent trees, throwing out leaves, branches, and shoots in their turn. Hence, a whole forest of mangrove trees are intimately connected with each other, and are thus so firmly rooted as to resist the most rapid tides and most impetuous current, They grow in wet places, and are generally covered with large quantities of oysters, here called mangrove oysters. They render creeks unhealthy, by retaining the mud and ooze and other putrefying substances among their tangled roots ; they also render them dangerous, by affording a secure retreat to alligators. The wood of this tree is extremely hard, and much used by the natives for building houses, as it is not so easily destroyed by the termites (white ants) as other kinds of timber.—*Winterbottom.*

How little the dividend-drawing public know of the dreary circumstances in which the toilers in these depressing regions live.

The traveller finds a subject of fascinating interest in watching the native pilot as he threads his course through an amazing labyrinth of waterways. In the Delta, channels open out in all directions, but the pilot is never in doubt; he presses steadily onward, not only by day but often far into the night.

On the lower reaches of the Niger no villages are visible from the steamer, and the only indications of human life are the men and women paddling their "dug-outs" under the shelter of the banks. These inhabitants of the swamps are scantily clothed, and their huge umbrella-hats of plaited palm leaves give them a quaint appearance. The villages are hidden in the back-bush wherever an acre or two of less swampy land affords an anchorage for a tiny cluster of huts. Little lanes of water, often invisible to the unobservant eye, connect the villages with the main stream. Sometimes the entrance is indicated by a "Ju-ju" house, or a primitive flag-staff, from which a fragment of white cloth flutters. The latter has also a religious significance but is not original, the custom being an innovation adopted in recent years by certain of the Delta tribes.

As we proceed up river the swamp gives place to higher ground and the banks become defined. Clearings in the forest are to be seen where plantains and bananas thrive. The increasing number and size of the villages, now built directly on the river banks, point to the fact that the country is well populated. One is struck with the lack of forethought exhibited by the natives when building these riverside villages. They are situated close to the water's edge, and, consequently, many huts are swept away during the annual flood. The swollen river, swirling along at a great pace, undermines the bank, causing large sections to fall into the water, carrying away at the same time huts and trees. The lesson of the year's disaster leaves no impression, and the native continues to build on precarious sites—as near the river as he can, presumably in order to be near his canoe, the river being the great (and often the only) highway to the markets. The huts are small and oblong in shape, the poorest in style and material in the whole country. They are constructed of mud and wattle, and thatched with palm leaves. Sometimes they are built on the ground, in other cases they are raised on piles to protect them from the floods. The local clay is of inferior quality, with poor building properties, and is unsuitable for building substantial walls similar to those erected by the people in the districts higher up the river.

The most important piece of property to the Delta native—as indeed to all natives dwelling in close proximity to the river—is the " dug-out " canoe. It is indispensable, providing, as it does, the only means of intercourse with the outside world. In the wet season no other mode of travelling is possible, and at times the native would be confined to the four walls of his hut were he deprived of his canoe. For the fashioning of a " dug-out," a tree is selected, by preference a mahogany (for cheap canoes bamboo or silk cotton trees are suitable), as near the water's edge as possible. From the main stem a log of the length required is taken, and this is roughly hewn to shape and hollowed out with native axes. The axe-work being completed, slow fire is applied to the hull, inside and out, and the rough parts made smooth. The canoes are of all dimensions, from those designed for a single paddler to those capable of carrying a dozen or more, with passengers and merchandise in addition. They are heavier and more cumbersome even than they look, and, from personal experience, I can affirm that they do not compare favourably with a rowing skiff.

Near Aboh the waters of the Delta converge into one main stream, and the river assumes an aspect worthy of its title, the " Lordly Niger." At the close of the wet season it is truly a mighty mass of water. Immediately the rains cease, however, it subsides at a remarkably rapid rate, and very soon sandbanks appear, and navigation becomes an intricate business.

As far as Aboh the inhabitants of the districts traversed consist chiefly of the Jekri and Ijaw tribes, but from this point the Ibo people predominate. The scenery has changed also. No more mangrove swamp is met with, and the country is higher altogether, though still continuing uniformly and monotonously flat. Magnificent trees lift their heads above the dense undergrowth, those particularly noticeable being the bombax (silk cotton), uroko (commonly called African oak), mahogany, cocoanut and oil-palms. Viewed from the launch, the country is extremely picturesque and often beautiful, but at close quarters its attractiveness quickly diminishes. The luxuriant living foliage springs forth from a tangled mass of dead and decaying vegetation, rank and reeking in the humid atmosphere; the home of myriads of creatures that creep and crawl. The "bush," as it is familiarly termed, is *not* the place to select for comfort and enjoyment.

A day's run north from Aboh brings the traveller to Onitsha, in the neighbourhood of which are seen the first signs of hilly country, a welcome relief from the depressing low levels hitherto encountered. Here it was that the present writer landed in September, 1900. The *Rattler* dropped her anchor just before midnight. The darkness was intense, and the pitch-black cloud-banks of an approaching tornado provided an appropriate setting for his introduction to "darkest Africa."

CHAPTER II

THE IBO COUNTRY

In 1900, Onitsha had not aspired to anything approaching its present importance, and it retained much of its primitive simplicity. The commercial centre of the district was at Abutshi, two or three miles down-stream, and the administrative quarters, first of the Royal Niger Co., and later of the Government, were at Asapa, on the western side of the river. To the north of the town, following the left bank of the Nkissi stream, on the site now covered with Government buildings, a large coffee plantation was laid out. Of the surrounding country, even of that comparatively near the settlement, but little was known. The existing maps were useless as none contained reliable data, the names inserted being based upon reports and conjectures. Some names were curious e.g. "Akpam" and "Nri." The latter certainly is a name well known over a considerable portion of the Ibo country. It is the name of a small town which is the headquarters of a priestly cult whose special functions are connected with the coronation of kings, hence "nri" men (priests) being travellers, were met with frequently. When asked whence they came the answer was a wave of the hand towards the east, and thus the name was given, in mistake, to the whole country lying east of Onitsha.

It is only during the last few years, i.e. since the British Government assumed the administration, that appreciable progress has been made in opening up the interior districts. At the time of my landing at Onitsha there was an attractive field for investigation in which the native could be studied in his primitive environment. The subsequent years have been equally interesting, but from another standpoint, viz., that of a spectator watching a nation passing through a period of transition. The process still continues, and the people and the country are changing at an extraordinarily rapid rate. The old conditions and landmarks are disappearing and modern developments will soon obliterate all signs of ancient history.

The limits of the Ibo country have now been approximately defined, and the territory apportioned into districts. A network of Government stations has been established, and trading and missionary interests shew evidence of vigorous prosperity. The Ibos are distributed over the greater part of the Central Province of the Protectorate and number about four millions, i.e., probably half the total population of Southern Nigeria.

In the Delta districts, and especially in the neighbourhood of Bonny and other coast towns, they are not indigenous. They consist chiefly of slaves under the control of "Heads of Houses." These slaves often outnumber the original inhabitants, and their language is of such vitality that "Bonny Ibo" predominates over the other dialects of the district.

From the coastline of the Bight of Benin, the Ibo country skirts the Ibibio, Aro-Chuku and Efik territories. After that its eastern boundary is formed by the Cross River. On the southern and western sides it stretches to the borders of the Ijaw, Jekri, and Igabo and other tribes, and then spreads across the Niger to the confines of Benin. After passing 6° 31′ N. Lat., it narrows in once more, and extends in wedge-like formation until its northernmost limits reach the boundary between southern and northern Nigeria, where the Akpotos and Munshis are the nearest neighbours.

The area covered by the tribe being so extensive, it follows that there is wide divergence in the physical features of the country. In the Delta regions the land is very low-lying. It is intersected by innumerable creeks and for a considerable portion of the year becomes a typical tropic swamp. The vegetation is rank, and the atmosphere humid and enervating. Clothes, if left exposed to the night air, even inside the houses, are quite damp by morning; rain falls in great quantities. As the sun sinks on a fine day banks of white mist roll up, enveloping everything in their damp and chilly folds.

In the neighbourhood of Onitsha the prospect is more pleasing. For the traveller striking inland in an easterly direction, the scenery improves almost immediately, and charming hills and valleys open out on all sides. The vegetation consists chiefly of scrub and jungle-grass with big patches of moorland here and there. Extensive and picturesque clumps of trees are scattered about, indicating, as a rule, the presence of towns and villages, or marking the sizes of burial grounds.

On these higher levels, high only as compared with the Delta, the soil is reddish and sandy, and, except in certain hilly spots, singularly stoneless. One has often seen holes opened out to a considerable depth without a solitary pebble being unearthed. However deep one penetrates, the soil retains its colour, and the only difference is the presence of more or less clay. It is of poor quality for agricultural purposes, and much labour is involved for which there is frequently no adequate return. The giant elephant-grass, the shorter jungle-grass and a variety called "Ata," or spear grass, flourish. This last is very exasperating to farmers and to anyone else desirous of cleaning the ground, because every particle of root is capable of vigorous propagation.

On the western side of the Niger the aspect is totally different. A large part of the country is covered with forest. It is on a lower level than the eastern side and is much more fertile. Great quantities of yams and other crops are raised and labour is richly rewarded. To provide sites for villages and land for agricultural purposes, clearings are made in the forest, and this has led to ruthless and wholesale destruction of valuable timber. The creation of a Forestry Department by the Government will, no doubt, do much to remedy this evil.

In porportion to what might be expected flowers are scarce. The most beautiful are the many varieties of lilies and orchids. Palms predominate amongst the trees, the oil-palm (*Elœsis Guineensis*) being of the greatest value. It flourishes in a greater or less degree, according to situation, throughout the Ibo country. The *Raphia Vinifera* and other varieties furnish the natives with copious supplies of palm wine. The cocoanut also abounds, together with many other species of palm. The uses to which the palm trees and their products are put by the natives are unlimited, every part being utilised in one form or another.

Compared with other parts of Africa, game is exceptionally scarce. Guinea-fowl and partridges are few and wild; buck of different varieties are to be secured occasionally as also buffalo. In some of the rivers and creeks the manitee flourishes. Hippopotami and crocodiles are common, though of late years they have exhibited a tendency to abandon the main river owing to the disturbance occasioned by the ever-increasing steamer traffic. Leopards are sometimes troublesome and there are several smaller species of the cat family. In bygone days there was a thriving market for ivory, a fact clearly attested by the arm and leg ornaments worn by men and women, and the magnificent "horns" carried by chiefs as part of their insignia of office. Nowadays elephants are almost extinct in the Ibo country and ivory is a very expensive luxury.

This scarcity of game is due, no doubt, to the fact that for generations every man was equipped with a gun—from the old flint-lock pattern to the more modern Snider, and, until quite recently, there was no lack of ammunition. The practice has been to kill bird and beast, without respect to age, sex or season. The people being well distributed, the result of this indiscriminate slaughter has been to denude the country of game. The hippopotami and the crocodiles fared better partly owing to the greater difficulties attendant upon hunting by water, but more particularly because the guns and ammunition were not of sufficient power to bring about any appreciable reduction in their numbers.

In appearance the people exhibit wide divergences due largely to local conditions. In the eastern districts they are inclined to be thin and scraggy. This may arise from a combination of causes. In the first place the cultivation of the land demands labour of a flesh-reducing character. Secondly, the yam crop is comparatively poor and meagre, and supplies must be eked out with cassava, beans, maize and other catchcrops. The appearance of a crowd of carriers, with their spare frames, spindle-legs and cucumber calves, often prompts the thought that the men must have recently experienced a period of famine. On the western side this is not the case. There the people are shorter and are of a stocky, thick-set build. They are disposed to be lazy yet they are passionate, and of a rash and fiery temperament, the result probably of an over-abundant supply of rich food.

Colour variations are prevalent from light olive to deepest black, and albinos are common. These freaks of nature are of unprepossessing appearance. They are not, however, treated as monstrosities; indeed the mother of an albino is usually gratified with her offspring. They are termed by the people " ndi-awcha," i.e., white people.

Skin disfigurements are very common, especially amongst the elder folk. These produce a pie-bald condition, the hands and feet being the parts chiefly affected. This is, I suppose, due to some form of disease which destroys the underlying pigment. I, personally, have seen but one certain case (and one other so reputed) of a child born with white patches on the skin.

The Ibo country lies within the recognised negro belt, and the people bear the main characteristics of that stock. Bridgeless noses and wide open nostrils are striking features, likewise the thick protruding lips and the powerful jaws. The shape of the skull repeats itself with astonishing regularity, this pecularity, perhaps, being accounted for by the process of moulding the shape of the head during infancy.

There are certain customs which rather point to Levitic influence at a more or less remote period. This is suggested in the underlying ideas concerning sacrifice and in the practice of circumcision. The language also bears several interesting parallels with the Hebrew idiom.

On the left bank of the Niger society is chiefly based on patriarchal lines. Every town, and, incidentally, every family or household, stands by itself. There is no combination between town and town. Although speaking the same language, and in times of peace intermarrying with one another, the nearest neighbours are still regarded as strangers, e.g., the people of Onitsha and those of Opusi do not reckon themselves as of one tribe, though a distance of less than five miles separates the two towns. With the exception of the king of Onitsha there are no kings in these parts. The solitary instance, tradition states, owes its origin to Benin. It is alleged that the kings of Onitsha were subject to the king of Benin and that recent holders of the title have been of Bini royal stock. On the opposite side of the river native rule was maintained by kingly authority. (*Vide* Chap. XXIV.)

It can be generally accepted, though not without reservations, that under native law land cannot be alienated from the family, the head acting as trustee of the property. Permission is freely given to others to cultivate land, or even to build upon it, but the "Head," and his successors, can always claim its restoration at will. The claim imposed is merely one of proprietary right. The occupier is seldom disturbed so long as he is prepared to acknowledge the ground landlord. Rent is not usually demanded, the tenancy being confirmed by the offering and acceptance of "ojji"[1] at the time permission to occupy the land is granted, and on more or less regular occasions subsequently. Amongst the people themselves land is sometimes sold, and in thickly populated centres parcels of land are owned outright by private individuals, in contradistinction to the more widely prevailing law which stipulates that all land is the property, not of private persons, but of the community. Even in the latter case, however, land is appropriated definitely for the use of recognised holders.

Personal property, including the wives and slaves, descends to the eldest son as heir, or failing a son, to the eldest brother or male relative. A wife ordinarily has no rights, either over herself or her possessions, not excluding her children. She is part and parcel of her husband's property.

[1] A small gift such as a fowl.

A Girl Wife

Belles of the Village

As a rule, when left to their own resources, the Ibos are a sober race. They manufacture no intoxicating liquor. The nearest approach is palm wine, which is allowed to ferment by natural processes. Palm wine is frequently heavily adulterated with water. When fermentation has reached a certain stage the wine is too much like vinegar to be enjoyable; even the old takers make wry faces when drinking it. It is almost a physical impossibility to get drunk on *fresh* palm wine. Men certainly drink themselves into a fuddled state, but this is probably as much due to the enormous quantities consumed at a carousal as to the amount of alcohol taken. To consume a similar quantity of tea would produce more serious consequences.

No method of distilling is practised; the Ibos have no knowledge whatever of this process. Drunkenness unfortunately, is on the increase, brought about entirely by the importation of foreign spirits. But for this traffic the Ibos would be second to none for sobriety. The opening up of interior districts affords opportunities for the expansion of the traffic, and the square green bottles are in evidence at all the markets. The introduction of spirituous liquors is a distinctly foreign feature. In many places it has already destroyed some quaint old customs. To be offered whisky, or German beer, when paying a call upon a native chief, is an innovation greatly to be deplored, especially when compared with the old ceremony of sealing friendships by sharing the kola nut. All the sentiment has departed, and, with it, the touch of reality that graced the ancient institution. This is denationalisation in one of its most pernicious forms.

Where water is plentiful the people are of cleanly habits, the women more so than the men. It is the women's business to fetch the household supply of water, and the visit to the stream provides an opportunity to bathe. The men are usually satisfied with a moderate amount of ablutionary effort, proportional to the supply of water at their disposal; the number of those who will exert themselves sufficiently to go to the stream solely for bathing purposes is not large.

Of sanitary ideas there is none, nor is there any sense of

modesty as the European understands the term. As regards sanitation, however, it must be remembered that the sun is a powerful purifying agent, otherwise the conditions would, in many places, be unendurable.

The word "morality" has no significance in the Ibo vocabulary. On the other hand, where the natives have remained untouched by outside influence there is nothing exactly corresponding to the "social evil" of European life. The Ibos, as might be expected, are not patterns of morality, but in their primitive state they are at least free from artificial vice and its attendant evils.

In the majority of Ibo towns a very clearly defined code of morals exist theoretically. Infringements of these laws may lead to severe penalties being inflicted, and cases are not unknown where infidelity on the part of a wife has been punished by the torture and death of both offenders. Extreme measures, however, were resorted to only when the aggrieved husband proved inexorable and rejected every offer of reparation. Instead of capital punishment the guilty wife was usually banished and her accomplice condemned to pay a fine which, in some instances, meant his being financially crippled for life.

The weather conditions of the Ibo country are very similar to those of the West Coast generally. They possess the merit, at least, of being regular. The dry season begins early in November, the rains concluding with a few heavy showers. Towards the end of December or in early January some slight rain will fall, ushering in the *harmattan*. This is a period of excessive dryness. A dull haze, caused by minute particles of dust, obscures the sun. The dry heat sets up irritation of the skin and nostrils and sometimes causes the lips to crack. During the day it is very hot and this great heat is succeeded at night by a very low temperature. Europeans find the weather distinctly chilly at night, and it is much too cold for the comfort of the natives. These conditions last from two to five weeks.

The *harmattan* is succeeded by the hot season proper, and the heat grows more and more oppressive until the end of March. The breaking up of the dry season is heralded by terrific tornadoes; wind, rain, thunder and lightning all being of extremely violent character. May and June are sometimes termed the "Little dries," i.e., the weather is mostly fine with heavy downpours of rain at intervals. At the beginning of July the wet season starts in earnest. A huge rainfall is registered between the beginning of July and the middle of October, from which date the rains gradually slacken, and the wet season ends as it began with a series of tornadoes; these being much less severe than those which prevail at the break up of the hot season. As regards climate, the Ibo country shares the unenviable reputation of the West Coast of Africa. In the past it has maintained its evil reputation and fully justified its claim to rank as part of the "white man's grave." Under modern conditions health statistics among Europeans have improved wonderfully. The great increase in the number of doctors, the judicious use of quinine as part of the daily rations, the wider knowledge of hygiene, and the short service system, have all conduced to a more satisfactory state of affairs. The climate itself is pleasant or the reverse according to a man's own temperament. One prefers the wet season, another the dry; both have their merits. The former is cooler but the conditions for travelling are frequently abominable. Rain falls in torrents, roads and tracks are converted into sluices, and one lives in a state of perpetual dampness. Outside the rain beats down mercilessly; indoors one must search for a sheltered spot, for few native roofs can resist the downpours. To retire to bed protected by a macintosh and a bath towel, and even by an umbrella, as one has had to do on occasions, is very amusing in the retrospect but very uncomfortable in actual experience. There is nothing more irritating, and no more effectual preventive to sleep, than the drip, drip, drip of water upon one's face or body.

In the dry season one is free from these discomforts, and camp can be made safely anywhere, but the sun and heat are liable to tax some constitutions rather severely.

The spell of the coast, whether it be exercised by the country, the climate or the people, is apt to weave itself closely into the life of the average European. Whilst in the West Coast he roundly abuses country and climate, he is never amiss in his calculations concerning the date of his furlough. When on leave, immediately the novelty of the home-coming has worn off, his mind involuntarily wanders coastwards once more. It is the "West Coast feeling," whatever be the causes which produce it.

There are, of course, unpleasant conditions to be endured by the resident in Nigeria, but only two that need be mentioned, viz., the violent tornadoes which sweep across the country with such destructive force, and, greatest of all nuisances, the insect pest. Mosquitoes, sand-flies, driver and white ants are positive plagues. In addition there are innumerable varieties of other insects which are increasingly active in their venomous attacks on man and beast.

These minor trials and afflictions, however, are not sufficient to counteract the fascination that draws the European so persistently back to the Ibo country.

CHAPTER III

THE IBO COUNTRY (*continued*)

For many years intercourse with the Ibos was limited to those dwelling in the neighbourhood of the factories scattered here and there on the river banks. The traders had no special interest or inducement to penetrate into the interior, for trade filtered through to them, and the river afforded every facility for transport. They had simply to select suitable centres, and there barter for the produce brought in by land and water.

Missionaries itinerated in various directions, but with no striking results. Eventually the lines of advance shaped themselves directly east and south of Onitsha on the one side, and west of Asaba on the other. There was no lack of reports from the interior. In the eastern hinterland the raiding expeditions of the Abams[1] were a fruitful source of fear, and the havoc wrought by the Ekwumeku [2] on the western side provided a topic for endless discussion in the streets and markets.

Nor were these fears groundless. Cannibalism, human sacrifices and other savage customs were real facts, and flourished within five miles of the outskirts of Onitsha, and no one would dare swear that the inhabitants of even that town were all entirely innocent! It is well within living memory that human sacrifices were offered, the death and burial of a king or notable chief being the most usual occasions.

At one period I was living in a tiny hut set up in the bush some five miles east of Onitsha surrounded by a number of towns. Between two of these there was a feud of long standing. At intervals war broke out in earnest.

[1] and [2] See Chapter XXII for a description of these Societie .

During the last campaign one party captured, and afterwards ate, seven of their opponents, whilst the other party secured only four victims. Regularly I visited the village of the attacked tribe, and was given a quiet, if not enthusiastic reception. The Chief, in whose house I would sit down, used to listen quite placidly to the conversation. He would recline upon the goat-skin thrown on the floor, or quite frequently he would use the occasion to grind up snuff. Leaves of tobacco were parched in a potsherd, and then ground with a small wooden pestle in a crude mortar. After perhaps an hour's discussion, the Chief invariably brought the interview to an end by declaring that he and his people would be quite ready to take heed to the words spoken on the one condition, that I would first of all assist them. It was always the same request. The enemy had secured three more men than his people had captured; if I would guarantee to arrange for three men to be handed over to balance matters, then they would be able to attend to other things. I might add that the account has never been settled to their satisfaction!

At that time I was accustomed to wander freely from village to village, very often unaccompanied. One morning I was walking alone when I came upon a bundle of sticks lying in the path; to this was attached a clean and fresh human skull, which I judged from the teeth and size to be that of a young man. It had been utilised as a fetish. It would act as a solemn warning to would-be thieves, and such a powerful "ju-ju" would ensure the owner finding his property intact, however long it was left on the road. It was in close proximity to this place that, as was well known, a cannibal feast had lately been held.

Amongst our lads there was a small boy whose father had been a servant to the Niger Company. Whilst carrying a message to Obushi, the father was murdered and his body disposed of according to time-honoured custom.

On one occasion I was resting outside my hut when a man of unprepossessing appearance came along and entered into conversation. His eldest son, then a small lad, had been placed by his father in the care of a missionary, in order that he might receive instruction. In the course of his remarks he solemnly asserted that it would be of great benefit to his son if he were provided with human flesh sometimes as part of his diet. He maintained that, if this were done, a proper man's spirit would develop in the lad.

The Royal Niger Company concluded many treaties with native chiefs and kings during their period of administration of the country. By these treaties certain rights were conceded to the Company, and they in return, granted among other considerations, a promise of protection. The people of Awkuzu had ever been a truculent crowd, and raided not only on their own account but went further, and procured bands of Abams to assist them in their predatory excursions. An appeal to the Company for protection was made by a town in the neighbourhood, and in due course troops were dispatched to cool the ardour of the disturbers of the peace.

The majority of the carriers employed for the soldiers were Onitsha men, and this is the story related concerning some of them. After some preliminary fighting, the troops entered Awkuzu and settled into camp. When all was apparently quiet a party of carriers considered the time was opportune for them to secure their share of the loot, and they went away bent on plunder. But the Awkuzus were wily men. They had anticipated the move and had planned a deliberate trap for possible looters. Some goats were placed in one of the compounds and the Awkuzus secreted themselves in the neighbourhood. Presently the gang of carriers arrived, attracted by the goats, and they walked right into the ambush. Some fought their way back to camp, but seventeen were left dead or alive, in the hands of the Awkuzu braves. The story is that of these the dead were eaten first, and later the wounded followed the fate of their comrades. Those who were uninjured were trussed up like fowls, and in this way kept until required.

Towards the south, cannibal tendencies assumed a worse aspect. All that has been said hitherto relates to the prevalent custom of feasting upon captives taken in war. In the southern districts a regular traffic in human flesh was carried on. Strangers were caught, or slaves purchased, with the deliberate intention of converting them into food. Human flesh was a marketable commodity, and a common article of diet. It is not long since a certain chief managed to get possession of one of his opponents against whom he had a grudge of long standing. He derived satisfaction from first lopping off the captive's ears and nose, and then flaying him alive. The carcase was eaten and the skin converted into a drum-head.

There is not a shadow of doubt that, could the history of the Ibo country be clearly traced, a host of suchlike stories would have to be recorded. I have become acquainted with many erstwhile cannibals, and quite good-natured folk most of them are. One week-end I was staying at a town a few miles S.E. of Onitsha. My quarters were very circumscribed, the only accommodation available being a tiny thatched lean-to shed against the compound wall, usually occupied by the goats and fowls. My boys and carriers shared the limited accomodation, lying at night alongside the camp-bed. After the evening meal, we settled down for the night, long before our customary bedtime; consequently the men chattered freely. Presently I became interested in the conversation, and amongst other items of news, gathered that they had all had a share in cannibal feasts.

At first they were reticent, but gradually they opened out and announced what they considered to be the choicest tit-bits; these, they affirmed, were the knuckles. They were strapping young fellows whom I had got to know sufficiently well to induce them to travel round with me. Since then they have all become Christians, and one is a very successful and much respected evangelist.

In the late autumn of 1900, an opportunity presented itself for extending our knowledge of the country lying west of Asaba. Our party consisted of volunteers from amongst the native adherents, and we proceeded through the country as far as a large town called Abwor (Agbor). At the time the king still regarded himself as tributary to his majesty of Benin (in spite of the fact that there was then no king reigning there), and was acknowledged as second in prestige throughout the district. The first evening that I walked about Abwor I found a shrine with a human skull upon the altar, and I ascertained that the same views were held as regards human sacrifice that were held in Benin prior to the expedition of 1897. In 1904 came the Rising of the Ekwumeku (commonly, but probably incorrectly, described as the "Silent Ones"). An immense amount of damage was done before the insurrection was quelled, whilst not long after, the massacre of one of the district commissioners, with his escort, ushered in a further period of trouble for the Government.

In such circumstances the carrier problem was a difficult one. Owing to the unsettled state of the country, it was not easy to persuade men to accompany one on journeys that took them far from their homes. Even when one got a following it was quite uncertain whether the men would stick to their task or desert, and one might find himself in an awkward and irritating predicament. On a certain occasion a compact was made between myself and another missionary. We arranged to leave our respective quarters on the same day, and for our routes to cut one another at a fixed point; my companions would then join his party and the canoemen who had brought him up the creek were to convey me down to Onitsha. The distance was not great, and soon after 2 p.m. (after some eight hours on the road), I arrived at the appointed spot on the bank of the creek. My colleague was to land a few miles further up and, as they returned down-stream, the canoemen were to look out for me. A couple of miles before we reached the creek, my companions, with the exception of one lad, struck northwards in order to intercept the other party. On arrival at the water's edge we looked for the canoe, but our expectations ended in complete disappointment, for it never appeared. I had no kit with me, our food was exhausted, and altogether the situation was rather humiliating. Hour after hour went by and the sun went down. Finally, we came across an old fisherman who, seeing we were completely at his mercy, agreed to paddle us down river, at his own price. He conducted us to his primitive landing stage, but no canoe was visible. In reply to our inquiry as to the whereabouts of his craft, he merely gave a curt nod in the direction of the water. He then waded out up to his middle, dived down and fished up his little " dug-out " from the bottom. It was badly battered, and before embarking the man had to plug several holes with clay. As the canoe was only intended for one, the added weight of two passengers was almost too much for it. It was a ticklish business getting aboard, and even more difficult to make headway. The ordinary canoeman never sits on the floor, but on the gunwale or the small flat stern piece. From start to finish my business was to bale out for, being so deeply laden, we shipped water at every stroke of the paddle. Darkness soon fell, and almost immediately we struck a submerged tree, and were only saved from disaster by the smart movements of our navigator. To illustrate the skill of these canoemen it may be mentioned that when it became dark our man—a tall and heavily built individual—carefully raised himself, stood up in the stern, and balanced himself with a foot on either side of the canoe. In this position he paddled with long sweeping strokes. He maintained this attitude for some four hours, only resting once when we were forced to run to the bank for shelter whilst a powerful breeze was blowing. When a strong wind blows, especially up-stream, the waters of the Niger are rough and dangerous for small craft.

On arrival at my destination, I ascertained that my colleague had fulfilled his part of the programme and had proceeded up the creek. Soon after landing, however, panic seized the men because they thought they were expected to act as carriers for the land journey. Hence, after depositing the loads, a rush was made for the canoe; they cast off from the bank and never rested until they were home again. My colleague fared worse than I did, inasmuch as the influence of the first deserters led to most of the remaining followers also leaving him, and he did not come in until a week later, all his plans having been frustrated, to say nothing of his having spent an uncomfortable time adrift in the bush.

The plan I usually adopted (and do still) when travelling in the Ibo country is a simple one. If but a short visit to a strange town was intended, I went accompanied by not more than two natives, one of whom would have some knowledge of English and be capable of rendering assistance should any language difficulties arise. For a more prolonged stay three carriers were added to the party, and we were seldom more than half a dozen in number. Such a small company aroused no suspicion, more especially because it was obvious to the inhabitants that we carried no fire-arms. Our numbers might have been reduced yet further, but there are no beasts of burden in the country, and therefore all loads have to be carried by men. Unless a direct invitation had been received from someone else I made a point of going straight to the house of the paramount chief and of putting myself under his protection. This plan was invariably successful. Having explained the reasons for our visit and allayed any suspicions he may have entertained, we were able to converse on easy terms. Immediately this stage was reached the chief would indicate that kola nut should be brought and once this was shared we were quickly on friendly terms.

The Ibo is very hospitable, and many of the chiefs are nature's gentlemen. Sometimes it came to our knowledge that we had ventured into what might have been awkward situations, but, personally, I noted suspicious features on but the rarest occasions. Being naturally of a highly nervous disposition, my mind was often assailed by imaginary troubles prior to starting on tour, but having begun the journey, these were quickly forgotten in the keen interest of the expedition. As all travelling had to be done on foot, by the time our destination was reached I was too fatigued to think of anything but food and rest. The depressing times, as already stated, were when we journeyed through a downpour of rain, and crept into camp miserable and chilly, with all our belongings soaked with water. Cheerfulness is a special grace in these circumstances. Matters improve, however, after a rest and food, and it is not long before the discomforts of the way are forgotten.

Contrary to the general rule of making a very early start I prefer waiting until after breakfast, and frequently choose the afternoon hours for travelling.

During my early days it was the custom to rise at an unearthly hour, strike camp whilst it was still dark, and get off as dawn appeared. This meant disturbed and curtailed rest, being nipped by voraciously hungry mosquitoes which had hunted all night for their prey, and bad tempers all round. It was too early to eat anything substantial, and yet one knew that not to do so meant reaching famishing point before the next meal was forthcoming. The mornings may be either chilly or oppressive, and everything is drenched with dew. Often and often one has been wet through to the skin within ten minutes of starting, and cold dew is distinctly uncomfortable. It also meant marching in wet clothes until the sun was well up to dry them. It occurred to me that this was anything but a healthy practice, and hence I tried starting at later hours. I now infinitely prefer setting forth at a reasonable hour of the day, after one has been able to partake of a substantial meal with some measure of comfort. The heat and glare are sometimes trying, but these drawbacks are more easily endured than the depressed and sinking feeling necessitated by early starts.

Travelling in this simple manner I was never once molested, and have never had cause to grumble at the treatment meted out to me at any of the places visited, however evil the reputations they may have borne.

CHAPTER IV

THE IBO VILLAGE

LIFE in an Ibo village is at once simple and picturesque. The houses, the general environment, the dependence upon local natural resources, and the contentment with the barest modicum of those articles which are usually regarded as indispensable in a household, all these, together with the easy-going spirit amongst the village folk, foster and maintain a life of extreme simplicity. Discontent with primitive conditions comes only with the introduction of novelties from the outside world, and then, like a child, the Ibo covets what he sees. Left to himself he neither needs nor desires foreign luxuries, but once the possibility of securing them presents itself, be they ever so incongruous, he will not relax his efforts until they become his cherished possessions.

A missionary has unique opportunities of becoming acquainted with village life, for from the very nature of things the soundest policy is for him to live in the closest communion with the people whom he seeks to influence. So it comes about that he enters freely into the life of the natives ; their huts are always open to him and he goes in and out more or less as one of themselves. In like manner they expect the missionary's house to be free to them, and to come and go as they please.

There is nothing symmetrical about the Ibo village, a fact which tends to make it the more picturesque. It would be thought that at least one point would be kept well in mind when fixing the location of a village, viz. a water supply. But in a great many cases this detail does not appear to have been taken into consideration when selecting sites. Again and again one meets people toiling to and from the supply situated perhaps from one to three miles away. With the exception of those actually situated on the banks of streams, it is usual to find the villages at a distance from water; indeed very often there is no adequate supply, the people simply dig catch-pits for the storage of surface water. In the wet season there is no lack, but in the dry months water is scarce and that stored in the pits becomes stagnant. In some districts the traveller must carry water, for he is likely to experience difficulty in obtaining any *en route* fit for consumption, and a bath is but an occasional luxury. Whilst travelling through such a district some years ago for three days we were denied the comfort of even a decent wash. For drinking purposes recourse can generally be had to cocoanut milk or palm wine. The former is preferable, as the natives dilute the palm wine very freely, and they are not particular whence the water for the purpose is drawn!

The huts are planted down just where the builders fancy, in all sorts of places and at every conceivable angle. The roads are adapted to the houses, and wind in and out between the walls in most bewildering fashion. In the evening time, when the setting sun casts its softened rays over the scene, the village presents a pleasing prospect, The terra-cotta coloured walls, and the thatched roofs, blend most harmoniously with the luxuriant foliage all around, the whole being topped by the graceful palms or shadowed by giant bombax and other large trees.

In the ilos (streets), the children are playing happily in the sand: a company of boys are imitating ju-ju ceremonies, and probably a bevy of merry girls are dancing with whole-hearted enjoyment. The men lounge round in a leisurely manner; a few of the younger, perhaps, engage in archery contests. In one corner a group of older men sit together deeply interested in a game of "okwe,"[1] a pastime common, I believe, throughout West Africa. The women and elder girls are engaged in work, but even they exhibit no signs of rush or worry. Some depart to fetch water, their large clay pots skilfully balanced on their heads; others are busy with preparations for the

[1] See Chapter XI.

evening meal. Little parties frequently sit in the street engaged in the tedious task of peeling "edde" (an edible root something like an artichoke in appearance, the leaves of which resemble those of gigantic arum lilies)—an occupation which affords a rare opportunity for gossip.

At a broad glance the whole scene is delightfully and charmingly picturesque, and it is advisable to follow the example of touring journalists, and be content with first and rapid impressions. These visitors have not the time for further investigation, and would not know where to look, or what to expect, even if they had. Should, however, inspection be made at close range, the visitor is liable to be quickly and rudely disappointed, for there is no attempt whatever to observe one single law of sanitation. The houses and compounds are swept diligently daily, and the women take infinite pains in rubbing the walls and clay floors, but all the rubbish and filth are simply cast down in any available spot in or about the compound and the clumps of bush between the houses; for all their attractive appearance, are little more than open cesspits.

The towns are divided up into villages or wards, and are spread over a wide area, a town often extending over three or four miles of country. There is no overcrowding in the interior towns. There is abundant space for each family to have its own house, compound and farm; in short, each household can be entirely independent of any other for all its needs. Every man understands the art of building and thatching. The materials he obtains from the surrounding bush. He puddles his own clay as near the site of the proposed building as he conveniently can, often in the compound itself. He and his dependents till the land and prôduce the main food supply. Fish and flesh are the only commodities likely to be sought from outside sources. If near a stream, the fish of which does not happen to be sacred, men and women trap or catch fish. Meat is not a common article of diet; it is a luxury to the Ibo.

Each village or ward has its own chief who enjoys the dignity and rights of a patriarch. He takes the lead in all public affairs, religious, social and political. Disputes are settled by him, and he used to preside at the trials of criminal offenders. He also, providing he has attained to the necessary rank, officiates at the sacrifices appointed for certain delinquencies, such as infidelity.

Every village has its own market-place, fetish-houses and public meeting ground. The markets are designated by the names of the day on which they are held, viz. "Ekke," "Afaw," "Oye" (Olie) and "Nkwaw," these corresponding to the four days of the Ibo week. The life of the womenfolk largely consists in a continual round of marketing and the preparation of food, varied by farm work in the season.

The fetish-houses are usually small and very crude; indeed they are neglected and allowed to fall into great disrepair, until some wave of religious zeal leads to their temporary restoration. The people do not appear to worry concerning the ju-ju. Wind and weather may play havoc upon it during the period that their fervour is at a low ebb, and, as a considerable number of these gods are composed of clay, the result is somewhat disastrous, especially during the rainy season. However, a little patching, at the admonition of the Chief, or at the time of some special crisis, satisfies the people, and they conclude that the god ought to be satisfied also. This is a mere statement of fact, not a point of sentiment. A charge is sometimes levelled at missionaries that they entertain neither respect nor regard for the native religion; but they probably understand the situation, and know the underlying currents of thought better than their critics, who too often trumpet forth their opinions, though some of them have never visited the country at all, and others have made but a "so-many-miles-in-a-fortnight" sort of tour. I remember a case in which a colleague was interrogated by one such visitor. An opinion was asked concerning a certain custom. My colleague answered that he could not commit himself to anything definite, as he had not been able to probe to the bottom of the matter. The visitor thought this strange, and went on to remark that he had *quite* a clear conception of the custom, underlying principle and all, as he had been asking questions for *the last two*

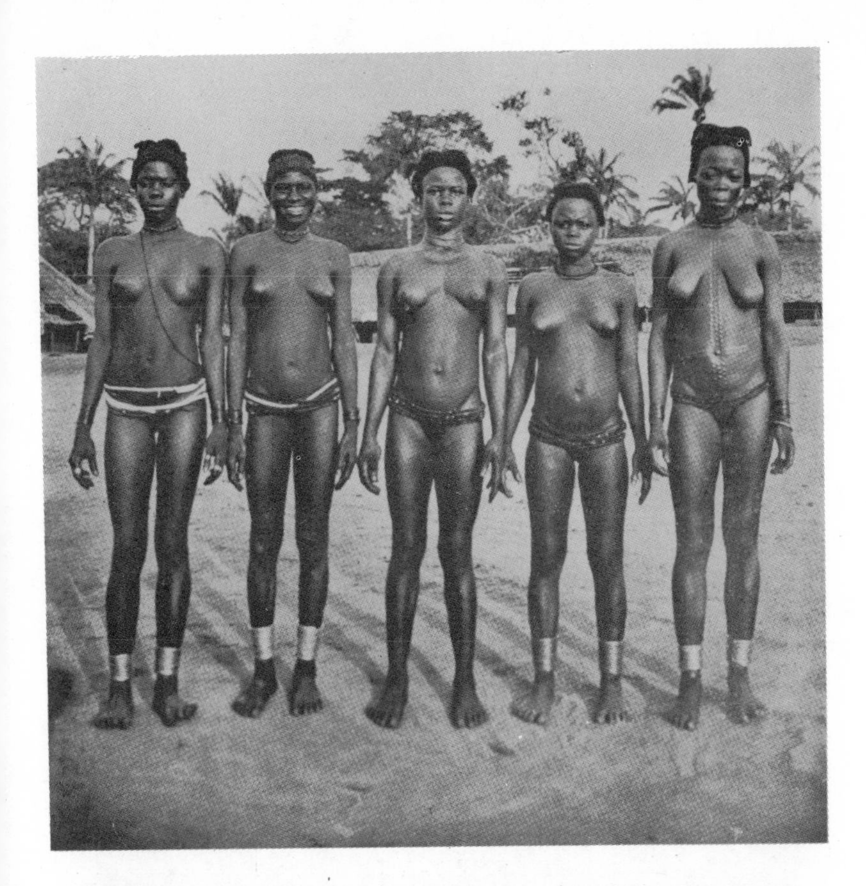

1. Girls from the Eastern Interior District preparing for Marriage
2. In Gala Dress

These girls are passing through the ceremony of Nkpu. They are wearing belts of tiny bells, and their legs are adorned with brass wire spirals, of which they are inordinately proud.

days ![1] My colleague replied that he had been working at the idea over a space of two whole years, and he was still far from being in a position to dogmatise on the subject under discussion.

The public meeting ground (Ilo), is a charming spot ; a large open space shaded by one or more Awbu trees. Beginning a few feet from the ground, these trees throw out, at right angles to the stem, huge wide spreading branches. As these extend they are supported by props. The leaves are large and abundant and the tree when fully grown gives an almost perfect circle of shade sometimes as much as one hundred yards in circumference.

These natural arbours eclipse all enclosed meeting halls. The crowd sits or lies upon the sandy floor, completely sheltered from the sun, each man assuming any attitude he pleases. Of course, fair weather is necessary to appreciate the advantages of the open-air conditions. The chief drawback is that the attention of the audience is apt to be diverted by every casual passer-by, and often some trivial incident will throw the meeting into hopeless disorder, and bring all business abruptly to an end. The people go off at a tangent on the slightest provocation —they are much like children and find it difficult to concentrate their minds for long together. Very similar conditions prevail in Hyde Park and other resorts of like character in England. It takes very little to attract the attention of the crowd, and the numbers fall off immediately anything transpires which shows the least promise of being more entertaining.

Meetings for many purposes are held in these open spaces: for the adjustment of differences between individuals or households : for the celebration of fixed feasts ; the offerings of common town sacrifices and on specially appointed occasions. Hundreds of people will assemble when an important question is under discussion, or a great function is in progress. Frequently the ilo serves also as the market-place, in which case it is the rendezvous of

[1] This student of native customs relied on a youth, an ex-labourer, as interpreter, whose knowledge of English was equal to a Standard II school reader !

great crowds of haggling buyers and sellers who create a din only to be compared to that of an English fair—minus the steam organs.

Having taken a general view of the village we now turn to a closer examination of the houses and compounds. These vary very much in different localities. At Onitsha the compounds resemble those in vogue in the Yoruba country, a fact which serves as an additional argument in support of the tradition that the chief inhabitants of that town are of Bini origin. The compound is rectangular in form. Against three sides of its surrounding wall, and occasionally on the fourth side also, small compartments are constructed round an open courtyard. The one entrance is on the side next to the roadway, and it is usually so diminutive that on entering caution is necessary if one wishes to preserve one's anatomy from knocks and scratches. The rooms are raised a foot or two above ground level. The courtyard being open, in the rainy season it frequently resembles a pond, but the greater part of the water quickly disappears through a channel cut through the main wall for the purpose. The walls of the building are of puddled clay, and the roof is constructed of bamboo or split palm stems, thatched with grass or palm-leaf mats.

East of Onitsha the distinct Ibo plan is adopted. Here the compound is enclosed with a boundary wall from four to ten feet in height, thatched to protect it from the heavy rains. The area enclosed depends upon the space available, and not on the social position of the owner. Inside this compound stands a collection of huts of irregular shape, anyhow and anywhere. Aspect, elevation and proximity to other buildings, are not considered by the Ibo. Very few of the huts are large; in most cases the back wall alone is carried up to the eaves; sometimes the ends, and always the front, being left open to admit air and light. The roofs slope down to within two or three feet of the ground, and are constructed of close rafters covered with a very thick and heavy thatch of grass. On the western side of the river the thatch consists of uma leaves tied on by their stalks. The roofs are very steeply pitched, a method born of experience of tropical downpours. The low eaves also afford entire protection from the sun. The floor is composed of beaten clay, raised a foot or two above the ground level. It is polished by the womenfolk with clay-water. To prevent it wearing into holes it may be studded with palm nuts (nkpulu ugwu-olo), a hard seed resembling a plum stone.

The furniture and adornments of the hut are curious. The underside of the roof is permeated with lamp-black, very dirty, but nevertheless a great preservative to the thatch, and a deterrent to mosquitoes and other undesirable insects. Suspended from the rafters are dozens of skulls of goats, cows, pigs, monkeys and maybe, human skulls also. These gruesome objects, filthy with smoke and dirt, are records of feasts and sacrifices. They are kept as a display of affluence rather than as fetishes, a custom comparable with the practice of mounting antlers and other trophies in English houses.

In addition, there are various articles indicating some of the habits and occupations of the owner ; wicker fish traps, flagons made from gourds and used in collecting and storing palm wine, native hoes and a miscellaneous collection of odds and ends. The fire is on the floor in the centre of the hut, and is seldom allowed to die out, it being kept alight by long logs of slow-burning wood. Near by is the master's pipe and a rough wooden bowl—polished by constant friction—used for grinding snuff. Usually there is no actual furniture other than a skin or two upon which the owner reclines upon the floor. Visitors usually bring their own chairs or skins if they require such luxuries. A special friend may be accommodated with a grass mat, a gin case, or a stool, and one has even had to make shift with half a cocoanut shell. This is not so uncomfortable as it is apt to sound, especially if the husk still covers the shell. An inclination to stoutness is likely to give rise to awkward situations, but happily deportment is of little moment.

Various patterns of beds are in use, movable and fixed. One of the former consists of a simple frame on four legs over which a layer of offolaw (palm-stems) is fixed crosswise. The immovable beds are supported by the two rear legs being sunk into the floor, and the two horizontal end pieces being buried into the side-wall of the hut; these also are covered with offolaw. Another variety consists of solid clay couches with a raised headpiece for a pillow. The native who objects to lodging on the "cold, cold ground" shows his ingenuity by making a cosy couch. A mound of well-beaten clay about seven feet by three feet, and two and a half feet in height, is banked against the inner wall of the house, and then the side is hollowed out in the form of an arch. In this cavity fire is placed and thus the bed is warmed through. On the death of a man of high social rank the corpse may be left on such a bed and the heat increased in order to dry and shrivel the body, and thus preserve it until satisfactory funeral arrangements can be arranged.

The head of the house has his own particular hut. Each wife has also her own which she shares with her children until the sons grow up, when they build themselves bachelor's quarters. Adjoining the chief's private apartment is the recess where the household gods are paraded, the family Ikenga occupying the position of honour. In front of the main building are one or more sacred ebwo trees which serve as a sacrificial grove. Just inside the entrance to the compound is a rude shelter for the guardian ju-ju of that particular house.

Cooking utensils are few and simple. In the vicinity of trading factories cast-iron negro pots are in great favour, but in the interior earthen vessels are employed. The fireplace consists of three stones or lumps of burnt clay, or if a back wall be available, and this is greatly preferred, two stones suffice. When a feast is in preparation, cooking operations may be transferred to the open compound, and, for public festivities, to the ilo itself. Considerable ingenuity is then shown in improvising temporary ranges. A narrow trench is dug running several yards in a straight line, and at intervals right-angled cross-cuts are made. The pots are balanced over the junctions where the cross sections cut the main trench, and firewood is pushed in on either side. Thus the number of cooking pots can be multiplied indefinitely.

Close alongside the hearth is the indispensable pestle

and mortar—heavy with cumbersome articles. The latter is hewn out of a solid block of urok timber, a hard wood similar to oak. The pestle is about $2\frac{1}{2}$ ft. in length and is of the same material, corresponding in weight with the mortar. *The Meal* of the day, i.e., the evening one, cannot be prepared without these utensils.

The head of the house keeps the awba, or yam stack, strictly in his own charge, and he hands out the daily supply. The rinds are hacked off, and the yam split into chunks. It is then cooked in a similar way to potatoes. When sufficiently boiled the blocks of yam are placed in the mortar, the pestle is dipped in water, and pounding begins. This is continued until the mass assumes the consistency of dough, and the resemblance is so close that the casual onlooker might mistake it for that article. The pounding appears to be a very simple business but it is really difficult, and a distinct knack has to be acquired. The pulverised yam is very sticky, and an inexperienced hand will pull the whole lump out of the mortar and roll it in the dust, thus rendering it unfit for use. One has never yet seen a European pound yam with passable success, and he also finds the labour very fatiguing, whereas the natives, men, women and children, are experts in manipulating the pestle.

Meantime another pot is stewing over the fire and this contains the soup or relish. It consists of water, purest palm-oil (that which is extracted from the outside flesh of the nuts), pepper, salt, herbs and smoked fish or meat, the last of nondescript nature and origin. When all is prepared the pot of soup is placed on the ground in the centre of the group of diners. Before each person is a ball of pounded yam called nni-ji, resembling an unbaked Cobourg loaf. A portion is pinched off the lump, rolled between the fingers to the size and shape of an egg, dipped well into the relish, and swallowed at a gulp. The pill, large as it is, causes no inconvenience to the Ibo. No attempt is made to masticate the food, and it disappears at an amazing rate. An enormous amount is eaten at these evening meals, and the native wants little more for the next twenty-four hours.

The head of the house dines alone in his private apartment, each wife in turn attending to his needs. He uses his own drinking cup, which he never allows out of his own possession. No other person must handle it; he has no wish for poison to be administered in his cup.

In the choice of meat the Ibo exhibits no fads. Usually he must be content with smoked fish. Domestic animals are scarce, and are seldom killed except for sacrificial purposes or for very special feasts. When any are killed, the carcases are hacked to pieces with axes and matchets, straight through skin and bones. Not the smallest particle is wasted, even the entrails being consumed. The blood is caught and allowed to solidify. It is then cut in pieces and cooked in the same manner as the liver. Wild animals are treated likewise, of whatever species they may be, large or small, young or old, diseased or otherwise. The only part shunned is the gall-bladder, the contents of which are believed to be deadly poison, that of some animals being much more feared than others. Leopards, monkeys, dogs, snakes, lizards, anything indeed that can be called fish, flesh or fowl is acceptable to the Ibo. Men have begged permission to shake the thatch of my house during the day-time in order to catch the small bats which shelter there. When thus disturbed the little creatures fly out, and are dazed by the light and, before they can recover themselves, they are struck down. Men have also made request to dig in the compound to unearth field mice. With the sole exception of the sacred python, snakes when killed are immediately tailed and headed—the tail being feared almost as much as the head, as it is thought to be capable of inflicting a poisonous sting. The extremities are buried on the spot whilst the still wriggling reptile is carried off to supplement the stock of food in the family larder. Those who have forsaken paganism include the python in their list of delicacies, the snake which is accounted sacred by the ordinary native. Rather late one night I had to pay a visit to the Institution dormitory to dress a sore foot for a lad. An extraordinary quietness aroused my suspicions and, at the same time, I was conscious of an extremely inviting odour. Upon investigation I discovered a little clandestine supper-party enjoying themselves greatly—a large python had been unearthed from its hole and killed, and the nest robbed of thirty-four eggs. Practically the whole of the snake and all the eggs vanished that night!

On another night, after we had retired to bed, we were disturbed by frantic screechings issuing from the fowl house. The result of our sortie was that a small python (7 ft. 4 in.), caught in the act of raiding the roost, came to a violent end. I wanted the skin, and said the reptile must be left till the morning. It was only with great difficulty that the boys could be prevented from cutting up and eating the creature that night, in spite of the fact that they had but recently partaken of a heavy meal.

One day one of the men shot a python some fifteen feet in length. Judging by his bloated appearance we conjectured that he must have had a substantial breakfast. It was owing to this, and the subsequent heavy sleep after the meal, that he lost his life. Imagine our astonishment when, after a surgical operation, we discovered that he had chosen a porcupine as his morning tit-bit, taking care however, to swallow it head first, the quills being thus pressed flat to its body and so preventing their business ends from causing uncomfortable internal sensations. But what amazed us more, and gives occasion for relating the incident at all, was the request of a gentleman present for the body of the porcupine (upon which the gastric juices had already been actively at work) to provide an evening meal! The python was taken in hand by the members of our compound and was pronounced "prime beef."

I was busy at work one afternoon when some men began to run and shout, and soon afterwards two of them came along with a slim black snake, six feet in length, killed in the act of stalking a chicken. The two men moved a few yards away, collected some dry grass and started a fire. The reptile, balanced upon a stick, was thrust into the flames and smoke until it was charred, but by no means cooked, and the men promptly devoured it. These snakes usually hunt in couples, so a watch was kept for the mate, and within a couple of hours number two had met with a similar fate.

Many attempts have been made to keep horses in the Ibo country, and a number have been brought down from Northern Nigeria, but they survived only a short time, owing to tsetse fly. As one of these neared its end, several natives sought to purchase it, but their offers met with indignant refusal and, instead, the poor brute was decently buried. But alas! it was not allowed to rest. Under cover of darkness the carcase was snatched, the natives strongly disapproving of the waste of so much good "beef."

After dark one evening I was strolling round and came upon a group of youths very intent on some business. On inquiry I found that shares had been taken up in the purchase of a dog. It was cut up into thirty penny shares, each youth taking one or more according to his resources. The native dogs, which are met with in every village but are not numerous, are of the pariah type, and are kept solely to serve as scavengers. They are small and scraggy and the refuse consumed by them is vile beyond description.

One might relate many examples, but these will suffice to demonstrate the Ibo's taste in flesh food. His cannibalistic propensities have been touched upon in a previous chapter. It will be seen that nothing comes amiss to the native. The limit is perhaps reached in those towns where even the evil-smelling, refuse-eating vultures are valued chiefly for their putrid flesh.

The Ibo village then, for all that is so picturesque, set in the midst of beautiful surroundings, and radiant with colour, is not the sweetest of places. But its failure to come up to expectations is due not so much to its natural environment, but is rather an illustration of the words:—

> "Where every prospect pleases,
> And only man is vile."

THE ENTRANCE TO A CHIEF'S COMPOUND

Guardian gods and a sacred grove are in front.

CHAPTER V

CHILD LIFE

THOSE who strive to combat infantile mortality in England are confronted with many difficulties, and probably the greatest of all are those arising from the ignorance, prejudice and superstition of the parents, though the last term may not be acknowledged.

When we inquire into the conditions of child life amongst the Ibo people, we soon discover that the methods adopted in dealing with young children are so drastic that it is surprising, not that many die, but that any survive at all. That so many do pull through demonstrates the infant's tenacious hold upon life.

From the very first the Ibo baby must run the gauntlet of all manner of perils, some the outcome of deliberate intention to injure, others the result of ignorance and superstition. In many parts if the infant fails to cry vigorously at birth, it forfeits its life, the omission being considered an evil omen. A similar fate befalls children whose mothers die before they are about six months old. The birth of twins is a calamity of the first magnitude, and spells disaster for them and the unfortunate mother. The underlying idea is that it has been ordained that mankind should propagate his species by single births, in contradistinction to animals; for a woman to bear more than one child at a birth is to degrade humanity to the level of the brute creation. Plural offspring is nature's law for goats and dogs; for a woman to imitate them in this respect fills the Ibo with unspeakable disgust. Mother and children are cursed and subjected to contempt and ill-treatment. The woman makes no attempt to defend herself or her children; she accepts the situation dumbly, and merely wonders why she, especially, has been selected for such dishonour. Her hatred of her offspring is as bitter as that of her relatives and neighbours. She turns from them with loathing and despair and, unless compelled, will make no effort to nurse them. It is believed that in some mysterious manner there has been an unholy alliance with an evil spirit during sleep, and the second child is the result.

With all haste the abominations must be removed. The children are thrust into an old waterpot without even a passing thought for the pain inflicted. Cocoanut fibre or leaves are thrown in to cover them, and the pot is then deposited in some lonely spot in the bush. The newly born infants receive no attention whatsoever. They are cast away at once, as unclean in the sight of gods and men.

It is astonishing how long some of the children survive after being treated thus; this extraordinary vitality being due, perhaps, to the fact that the umbilical cord is not severed.

In one case of castaways with which I had to deal, they had been lying a whole night, and the greater part of the next day, in the bush—at least sixteen hours. One died from injuries either deliberately inflicted or received when being forced through the neck of the pot; the other, and uppermost, child had escaped serious injury and has since grown into a sturdy boy, mother and child having been kept under supervision for some months at the medical mission.

This method of dealing with twins is reckoned to be the only one open to the parents, as by acting thus they hope to avert further calamity. To permit the children to live would amount to a direct challenge to the malignant spirits, and the parents, and indeed the whole community, would be exposed to all manner of dangers.

There is no alternative for the Ibo but to cast them out. This is the kind of custom that legislation finds very difficult to eliminate, as the influence of the supernatural is much stronger than that exercised by human instrumentality, and it is in such circumstances that missionary effort can and does play an important part in the evolution of the savage.

Polygamy is the recognised rule, and some of the marital customs which arise from this institution are peculiar, e.g. it is an unforgivable sin for two wives to give birth to children on the same day. As with twins, mothers and children are made to suffer the full penalty for such misdemeanours.

No provision whatsoever is made preparatory to the birth of the child. The prospective mother continues her daily round in the most unconcerned manner. Consequently it not infrequently happens that the child is born at an inconvenient time and place, perhaps whilst the woman is at the farm or by the roadside during the journey to or from market. When confinement takes place at home a native midwife may attend, and she is assisted by the grandmother of one of the parents (the maternal one preferably) or by some other ancient dame. For the first day or two after birth the mother does not nurse the child. The women declare that the first milk is "bitter" and quite unfit for the child. To test the quality of the milk ants are used. A small quantity is expressed and placed on the ground. If the ants refrain from tasting it or, if they consume it and death follows, then it is assumed that the milk possesses poisonous qualities. If they take it greedily then it will prove to be wholesome food for the child. Instead of the mother nursing her child from the hour of birth the old woman in attendance attempts to suckle it, a custom as disgusting as it is fickle.

Coverings for the newly-born infant are not forthcoming. In the tropics this is not a serious matter, but still the cold clay floor does not improve the chances of the child any more, perhaps, than its being held in, and afterwards washed in, cold water, immediately after birth.

The babe must always sleep with its mother. The introduction of a crib by the wife of a West Indian missionary raised very grave doubts as to whether she cared for her child. To put the baby "upon a shelf," as if it were a common utensil, was utterly incompatible with the local ideas of affection. To neglect the child thus showed a complete want of love, and a scant respect even for duty.

The rite of circumcision is usually performed on both boys and girls between the third and eighth day after birth. The time, however, varies in different towns, the operation being often postponed until the age of puberty is reached. It is the common practice to postpone the rite on the western side of the Niger. No religious rites whatever accompany the operation, which is performed by both men and women without restriction.

Naming the child is an important function. It is a mark of honour and respect to be invited to give a name, and the privilege is usually reserved for one of the elder relatives. Two or more names may be given, the first almost invariably taking the form Nwa (child, in combination with the name of the day on which the child was born, e.g. Nwa-ekke—the child of Ekke day). The second name is suggested by the display of some characteristic trait, or some resemblance, fancied or otherwise, to a deceased member of the family. The Ibo believes that all children are reincarnations of beings who have already passed through a lifetime in this world; hence a man will point to a little girl and gravely inform you that she is his mother reborn into the world.[1] The child will consequently be given the name of the relative it is supposed to resemble, and as such will receive a joyful welcome back to earth. It is a time of great rejoicing and feasting, and large quantities of palm-wine are consumed in celebrating the occasion.

When there is a dedication of the child it takes place on the same day as the naming. Ordinarily this rite is confined to boys. The "dibia" (medicine man) detects some sign which convinces him that this baby is a reincarnation of a former dibia and hence, *ipso facto*, he must be dedicated to the medical cult. The boy lives with his parents until he is about eight years of age, and is then transferred to the care of the dibia. As he grows up he is gradually initiated into all the mysteries of the profession. This is the manner in which the ranks of the dibias are recruited.

[1] See also Chapter X.

Besides a supposed resemblance to a departed dibia, and the consequent dedication to that service, children of either sex may be devoted to the "alusi" (idols). This is always the case when a child is born within the precincts of an idol house. Such births may occur, as already stated, when the mother is unable to reach home before confinement. The child is claimed by the priest on behalf of the alusi and is consecrated (married) to it for life.

The cutting of baby's first tooth is a source of keen interest to the community and of serious anxiety to the parents, for upon it hang the issues of life and death for the child. Should it pierce the lower gum, then all is satisfactory, and it is the signal for great rejoicing and mutual congratulation. On the contrary should it prove to be an upper tooth, the omen is bad and the child's fate will be similar to that of twins. The unfortunate child, now a few months old, after being thrust into the waterpot, is thrown into the " bad bush " and is condemned to endure terrible agony before death ensues.

The prevailing superstitions instigate the people to commit these foul deeds, and in their religious beliefs the root principles for these customs must be sought. It is owing to their anxiety lest they themselves should offend, and, therefore, suffer at the hands of the evil spirits, that they are prompted to sacrifice their offspring. They simply obey the dictates of fear.

Babies are handled in a very crude fashion. To lift a child it is grasped by the forearm, and swung up into the desired position, yet in spite of this apparent carelessness, shoulder joints do not appear to suffer and the children themselves show no signs of pain.

Hot water is used for the morning bath for very young babies, the idea being that this will assist in the massage and limb-stretching operations. Occasionally the proceedings are distinctly curious, and I cannot do better than give the following description, culled from the observations of the missionary in charge of the Twin Rescue Home at Onitsha. This account will further illustrate the Ibo ideas on the management of newly-born babies. The mother sits upon a low seat with her apparatus handy. This consists of a small cooking pot, containing liquid in which a certain herb has been stewed, and a bundle of fibre obtained from a native loofah. She places the baby upon its back in her lap, and then applies the concoction internally and externally. For the internal application the left hand is placed funnel-wise at the corner of the child's mouth, with the little finger pressing on the nostrils. It is thus forced to keep its mouth open in order to breathe, and the liquid is then allowed to trickle through the curved hand into the mouth, and thence down the throat, the poor baby, meanwhile, protesting as vigorously as its restricted opportunities will permit, and appearing to be in imminent danger of suffocation.

The child having been forced to swallow the dose, the loofah is now dipped into the liquid and strenuously applied to the body; the bones of the skull are pressed together, and the spine and limbs are massaged in a more or less methodical manner.

The ablutions completed, the mother blows into the eyes, nostrils, mouth and ears with a force one would think must produce paralysis of the tiny brain. Finally, streaming wet, the babe is put down to rest, sometimes on a banana leaf beside the fire, sometimes on a piece of cloth, and often simply on the bare floor with nothing but a rough pad beneath the head. This treatment—Spartan though it be—is nevertheless beneficial, for the children thrive under it, and in cases where European and Ibo methods have been practised simultaneously on two infants, the greater success of the native system has been clearly demonstrated.

For children's disorders native remedies are applied with varying effects. Suffice here to give one prescription noted down by the superintendent of the Home, viz. that adopted in the case of a wasting infant. "Seven ants cut in halves, mixed with proportions of red pepper, chalk, red ochre and palm-oil; this preparation to be well rubbed into the body, when the tiny insect infecting the skin will come out in the semblance of small white hairs. It must be stated as a simple fact—neither for nor against native medicines, that very beneficial results have followed this treatment. After a few applications the child has visibly fattened, whether from the effect of the remedy or of the massage cannot be confidently asserted."

For babies in good health the morning (warm) bath is followed by massage and stretching of the limbs. The muscles are vigorously squeezed and the joints well stretched; the nose is also pressed and pulled to induce it to assume what is considered the orthodox shape. Water is poured into the child's mouth and nostrils, and often the baby is held by the ankles and, upside down, is shaken in order, so it is alleged, to drive the water to all parts of the body. After food has been taken it is a common custom to toss the child, throwing it into the air and catching it again. This is done with the idea of providing healthy exercise after meals. Little children are taken by the ankles and swung round in circles, chiefly for amusement. Small boys are tossed and swung round also in order to develop fearlessness. One of the objects of half choking the baby by pouring water into the nostrils, is to prepare it for the first sensations when learning to swim.

As the young native mother is expected to carry out the full household duties, including the perpetual marketing, she must needs carry the baby about with her, or leave it in the care of others. If she decide for the former plan, in the more civilised centres the woman takes a loin cloth in her hand; then leaning well forward she swings the baby—with its arms and legs outstretched—across the lower part of her back. The cloth is then thrown dexterously over the child and the ends brought round to the front, pulled up tightly, the edges rolled, and the ends tucked in. The baby appears to ride in a precarious manner, but in reality is held quite securely, and in this position it rests and sleeps as peacefully as in a cot. The mother's hands are perfectly free and, with a little assistence in raising or lowering her basket, she will carry a heavy load upon her head to and from the market.

If not going any appreciable distance, the mode of carrying a child is to swing it up by the arm, and to place it astride upon the hip, the infant assuming a semi-recumbent attitude and clinging tightly with one hand. The child is usually suckled whilst in this position. When a woman decides to leave her child at home, it is put into the care of one of the younger members of the household; where possible a boy-nurse is chosen for a boy, and a girl for a girl-baby. As the Ibo mother does not concern herself about regularity in feeding the child, she goes on with her occupation regardless of the needs of the baby left at home. The youngster who has charge of it manages very well for a time. When hunger begins to trouble the baby, and it asserts the fact in the usual manner, recourse is had to the water-cure for crying. Every time the child begins to cry, the nurse promptly pours water into the open mouth, and the process is repeated as required until the mother returns.

There is no fixed time for weaning—in fact, the custom does not really exist, infants being naturally fed until they themselves refuse the milk. In this connection it should be noted that it is contrary to the custom of the Ibos for a woman to bear a child until the interval of at least three years has elapsed since the birth of the previous (if still living) child. Hence the infant is suckled for a considerable period after it has begun to run about, indeed, it behaves very much after the manner of the little goats running about the compound.

Parents manifest deep fondness for their children, What appears to be inexpressibly cruel on occasions does not arise from savage, inhuman propensities, but is the logical and inevitable outcome of their creed. In their earliest years the children are very attractive, with pleasant features, chubby faces, and large dark liquid eyes. When quite young the predominant peculiarities of the negro type are not pronounced. Children are priceless possessions, and no man can have too many; the more he has the more will he be respected and envied by the community. Between actual brothers and sisters, and between children of the one father but by different mothers there are strong ties of affection. Each must, and will, help the others always, and by all means. The mother's love for the child, and vice versa, are perhaps the most remarkable elements in the family relationships. The son may not always treat his mother kindly—although not to do so is abhorrent to the Ibo mind and very seldom indeed is the mother neglected or treated disrespectfully—but the son never forgets his mother. Invariably she is the first in his affections, and she is his confidante in all the serious affairs of his life. In times of danger the mother is thought of before even wife and children. Wives are always to be had; he cannot get a second mother!

From the age of about three years, the Ibo child is reckoned as sufficiently advanced to be left more or less to its own devices. It begins to consort freely with children of its own age or company (otu) and to take its share in work and play. Boys and girls soon separate, each sex being intent on its own games and occupations, the one quite independently of the other. The lot of the boys is preferable to that of the girls. Pleasure and enjoyment are the special prerogatives of the former as befits the future lords and masters. It is sufficient for the girls that they minister to their male relations: that and the bearing of children are the sole reasons for which they are created.

The open street (ilo) is the children's playground, a spot well suited for the purpose, as it is generally covered with fine sand several inches in depth. Huge trees afford abundant shelter from the sun, and the absence of all but pedestrian traffic secures for the little ones playgrounds where they can pursue their pastimes in perfect safety and enjoyment. It is a charming sight to watch the children playing in the sand amidst the sunny glades. Clothing is superfluous and, therefore, conspicuous by its absence; the children being thus quite unhampered in their movements, and free from all anxiety as to the ripping of garments.

At an early age the boys engage in regular exercises, of which there are many forms. They obtain little bows and arrows, and they exercise their skill on small birds and the multi-coloured lizards which dart about in all directions. A common form of sport is that of turning somersaults, both by means of a primitive spring-board and without artificial assistance. The spring-board, though simple, is very effective in operation. It consists of the butt end of a large palm frond fixed firmly in the ground, at a slight backward angle. The lad takes a short, swift run, and brings one foot down sharply on the tip of the palm stem, and this, being very elastic, shoots the boy into the air, and he lands on his feet some distance away, having turned a complete somersault *en route*. It is quite fascinating to watch a string of lads following one another in rapid succession. Many become very expert at the game and after a time dispense with the spring-board altogether. Small boys soon begin to imitate their elder brothers in wrestling and dancing. The result of all this physical outdoor exercise is that the muscles are well developed and the lads become strong and wiry.

In the season, boys accompany their elders to the farms, and get an insight into the business of raising produce, the amount of work actually done by them varying according to the disposition and circumstances of the parents. They are also called upon to help in building operations, the task usually allotted them being to carry the lumps of puddled clay from the pit to the builders. They become useful whilst still extraordinarily young, assimilating a wonderful stock of practical knowledge. They become familiar with certain aspects of bird, animal and plant life, but cannot be characterised as observant of things unconnected with their own personal affairs.

The women and girls are not so free, though they enjoy themselves well enough in their own way. Almost as soon as they can walk girls take a share in the household duties. They begin by carrying water, collecting firewood, rubbing floors, assisting in the preparation of food, and then, later on, accompanying their elders to the markets where they are initiated into the technicalities of trade.

It must not be assumed that the life of a small girl is an unhappy one. It is true that girls early develop a measure of stolid independence, or rather the responsibilities of daily life are taken up seriously at a very early age, but they have their amusements and pastimes, and are quite capable of enjoying themselves. They are especially fond of a certain form of step-dancing. The partners face each other, beat time by clapping their hands, and the one must anticipate the movements of the other and be ready to respond. Failure to meet the correct movement is hailed with shouts and laughter by the assembled company, and a new partner comes in to try her skill.

In the native home-life there is nothing of the nature of discipline. The children do exactly as they choose and are only punished when they have been exceptionally aggravating. This laxity does not improve their morals, and there are incidents of child life which are sad to contemplate. But little attempt is made to check the children, and it is quite a new experience for them to come under school discipline, and there, in another atmosphere, to learn to bring their natural impulses under control.

CHAPTER VI

COURTSHIP AND MARRIAGE

Marriage is a most important event in the Ibo's life. From the time that boys and girls are capable of thinking for themselves, marriage is set before them as the one object to be attained. During the earlier years it does not assume a serious aspect, but question any boy or girl, and the answer is certain to be that, in due course, they must marry. Celibacy is an impossible prospect. Unmarried persons of either sex, except in special cases, are objects of derision, and to be childless is the greatest calamity that can befall a woman. Hence a very high value is set upon marriage.

Courtship, as such, does not exist. The word "love" is not even found in the Ibo language. The nearest approach to the idea is "ifu nanya," i.e. "to look in the eye" in a favourable manner. The verb "to hate" is constantly in use, and there is an expression "to look in the eye" which implies the reverse of love. I had a very practical demonstration of this some years ago when travelling through a strange town. I believe it was the first appearance of a white man in that particular spot, and for a few minutes there seemed to be imminent danger of unpleasant experiences. Our party consisted of four, three natives and myself, and as we pursued our way along a tortuous bush track, we suddenly rounded a corner and found ourselves on the edge of a large open square. The hubbub indicated that we had wandered into a market, but before we had opportunity to take note of our surroundings, an excited crowd of men, bristling with spears and guns, hustled us apart and hampered our movements and observations. Eventually I managed to cross the market and later rejoined my companions. On putting the question, "Why did you leave me alone in the crowd?" the answer was immediately forthcoming, "Because the men—they look us." It was a most telling illustration of the text, "And Saul *eyed* David from that day forward."

Love, then, usually has no part to play in native courtship. Later a substitute for love may develop consisting of a certain amount of affection or favour bestowed by the husband upon his wife. After marriage the woman is ranked with the other property of the husband with a proportionate value attached, but little greater than that of the cows and goats. Ordinarily the betrothed girl raises no objection to the prospect of marriage, but occasionally one will refuse to follow the intended husband in spite of entreaty or applied persuasion. In such case any expenses incurred by the man must be refunded by the guardian of the girl.

Parents of the richer class often select a wife (or wives) for a son whilst he is still quite a boy, irrespective of his wishes or inclinations; he probably is not even told of the transaction until it is an accomplished fact, and the girl is presented to him as his wife. In the majority of cases the young man makes his own choice. He happens to meet a girl who attracts his attention, and he immediately institutes inquiries as to her parents, and whether she be already engaged or not. If she is free he endeavours to elicit, through her friends, information concerning her capabilities in cooking, trading and other useful and profitable accomplishments. He also enquires about her character, whether she be of good temper, quiet, industrious and so forth. Should these investigations prove satisfactory, he lays his case before his parents or his confidential friend, for he cannot make the first advances personally. This intermediary proceeds to open up negotiations. A visit is paid to the girl's home, and a bottle of gin or a pot of palm wine offered as "ojji" (kola). If the present be accepted, friendly relations are established, but no mention whatever must be made of the contemplated marriage. Several similar visits will ensue and more presents be offered to all who can claim any sort of kinship to the girl. Finally the real business is broached to the intense surprise of the girl's relatives! "She is very happy where she is, and we should be miserable without her. She is so intelligent, and so useful, we cannot spare her!" When, at last, these preliminaries are over, the girl is called in, and asked if she has any objection to the proposal, and then, after a long palaver, the amount to be paid as dowry [1] (head-money) is fixed. In the old days the price was reckoned in cows, goats and cowries. This dowry money is a specified amount: any presents given are additional, and quite irrespective of the dowry. Nowadays the price is sometimes stated in English cash terms. It varies in value from £2 to £50 according to the township, social rank, age and personal qualities of the girl. Cows are reckoned at an all-round price of £5 apiece, and hence the sum named would be in the terms of cows (and goats, valued at say 10s. apiece). Only on very rare occasions is the whole of the dowry money paid down at once; it is never done except there be some special reason. For one thing the girl has not reached a marriageable age, as a rule. The usual practice is to pay by instalments spread over months and even years, in fact, right up to the very day on which the man wishes to take his wife permanently to his own house.

This taking of the bride permanently implies that she has paid temporary visits to the man's home, and this is the actual case. From the moment that the first instalment of the dowry has been paid the girl is reckoned as the man's wife. There are no such intermediate words as "betrothal" or "engagement." As soon as matters can be arranged the custom of "uri" must be observed. This consists in the girl being sent to the parents of the affianced husband, when she is introduced to all his relatives. It is somewhat of an ordeal, as some of the man's kinsfolk do not hesitate to comment freely on the debutante into the family. Her general demeanour is subject to close observation, and her domestic qualifications criticised. If the

[1] The term "dowry" is to be interpreted throughout in accordance with West African usage, viz. as money paid by the prospective husband for his wife. "Head-money" would be the more accurate term.

girl be quite young when she is betrothed she will continue to make annual visits to her prospective parents-in-law, staying with them for about one month at a time. In good homes she will be carefully guarded, but in a great many cases the girl, to all intents and purposes, becomes actually the wife of the man to whom she is betrothed, during the period she is residing with his parents. Amongst young people, morals are not very rigid, the only real stipulation being that a girl must have no intimate relations with any other man prior to the first visit to her intended husband. After that is over, she is more or less free to select her own friends, and invariably does so. Should a child be born in the waiting time before actual marriage, it is the property of her betrothed husband.

In due course the marriage takes place. The man himself may inform the girl's guardians that he is ready to pay the balance of the dowry money, or, as often happens, the guardians give pointed hints that, as the girl is now fully grown (in their estimation) it is time for the bridegroom to fulfil the marriage contract. On the appointed day a feast is prepared—copious supplies of gin or palm wine forming an essential feature - at the expense of the bridegroom. In the presence of the relatives and others chiefly concerned, the final instalment of the dowry money is handed over; this transaction constitutes the marriage, and the pair are declared man and wife. The bride receives presents from her relatives consisting of cooking utensils and, in better class circles, perhaps a couple of goats and some fowls as a contribution towards the working capital of a married woman. A rich father will also make his daughter a grant of one or two slaves to act as her personal attendants. At the conclusion of the marriage feast the bride may accompany her husband to his house, but it is more usual for her to be led by some of her girl friends to his home after darkness has fallen. In some parts there are no marriage ceremonies, but the girl simply joins the man at his house as soon as the first instalment of the dowry is paid, and they are acknowledged as man and wife. The great festivities are deferred until the birth of the first child.

These are the broad outlines of courtship and marriage as they exist.

Although so much is done by the parents or guardians, there are many little dodges on the part of the young folk which save the courtship from being an utterly cold-blooded business transaction. The village belles are not unversed in the arts of coquetry. They take particular pains to attract the attention of eligible young men, and do not hesitate to advertise their personal charms. Cleverly drawn freehand designs are traced over the body from head to foot, and extra care is exercised in the plaiting and adornment of the hair. On gala days every available ornament is brought into requisition ; strings of beads of a particular kind worn round the neck and waist, bracelets of ivory or cowrie shells and leg ornaments. These last are mostly of two patterns ; they are either simple rings of graduated sizes, or immense and heavy plate-like brass anklets. The girls revel in dancing and seize every opportunity of displaying their charms.

The young men are equally vain, rather more so in fact. They array themselves after their fashion, and, like the girls, their main object is to display their fine points of physical development. Their only garment is an awga-daw, a strip of cloth dyed red with camwood stain, and tightly rolled, and worn as a very meagre loin cloth in a style peculiar to the Ikolopia, i.e. " young bloods." Just below the knees, and on the biceps, are choice circlets of ivory. The hair is plaited in tails, and in some districts this plaiting of the hair has a recognised significance.

The Ibo registers no account of years and none can state his age. In lieu of a birth certificate, they refer to their otu (company). This indicates that this one, and that one and others were all born the same year. If inquiry be made as to the age of anyone, all the answer given is that he or she is a member of such and such a company. When it is remembered that Ibo women bear children at fairly regular intervals of three years there is a certain amount of reliability about this otu system. On the other hand, it means that all girls in any particular company, being about

PREPARING FOR MARRIAGE
Girls with recently cut Mbubu marks

the same age, are reckoned as fit for marriage at the same time, whereas it does not at all follow that all have attained to an equally advanced stage of development. It can be assumed that under normal conditions girls are married when about fourteen years old, the first signs of puberty fixing the minimum age. In the districts with which I am most familiar, all the girls of marriageable age go into "nkpu" together. This is a peculiar custom, the object of which is to announce the fact that these girls will be entering the marriage state during the ensuing year. Considerable preparations must be made for the proper observance of this ceremony. Six months prior to the formal entrance into the nkpu state, the girls take up their quarters in separate apartments. They must not venture out into the open during daylight, though they do not hesitate to wander forth after dark! They do no work whatever during this period, and are provided with more food than they can possibly eat. The only occupation they have at this time is the preparation of camwood dye wherewith to stain their bodies. Poorer girls have to reduce the time for this fattening process to four months, as they cannot be spared so long from work, nor can the parents afford the unlimited supplies of food for the full period. Some of the girls grow grossly fat and heavy, and all exhibit signs of over-feeding, but when on parade they receive honour in proportion to their size, and the fatter they are the more pleased and proud are their future husbands.

The final festivities are spread over some seven days. The less fortunate girls must content themselves with little more than an extra plaiting of the hair and a plentiful use of camwood stain; those in more affluent circumstances are able to make a grander display. They wear no clothes whatever. Their bodies are smeared all over with vermilion red and they are decorated with ropes of tightly-twisted cloth or threaded cowrie shells. One or more tiny brass bells are fastened to the cloth or cowrie-shell waist-band. Rings of brass adorn the legs, graduated in size from the ankles to just above the knees. The coiffure is a very elaborate affair and requires unlimited patience and skill to arrange in the correct style. In the centre the hair is worked up with a mixture of clay, powdered charcoal and palm-oil until it becomes a sticky mass. It is then moulded into a shape resembling the central crest of a Roman helmet. The centre comes well over the middle of the forehead, and it extends backwards into the nape of the neck. Below the main erection and on either side delicate patterns are traced with tiny plaits of hair curled into small coils and then plastered down flatly to the head. Finally the high centre has its sides embellished with mother of pearl or bits of brass: the pieces (about the size of shillings) being sewn in with hair. The tufted end of a cow's tail mounted on a leather handle is carried, together with one or two small mirrors, set in handled frames, carved specially for the purpose.

The nkpu girls are attended all through the round of festivities by maids of honour, and these also are smeared red with camwood dye, the fashion being to use as much paint as possible, from the crown of the head to the feet. In cases where the girl's parents can afford it or where the affianced husband is a man of means, a goat is slain as a preliminary on the first day of the carnival. To advertise this mark of affluence the kidney fat of the goat is laid on the head of the prospective bride and fastened securely thereon with finely drawn strands of fibre. The mass of fat is spread completely over the high central decorated portion of the hair, and there it remains until the ceremonies are concluded, it having in the intervening days become putrid and disgustingly filthy.

When the bride-elect has finished her elaborate toilet she sallies forth and joins company with other girls observing the nkpu custom, and together they parade the town with their maids of honour in attendance. These latter carry large fans wherewith to refresh their ladies after the bouts of dancing in which they indulge. Dancing amongst the Ibos is apt to be a very exhausting business, and the nkpu girl does not spare herself in her efforts to win the plaudits of the spectators. If she succeeds in pleasing them, the basket or calabash placed at her feet for the purpose receives a contribution of cowries from the bystanders as a token of their approval. These are useful, and are also an expression of the crowds good wishes for her married life.

There is another custom to which the bride-elect must submit before the actual marriage can be consummated, viz. cicatrization. This consists of very rough tattooing over the front part of the body, generally in the form of a cross, made with triple lines of mbubu or ebubu (small raised lumps or blobs). The presence of such cicatrices indicates that a woman is already married or preparing to enter that state. For conception to occur before this ceremony has been fulfilled is an abomination, but it does not prevent it happening all the same, and it often falls out that the girl is hardly through the nkpu celebrations before she becomes a mother.

At some time just prior to marriage the bride-elect must appear before one or more women, specially appointed, whose function it is to instruct her, and impress upon her the rules governing marriage and the married life of a woman, according to the etiquette of the town. It will be made clear to her what things are permissible and what are "nsaw" (forbidden) and she is enjoined to observe these regulations strictly.

As soon as the marriage is completed, and the bride has come to her husband's house, custom compels her to confess the misdeeds of which she has been guilty since the days of her betrothal. She is bound to divulge the name of any and every man with whom she has been on terms of intimacy. This confession is first made to the umuada, i.e. the female relatives of the husband. The confession takes place before the idol awfaw, an idol which is kept in the house of the head of the whole family. The woman, holding a fowl in her hand, makes her confession before the idol, and then the fowl is killed, and its blood poured upon the awfaw in expiation of her misdemeanours. The husband is satisfied with her confession and sacrifice. He then calls the men who have been named as accomplices in order that reconciliation may be made between himself and them. This is accomplished by the offenders offering the prescribed sacrifices and paying fines, if any should be assessed. Finally all eat kola nut, and drink palm wine together to signify that the reconciliation is complete.

If, in due course, no children are forthcoming as a result of the union, serious differences arise between husband and wife, each mutually accusing the other of being responsible for this state of affairs. Should matters continue so, the wife is at liberty to cohabit with another man in order, if possible, to secure the desired result. Should any children be born in this way, they are recognised as the property of the husband, just as if he were the actual father.

There are a few instances where young people do not marry. On the western side of the river the kings were wont to employ eunuchs in their establishments, and as many of those were appointed as were deemed sufficient to supervise the wives in the household.

Again on the western side of the Niger, and in some parts of the eastern side, one or more daughters are retained at home for life. These are kept at home solely for the entertainment of guests. At Ibwo, for instance, where there is a family of five children or more, if the last be a daughter she is devoted to the house. Her face is tatooed with peculiar "ichi" marks and she is not allowed to marry, nor to reside anywhere but at her father's house. Children born from the various liaisons between her and her father's guests become part of her father's household.

Cognate with courtship and marriage is divorce. This is not a complicated business and depends very largely upon the mere whim of the man. A woman cannot divorce her husband; she is his property, duly paid for, and she cannot take action against her lord and master any more than one of his cows or goats.[1] Being, however, a creature endowed with human susceptibilities a woman with a little more spirit than usual may object to the condition of affairs under her husband's rule. Failing to obtain redress of her grievances, she returns home to her people. Should

[1] The custom varies somewhat in different parts of the Ibo country. In the Southern Districts a woman is considered to have fulfilled all obligations, pecuniary and otherwise, as soon as there are two of her children running about the house. If the husband gives her cause for complaint he is liable to lose her; she is at liberty to forsake him and go to another man, in which case the original husband has no means of redress.

the husband desire it he can demand her back from the relatives, and she will be forced to return. The feelings of the woman are not consulted; she has no rights to be respected, and if she acts contrary to the law of the land she must bear the consequences. The husband, however, may not desire to see her again, in which case the whole of the dowry money paid for her, plus any other expenses incurred, must be refunded on demand. As this has already been spent by the woman's relatives they manifest great reluctance in collecting the sum and, therefore, a woman who ventures to return to her relatives is liable to receive but scant sympathy from them. She is accounted a nuisance, and they will do their utmost to persuade her to return to her husband, and will, failing to attain their object by persuasion, not hesitate to resort to forcible measures.

Should the husband be the aggrieved party he orders her to leave the house, or promptly drives her out, at the same time throwing her cooking pot and one or two other personal articles after her. This procedure constitutes permanent divorce, and the action of the husband will be upheld by native law. The wife, so treated, is deprived of all property and also of her children; indeed neither ever were hers. Her only possessions are her cooking pot, market basket, and a few other small articles pertaining to the domestic side of the house. She may go where she likes, and live as she pleases; the husband ceases to take any interest in her or her affairs from that day forth, with one exception, viz. that should another man express a willingness to marry her, the original husband immediately claims full dowry money for her. Although he has cast her out like an old garment, yet she remains still his property, and he never relinquishes the hope that sooner or later, he will be able to make a profitable deal out of her re-marriage.

CHAPTER VII

IBO MEN—YOUNG AND OLD

THE controlling factor in the careers of both men and women is the state in which they are born. Everything turns on the point whether a man be bond or free. To the free-born youth all things are possible, and all ranks of society are open to him. On the other hand the slave has no rights, and whatever success he may achieve in any department of life depends entirely on the goodwill of his master. In this chapter we shall confine ourselves to the ordinary life of a free-born youth.

Freedom by birthright is a very valuable asset. Privileges and favours ensue as a matter of course, and benefits accrue from the earliest days. Between boys and girls the comparison is all in favour of the former, the latter only counting as a useful accessory in the life of a man. From the outset a youth assumes the positions of a " lord of creation " as his rightful heritage. He quickly recognises the distinction which free-birth confers upon him, and though he fraternises freely at ordinary times with the slave-born, yet he never, for one moment, loses consciousness of an inherent superiority ; it is ineradicably ingrained in his very nature. The life of an Ibo lad is also greatly influenced by the locality in which he lives. His fellow-townsmen may follow an acknowledged profession, or they may be simple farmers, fishermen or traders. The men of Awka, for example, are renowned throughout the Ibo country, and even beyond its borders, as clever blacksmiths, and they traverse the country from end to end plying their craft. These men make extended itinerations annually, a large number of towns being visited. Again the men of Nri are the priests whose presence is essential for a valid celebration of the ceremonial rites in connection with the coronation of kings, and they travel far and wide in the performance of these priestly functions. The men of Uniu-di-Awka journey from place to place practising the art of cicatrisation, they being recognised experts in the cutting of ichi or tribal marks.

A lad brought up in such a town naturally adopts the profession of his fathers. He has abundant time for recreation, as the native works only at such times as happen to be convenient to him, but the apprenticeship starts from the earliest years. As soon as ever possible the lad accompanies his elders on their journeys. Rarely is any reluctance manifested, for he knows well enough that if he is to secure any honourable position in life he must make money at all costs. In some places custom forbids even the wearing of a loincloth until he has entered the first degree of titular rank, and title-taking is expensive. Rich fathers usually provide the wherewithal to meet the cost of the lower titles, as much for the sake of their own dignity as for the benefit of the boys, but, as a rule, the youth must win his own position.

Where the men practise a useful trade—as at Awka—the majority find no great difficulty in raising the necessary funds to enable them to pass through the lower degrees of titular rank; but where farming or fishing are the prevailing occupations, but few secure the much coveted honours. As a matter of fact in a great many cases the methods adopted to collect money for the purchase of titles will not bear scrutiny.

Play and work, then, go together from the earliest days, the former predominating except at particular seasons. Up to the age of ten or twelve the boys run about in nature's garb, and are only distinguished from the other young animals in the compound by the fact that they are human. Given good health, the Ibo boy has a thoroughly happy time. Whilst enduring the infliction of yaws or kraw-kraw, he has rather a miserable experience, it is true, but having survived that stage, he allows very little to trouble him. These loathsome diseases, yaws and kraw-kraw, are deliberately induced in children by inoculation in their early years, as the natives believe no person can escape them, and that the suffering to be endured is much less in childhood than in adult life, hence the practice of inoculation. Boys associate freely with their elders, but for games they consort with their own company (otu). Their chums are always boys, and the friendships formed in boyhood's days continue throughout life. Young men do not drop each other after marriage; the wife never displaces her familiar friend. The man still turns to his old companion for counsel and as the one to whom he can confide the thoughts of his heart.

The only woman a man really trusts with his deeper confidences is his mother. No man with his wits about him would so compromise his dignity as to put himself in the power of a wife! How, too, can a woman be expected to enter into the ideas, pursuits, and affairs of men? Consequently it would be pure waste of effort, as well as folly, to discuss serious matters with womenfolk. It follows, then, that the lives of Ibo men, generally speaking, run on lines quite distinct from those of the women.

Increase of stature, the handling of tools and implements, and knowledge of the ways of men advance simultaneously. The school is the world in which the boys live day by day. By the time a youth is from twelve to fifteen years of age he has become expert in the occupations practised by his elders, and he can take a full share in any work he is called upon to do. He knows how to build, to use the hoe and the matchet, and generally to take his place as a useful member of the family and the community.

The majority of Ibo men are accustomed to work at intervals only, i.e. when necessity compels. The dry season is devoted almost entirely to leisurely pursuits. Towards its close a few casual visits are paid to the neighbouring jungle to collect supplies of ripe grass for thatch-repairing. Immediately after the grass harvest, the bush is fired and burned without discrimination, especially in such parts as are selected for cultivation. For some four months these are the only attempts at anything in the nature of real work by the men. The youths amuse themselves in various ways; the young men (Ikolobia) engage in archery contests, wrestling and other forms of sport. The old men gossip and play okwe, this leisurely life being enlivened at fairly frequent intervals by feastings or drinking bouts.

This sort of life is apt to become insipid to the young bloods, nor does it bring pecuniary benefit to them. Therefore recourse is had to fighting as an outlet for their energies. This provides action and excitement, possibly the materials for a feast, and pecuniary benefits in the form of loot. The business is easily and quickly arranged. Young braves lie in wait for stragglers from a neighbouring town, kill or capture one or two, and thereby start a feud. Throughout the remainder of the dry season raiding will be the sport in fashion, each side generally getting about equal profit from the contest. Much less damage is inflicted than the noise and excitement would lead one to expect. If the combatants have not satiated themselves, or come to terms by the end of the dry season, hostilities are postponed. With the approach of the rains, a truce is declared, both parties recognising the obligation to attend seriously to farming. To neglect this work involves the hardships of famine, which none of the combatants has either the desire or intention to endure.

The first tornado of the season is the signal for great activity for all, young and old, men and women. For a short period all work with intense zeal and energy on the farms, beginning at daylight and plodding on without rest until noon. A month of steady work brings the farm into good order, and the majority of the men-folk do not suffer from over-exertion during the next five or six months. A few work on the farms, putting in sticks for the yam vines, and later in uncurling the vines and training them to climb the sticks properly; also in earthing up the roots; but the women-folk are expected to do the greater part of the weeding and other necessary tasks whilst the crops are maturing. At harvest time the men go forth to gather in the crops and carry the yams home to be stored. When the operations in the fields are at an end and the yams and corn safely harvested, a regular time of feasting follows, commencing with the "iwa-ji" (new yam feast). Betweenwhiles the men are engaged in tying the yams, one by one, to open upright frames in such a way that wind and sun may have free access to them. Yams rot very rapidly if left lying on the ground. The yam-stack stands in a secluded part of the compound, and is penned off with a stout fence and the entrance padlocked, and no one may enter but the owner. He, himself, usually deals out the daily supplies for the household, and woe to anyone found loitering in close proximity to an awbwa, or caught in the act of robbing it.

Should building operations be contemplated, the clay for the walls must be excavated and puddled during the time of the rains. In many parts of the country clay cannot be puddled at any other time, as water for such purposes is not available. In the dry season, mud-treading, as it is commonly called, is entirely the work of men ; it is never delegated to women.

A lad shares the house accommodation with the other children of the family until the age of puberty. At this stage in his life he is allotted separate quarters which his father may provide, but which he more likely has to build for himself. It is a tiny bachelor apartment, where he sleeps, stores his treasures, and receives his special friends. When a man marries he usually starts a compound on his own account. To a certain extent he settles down in life, and if of an easy-going disposition seldom worries deeply about anything; but if he be of an ambitious turn of mind, he will apply his energies to secure a position of rank and power. He will begin by the multiplication of wives, or by taking up more advanced titles. Both are expensive affairs, but they are also investments. The initial outlay in procuring an additional wife is recovered by increased profits from trading, and, as a duly qualified member of the society which confers a specified title for cash, he receives his share of the entrance fees paid by all new members—a dividend that never decreases. A favourable beginning having been made the man steadily pursues his course and endeavours to obtain the remaining higher degrees of titular rank. The system of native "titles" is worthy of special study, and is dealt with at greater length in a later chapter (XXIV). Every free-born youth on arrival at full age (puberty) becomes a recognised citizen and is bound to bear his share in all that pertains to the welfare of his town in times of peace and war. He must contribute to the public feasts and pay taxes levied for religious, social or other purposes. He must give his services in times of special need, and also subscribe his allotted share towards the maintenance of the dignity of the paramount chief, as well as serving the head of his own family. This service may be rendered in money, as when the chief is desirous of proceeding to a higher title or is erecting a new house. He will also co-operate in building schemes and in farm-work—all such service of course being given gratuitously. Ordinarily a son is at his father's disposal one day per week, i.e. every fourth day.

The professional men, as already noted, travel extensively during the greater part of the year. When they return with their gains, a regular round of title-taking and feasting ensues. Enormous quantities of palm wine and, where procurable, gin are consumed, very often both. The amount these men are able to drink is prodigious. Equally astonishing is the rapidity with which the liquor disappears. The one who cannot drink his four to six consecutive bumpers of palm wine, or a measure of neat gin at one draught, is regarded as unworthy to mix with men ; he is still in the apprentice stage. I have been present at assemblies and have watched the men range themselves around the pots and demijohns of wine. There is no talking or sound of revelry at this stage. For the most part they sit in silence, all eyes turned towards the pots, the whole proceeding apparently being a serious business needing concentration and endurance, and it is a gross breach of etiquette for any member to depart or shirk his turn until every vessel is drained. One of the party acts as potman, and the cup, horn or calabash is passed to each in turn in order of seniority, and round and round the cup travels until the whole supply is consumed. They scarcely seem to drink ; the liquid simply disappears as though poured through a funnel. I allude here to fresh palm wine or, at any rate, such as is not more than twenty-four hours old. When allowed to ferment, it is too bitter to be a popular drink, and though seldom refused, it is not taken with great relish, and the consumption is limited to very small quantities as compared with the fresh wine. Where gin is the standard drink, regular drinking clubs are sometimes formed. It is not an uncommon practice for men to chew raw pepper in order to harden the palate, and thus enable them to endure the burning sensation of neat spirit without undue inconvenience. Gin-drinking is naturally much more prevalent in the coast districts and in the river-side towns lying between the sea and the prohibited area line than in the upper Ibo and back bush districts, where the people rely chiefly on palm wine; but they all prefer gin whenever it can be procured. (Cf. Chap. II).

The men, young and old, are quite as fond of bodily adornment and display as the women; in fact, they outrival the women in vanity and conceit. The young men are partial to circlets of ivory worn just below the knees, while the old and rich men carry a whole series of them on the arms. On the western side of the Niger, chiefs often wear huge ivory anklets also. Necklaces of elephants' "eye-brows" (really whiskers or tail hairs), corals and one or more aggry beads threaded on a string are always fashionable. The garments donned on a gala day baffle description; they are many and various, often ludicrous and always incongruous.

For the Ibo man the necessities of life are very few. After securing his hut he has need only to make sure of his implements for tilling the soil, fishing, or for practising his trade. He values any article that will serve as a garment or that can be made to hang on the body somehow. He also regards the possession of a few fowls and a goat or two as essential to the completion of a household, and, if he be a man of rank, some cows. A gun is his greatest treasure, however, and the Ibo will do anything to procure one. The multiplication of wives and an abundance of children are visions which every young man sees and hopes to realise in due course. In addition to money, in the form of cowries, brass rods or English cash, all sorts of articles are objects of value, e.g. odd pieces of rusty chains, empty (and dirty) old demijohns and old iron cannons, the last being in great demand for second burial ceremonies. In the house of one old chief of my acquaintance there is a miscellaneous collection of old iron, the supreme place being given to the stump end of an old bedstead which is now scarcely more than a pattern in rust. Toby-jugs of more or less ancient date, monkey-bottles, earthenware soup-plates, dishes and ornaments are all held in high esteem, and in past days were very expensive objects of art because of the long distances they had to be carried and the continuous risk of loss by breakage and theft.

The eldest son succeeds absolutely to all property of his father. He takes over all the household effects, also his father's wives, and, with the exception of his own mother, he treats them as his own wives. He may keep them all, or he may dispose of some to other men for the sake of the dowry money. If the women are old, however, they settle down quietly to their own devices in the compound, and are not often disturbed by the new head of the household.

But he not only inherits his father's property; with it he inherits his father's liabilities and also any which may have been handed down from his grandfather. The settling of ancient debts—perhaps three generations old—is a very intricate business, and a young man may find himself in an undesirable, and even critical position, owing to his being suddenly confronted with a debt contracted years before by his grandfather, the repayment of which has not become easier by lapse of time—the money-lender sees to that.

Under the old conditions of affairs, i.e. before civilian influences made themselves felt, old men were treated with great respect, and the chiefs were held in the highest honour and were accorded implicit obedience. Any infringement of the rules of etiquette towards them met with severe reprisals. At the same time fathers exercise very slight control over their sons, and discipline is utterly lacking. For a father to chastise his son, is quite unusual; most fathers would not entertain such a proposal. They will not punish even in cases where their offspring thoroughly deserve a sound thrashing. One has known instances where boys have been terrors to the household and still the parents would not take a strong line to bring the young rascals to order. The explanation is that the father stands in mortal dread lest he should incur the lasting displeasure of his son—especially of the eldest one—for on his son depends his own salvation. If his son hates him how is he to be given an honourable and worthy burial? With what marks of distinction will he enter the "Land of Spirits" if his son remain at enmity with him? This being the case, the father endures the misdemeanours of his son rather than risk incurring that son's displeasure, and thereby putting in jeopardy his status in the future life.

Mention has already been made (Chap. V.) of the great mortality amongst children. The law of the survival of the fittest continues to operate in later years, and the susceptibility to fall out of the ranks is very marked amongst the youth of the country. It is extraordinary how the young people die off, pneumonia and dysentery being responsible for great numbers of deaths. Those who do survive are blessed with sound constitutions and there are many very aged people amongst the Ibos.

During the progress of special functions one watches the ancient cronies with mixed feelings. They attempt to dance and show off their paces as if they were still lusty young athletes, in spite of their uncertain gait and tottering steps. Old men who normally do little but eat, sleep and gossip, on these public occasions prance about, flourish their spear-headed staves, strike them viciously into the ground, and assume the fiercest of expressions, and will exert every ounce of their well-nigh spent force in order to demonstrate that they are still worthy of their place. Their object is to insist on the spectators recognising the fact. The display would be sublimely ridiculous were it not so woefully pathetic. Then comes the end. At last the old man is quite played out and he simply dodders along until the spark of life departs. He has lived his life, perhaps on the whole a peaceful one, but not lacking in exciting episodes, and certainly without the restraints and worries that civilization inevitably entails. He has probably never experienced the pressure of circumstances. Every aged veteran can relate his stories of the brave days of old and his tales of high adventure. It is doubtful if one could be found whose hands have not been steeped in blood. In his day he has lived fast and loose; probably he has been slaver and cannibal, and now he resigns himself to the inevitable and waits patiently the hour to join his old comrades in the spirit world. His last solemn wish is that the funeral rites shall be on such a scale that he may be spared all feelings of shame when he meets his former companions. He desires to have such marks of honour paid him at his death as will be equivalent to those he has enjoyed in life.

CHAPTER VIII

IBO WOMEN AND THEIR WAYS

As in the case of men, the question whether they be free-born or not largely determines the position occupied throughout life by Ibo women. It concerns them chiefly in the matter of marriage, inasmuch as, in most parts, a free-born youth will, on no account, take a slave woman to wife, although it is not unknown for a man to redeem a slave in order to marry her. A woman in a state of slavery, whether by birth, capture, or purchase, is in a very unenviable position. In this chapter we shall touch upon the lives of free-born women only. Bond and free have one characteristic in common, viz. they are the burden-bearers of the country. Women have but few rights in any circumstances, and can only hold such property as their lords permit. There is no grumbling against their lot; they accept the situation as their grandmothers did before them and, taking affairs philosophically, they manage to live fairly contentedly.

Passing from the infant stage, girls immediately enter upon a life of service, and are allowed such a share in feminine affairs as their size and strength allow. They are little more than babies themselves when they are given the care of the younger children. From the age of four they begin to acquire the art of balancing articles on the head. Carrying a tiny waterpot they accompany the elder girls to the spring. By the time they are nine or ten they are regularly employed in fetching supplies of water. They take part daily in such duties as the sweeping of the compound, the rubbing of the house, the collecting of firewood, and the preparation of food.

Soon after daylight the womenfolk leave the house in

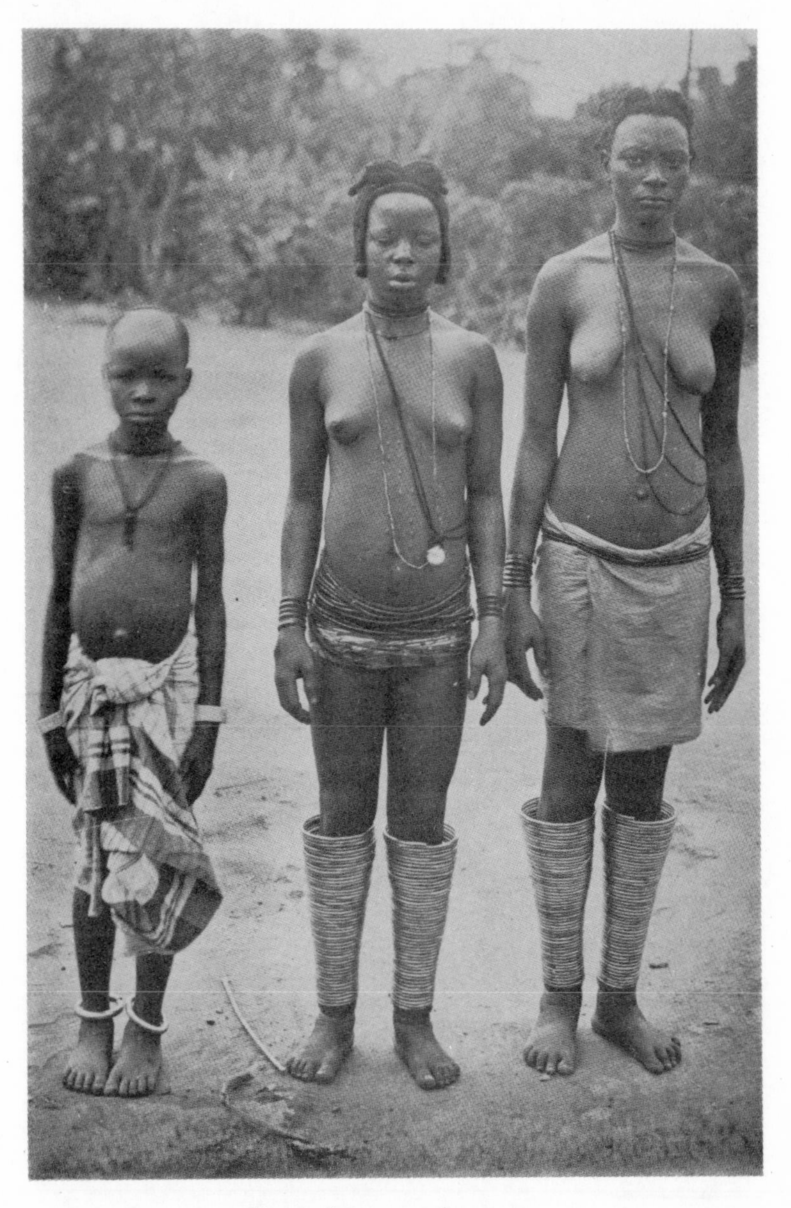

Three Stages of Girlhood

The graduated brass spirals on the legs are very heavy, and bandages are wrapped round the ankles to prevent chafing.

order to bring in the morning supply of water. This may occupy anything up to two hours or even more, according to the distance they have to travel, the supply sometimes being a long way from the village.

They next proceed to clean up the house and compound. The floors and walls of the huts are composed of reddish clay beaten hard. By persistent rubbing a polished surface is obtained, the process also acting as a preservative. The men build the walls ; the women finish them. Some rich coloured earth (upa) is taken from a pit and rubbed through the hands with a copious supply of water. A piece of rotten banana leaf is rolled into a pad and with it the liquid is freely applied to walls and floor, and the whole thoroughly well rubbed. If the wall be rather new or rough it will be worked down to an even surface with pieces of cocoanut shell, but once a smooth surface is secured it is only necessary to polish with clay water. Some of the houses are beautifully polished and are quite works of art. Women of artistic temperament take an immense amount of trouble and stain the walls with striking colours, washing in a variety of patterns with wide sweeping movements. Considerable ingenuity is shown, and no little skill, in manipulating the primitive pad in order to produce many of the coloured designs. Of course, these decorative schemes are not daily affairs ; they are reserved for days when there is plenty of time for the purpose. The daily morning rub covers only the floor of the house and any parts of the walls that may happen to be soiled.

Domestic occupations being accomplished, the little girls are free to play and revel in the sand and sunshine for the greater part of the day. When they get tired they curl themselves up in a shady spot and go to sleep. On market days practically the whole female population move to the market-place, either to trade or to enjoy the general entertainment such gatherings afford. Ibo women cannot keep away from the native market any more than English women can be kept away from Regent Street. They are the most inveterate bargain hunters ; indeed, marketing, together with the preparation of food, constitutes the chief occupation—nay, the very life, of the women. They haggle over prices in a manner which suggest that the contest will be decided by blows. On all sides shrill strident voices are raised to the highest pitch, every word being emphasized with violent gestures. Goods are handled, examined, approved or condemned and sometimes thrown down again, to show contempt for the price demanded, and altogether the market appears to be a veritable pandemonium. No article of any value has a fixed price; exchanges are arranged only after long bouts of bargaining. Small perishable commodities are the only items that are cleared off without much fuss towards the close of the market.

Practically the whole of the trade in the Ibo country is in the hands of thc women, and they are extremely capable. The more expert a woman proves herself to be, the more is she appreciated by her husband. Ability in this direction is always a desideratum in a man's choice of a wife. The apprenticeship begins early as already noticed, viz. from childhood itself. On arrival at full age the girl is provided with her own basket, and she begins to trade more or less independently. In the domestic affairs of life it works out that the men-folk hold themselves responsible for the yam supply, whilst the women provide all the extras, fish, oil, peppers, and other luxuries; they are the purveyors of the salt and savour of the men's lives!

Ibo women are but little concerned with dress, and in this respect they differ rather from the men. The reason is twofold. In the first place women's apparel is never found in any interior market and but very recently at places where there are trading factories. In the second place the men always put an embargo on feminine apparel, and, until recently, have deliberately barred the use of clothing. On the western side of the Niger the fashion is a small white loin-cloth and a sort of shawl thrown loosely round the shoulders, both woven by the women themselves from native-grown cotton. Sometimes the cloth is of sufficient size to cover the body from just beneath the armpits to the knees. On the eastern side it is the custom for girls to go entirely naked up to (and sometimes after) marriage. In places like Onitsha and Asaba the girls now refuse to comply with the injunctions against the use of dress, and, as the country is opened up, they will become obsolete altogether. In certain parts the women, old and young, rich and poor, married and single, pass their whole lives in a state of nudity. On reaching the age of puberty a piece of fine cotton string is worn loosely round the loins to indicate the fact, and this is later discarded for a more permanent circlet of spring-coiled brass wire (called awna-idide, i.e. brass worm). After marriage a shred of cloth is added and this completes the outfit. Later the awna-idide is exchanged for a string of black beads of a particular pattern called the "nkpulu-ife." This is never removed as long as the woman's husband is alive, except for purification purposes, and even this is not essential.

On the other hand ornaments are highly esteemed even when they are in the nature of inflictions, and the wearing of them entails actual suffering. Most towns have their own peculiar fashions in this respect. In the neighbourhood of Nleggi no woman is happy till she is the proud possessor of a pair of enormous brass anklets (awbwa). These are beaten out of solid bar brass and then fixed round the leg by a blacksmith, and a smith is required to remove them. Once hammered on they are permanent evidences of deluded vanity, and from that hour the wearer can never again stand, sit or lie in a normal position. These plate-like ornaments may be anything from nine to fifteen inches in diameter. When walking one leg must be swung clear of the other in a semicircle, partly in order to swing the weight, and partly to prevent one foot tripping over the anklet of the other. It is a curious spectacle to watch a procession of women wearing these atrocious ornaments. The anklets are kept highly polished and flash brightly in the sun as the wearers move along with the extraordinary swinging gait entailed by the cumbersome brasses. In well-to-do families quite little girls are burdened with anklets of a size considered suitable for their age. In due time the smaller anklets are removed in favour of full-sized ones. The striking feature is the dexterous way the women clear their feet in walking; they rarely clash the brasses one against the other.

More widespread are the brass leg rings. For the complete outfit these are graduated in size from the anklet upwards, the number of rings being dependent upon the size of the girl. Up to a certain age the rings must finish below the knee; at full age they must extend above the knee. These spirals (nza) are made from the brass rods common in some districts as currency. The rods are welded together and turned into spirals—each being slightly larger than the one below, the top one having a diameter of about nine inches. One set of nza that I examined contained thirty-five rods to each spiral and were many pounds in weight. These are worn prior to marriage—never after. Further, they are worn at certain seasons only and then but for short periods, the chief times being when the young lady is particularly desirous of exhibiting her graces! She spends much time at the waterside scouring the brasses with leaves and sands. This is done daily as the brasses tarnish very rapidly in this climate.

But the most valuable, and the most prized of all forms of ornaments, are the anklets and bracelets of ivory. These can only be worn by rich women or by such as are of high rank. They are simply sections of huge elephant tusks. The anklets are about nine inches in depth by from two to three inches in thickness; the bracelets vary in size, some being large and clumsy. Once these are on the limbs (they are forced over feet or hands after a course of powerful massage with oil) they are not removed till death. Young women during their course in nkpu sometimes wear ivory bracelets right up the arm, but this is quite a temporary arrangement. With the older women these ivories are priceless treasures, and they will endure any hardships in preference to degrading themselves by selling them, however great the inducement may be.

In all cases the anklets are very heavy and it is astonishing that they can be endured at all. To prevent sores from chafing, old rags are bound round the ankles.

There are other smaller ornaments, but all more or less alike. Copper bracelets and anklets are common, though worn by men more than women. Necklaces are always fashionable, the most usual being a single string on which one or more aggry beads are threaded, and necklaces composed of elephants' hairs or imitations thereof. Occasionally hair pins of burnished iron are worn, more especially in communities of which the male members are blacksmiths.

The only possessions that can really be labelled as the property of a wife are her waterpot, market basket and calabash, together with her cooking utensils, and all the vegetable called koko (edde). She helps to purchase other household requisites and has free use of them ; she may also accumulate extra things in her own corner. On her death her eldest son, not her husband, will inherit these personal items. As long as both she and her husband live she must continue to provide her due proportion of food for him in conjunction with the other wives. Where husband and wife live happily together the former will, at intervals, present his wife with a piece of cloth as a mark of special favour.

A wife is granted a certain amount of private accommodation in the compound, usually to the extent of a hut for the use of herself and her children. At the same time her happiness and prosperity rest entirely on the goodwill of her husband. She fears her husbands gods, but may not touch or worship them. Her own objects of worship, as will be noted later, are of the most primitive character, consisting of little more than lumps of shapeless clay.

The women take their full share in farm-work, assisting in turning the soil and moulding up the yam beds. After the yam seed has been set they hoe up the weeds and keep the farm in order. They tend their children, trade in the markets, prepare palm-oil, and manage all domestic affairs. Hence, in one way and another, the women find sufficient work to keep them well occupied, but it is very seldom that they show the slightest disposition to hurry over anything ; they take life very leisurely, and what is not done is quietly left undone. On the whole the women are cheery and bright but their lives run in a hopeless groove—the outcome of generations of monotonous routine. As children, no marked difference is noticeable between boys and girls as regards capacity for learning, but after the age of ten or eleven the girls are so much occupied with their daily tasks that they have little time or inclination for intellectual pursuits. Moreover, the rigid conservative habits of their relatives and friends are a strong restraining force against the adoption of new ideas. Unless a girl can read before she is twenty it is safe to assume that she will never learn at all. This will serve to illustrate the uniformly low level of intellectual attainment with which Ibo women are satisfied. On the other hand they are endowed with a sense of humour and readily respond to a joke. The most striking fact perhaps about the women is that they are all so extraordinarily alike. They are intensely conservative in their habits and ideas, and to know one is to know all. Ibo women select their companions from their own sex, as do the men, but each has her own particular male friend, independently of her husband, with whom a more or less clandestine relationship is maintained. In all the ordinary affairs of life, however, women consort with women. When passing to and from market, or fetching water, they go in companies, invariably walking in single file. This habit arises from the fact that it is considered unsafe to travel alone, and also from the nature of the paths which are too narrow for two persons to walk abreast. The old custom still prevails even on the good trunk roads that are being constructed in the country. The women have their own clubs or societies. On one occasion I had the opportunity of watching a crowd of women making preparations for a meeting. The peculiar feature about it was the fact that they were dressed up as men; they wore men's hats and, in some cases, coats; the breasts were bound down close to the body by crossover straps and each member flourished a cutlass in her hand, and in every way they could they imitated men. In every town there is a sort of committee of women which controls all women's affairs and exercises great influence in various directions. The leader is chosen, and a ceremonial crowning is performed by a nri (priest), similar to the coronation rites observed in the making of a king. The woman chosen is known as the "awmu," a title equivalent to queen. She is never the wife of the king. One does not often see the crown nowadays; instead a man's hat is worn; no other woman may wear a hat. She is assisted by a limited number of members who take precedence according to age and rank, all of them having taken one or more titles. In the markets the awmu usually sits on a special stool, in a corner reserved specially for her, wearing her hat, and probably with chalk rings around her eyes. She receives queenly oblations and many tokens of respect in the way of small gifts (ojji).

The committee further controls everything in the town relating to women. In judging cases where both men and women are involved the chiefs must call upon the members of the committee for their opinions and assistance. The committee makes its own laws for the women of the town irrespective of the men. The chief wife of a man attains automatically the rank corresponding to that of her husband. Every degree to which he advances is bestowed simultaneously upon his wife; as he adds an additional title-cord around his ankle so the chief wife must add a similar cord around her ankle. Any neglect to observe this custom leads to friction, as the wife is then charged with failing to uphold the proper style and dignity of her husband.

Hairdressing is almost exclusively confined to women: and the results are much more elaborate than anything attempted by men. The fashion for prospective brides has been commented upon in Chap. VI, but that deals with a particular instance only. Locality fixes the mode, and age limits the period during which a woman takes special pride in her hair. The hair, in itself, signifies much and great pains are taken to secure a flourishing growth, as it is reckoned to possess great powers of attraction for the opposite sex. Until the age of self-consciousness and personal vanity is reached the hair receives but scanty attention, but between this age and until a few years after marriage many Ibo women exercise all their arts, and spend much time in hairdressing. In middle age and later life such vanities are cast aside and they revert to the natural woolly-headed state. Plaiting is a pronounced feature in the majority of styles and this is more or less highly developed according to local taste. Very few hairs are taken at a time and these are pulled and stretched, and then very tightly plaited into a threefold strand. The plaits are well rubbed with a mixture of powdered charcoal and oil, and then they are plastered into position on the scalp. In some parts this is the mode; in other parts after the plaiting process, the hair is combed out into puffs. In any case the arrangement is elaborate and evinces considerable artistic skill.

In connection with trade, farm-work and the water supply, women are called upon to carry heavy loads. They are borne upon the head except at times when the hair has been specially dressed as stated above, in which case the burden is carried on the shoulders. On the western side of the river a king's first wife must not carry loads upon her head. This exemption distinguishes between her and the other women. The women on the whole are strong and sturdy. When young they are very graceful and upright, a trait largely due, no doubt, to this custom of balancing loads upon the head, and promoted by the practice of lying flat on a hard surface when sleeping, usually without any other pillow than the forearm. Old women enjoy the doubtful privilege of being allowed to use a half-section of the husk of a cocoanut as a pillow.

After marriage the women deteriorate in appearance at a remarkably rapid rate and often look old by the time they reach their twenty-fifth year. They are inclined to become stout and slow-moving, and soon settle down to their humdrum existence. Between twenty-five and forty-five there is but little noticeable change, and even after that age it is difficult to discriminate until the white hairs begin to manifest themselves among the black.

Women often live to extreme old age. They continue their labours as long as strength permits. As a rule their declining days are spent in leisurely quietness, for they are generally respected and are seldom in danger of losing the affections of the younger members of the family circle.

A Proud Trio

Prospective brides of chiefs. The necklaces are of leopard's teeth and aggry beads. The staves and ivory bracelets are loans from their future husbands.

CHAPTER IX

POLYGAMY AND SLAVERY

Polygamy. This institution is inseparably bound up with the family and social life of the Ibos and, without exception, touches the lives of every man and woman in the country. Polygamy is favoured and fostered equally by men and women; in some respects the latter are the chief supporters of the system. It is well to remember this fact, especially in dealing with any attempt to solve the many problems that arise from the custom. The ambition of every Ibo man is to become a polygamist, and he adds to the number of his wives as circumstances permit. They are an indication of social standing and, to some extent, signs of affluence; in any case, they are counted as sound investments.

Whilst polygamy is recognised as an integral part of the social economy of the Ibos, yet in actual fact one wife only is specifically acknowledged. In native law the first wife alone is granted the position and rights of a legal wife. She alone bears the title of "anasi" and, in virtue thereof, is accorded a measure of respect vastly superior to that given to any of the additional wives. Her standing also endows her with a powerful influence over the life and affairs of her husband.

She, as anasi, is the priestess of the gods "ekwu" (small conical arrangements of moulded clay). These are kept in the apartments where she reigns supreme and none but she may serve them; it is her personal and sacred right as first and only legal wife.

In all public affairs, such as the taking of title, festivals, dancing and so forth, anasi enjoys privileges which are totally denied to all the other wives. On these occasions she only is recognised and is embraced by the husband, and she receives equivalent honour and respect with him, the other wives remaining quite in the background.

During the celebration of feasts to the "ilaw maw" (spirit worship), the husband will offer no food to the alusi (idols) other than that prepared by anasi. In every way the distinction between the first wife and the others is clearly defined, showing that, in principle, the Ibo recognises but one legal wife.

The first wife is obtained either by direct payment of the dowry by the man himself, or is a gift from his parents. In the latter case she may be years older than the lad and be the mother of several children before he is old enough to fulfil the functions of a husband.

A first wife retains her position throughout life; she dominates the household and has more or less control over all other wives who may be added to the establishment. The second wife may be taken at the instigation of the first, and with her active co-operation, or the man may act on his own initiative. This generally follows after the birth of the first child. It is not only a matter of disgrace, but an actual abomination (nsaw), for an Ibo woman to bear children at shorter intervals than about three years. Should she be so unfortunate as to do so the first child is in danger of being cast away and abandoned on the ground that it would be a hindrance to the second. The idea of a fixed minimum period between births is based on several sound principles. The belief prevails strongly that it is necessary for this interval to elapse in order to ensure the mother being able to recuperate her strength completely, and thus be in a thoroughly fit condition to bear another child. Should a second child be born within the proscribed period the theory is held that it must inevitably be weak and sickly, and its chances jeopardised, as no mother is considered capable of nourishing two children simultaneously. Artificial feeding is unknown, hence there can be no relief for the mother from the duty of suckling her child. There are herds of cows and goats, but neither are ever milked, and, if they were, the Ibo would not make use of the milk, the very idea being disgustingly repulsive to the native mind.

The result is that, after the birth of a child, the wife is not supposed to cohabit with her husband for a lengthy period, and theoretically (but by no means in fact), they live separate lives. This state of affairs does not satisfy the man and he seeks to remedy it by procuring another wife. This action will engender no jealousy on the part of number one; indeed, as stated above, she most probably suggests the idea, and will gladly assist in raising the dowry money.

There is another aspect of the case for polygamy, viz. that a woman is not content to remain the sole wife of a man. An only wife considers herself placed in an unenviable and humiliating position. It is also lonely, as the sexes are not companions one to another. Again, as the sole wife she has to bear the whole of the domestic burdens of the household, and that prospect does not appeal to her. Therefore, for the sake of companionship, and to secure relief in her daily tasks, the first wife will willingly render assistance in bringing a second into the establishment. The average number is from three to five. Some men, perforce, must be content with one, whilst rich men, and especially kings and chiefs, will increase the number up to twenty and, in certain instances, they have numbered nearer two hundred. The great point to bear in mind is that the system is supported by both sexes.

In order for polygamy to exist at all there must be more women than men. This, no doubt, is the case, but the system does not depend upon that fact. Whether more girls are born than boys is rather a matter of speculation than of exact observation, and I am reluctant to express an opinion, but from personal experience I am inclined to affirm that girls do preponderate. In almost every household visited one is struck by the number of girls as compared with boys. Then from the age of ten upwards the liability to death is greater amongst males owing to war, dangers encountered whilst travelling, and such-like causes. Hence were monogamy the rule a large number of women must, necessarily, remain unmarried. No Ibo woman would tolerate that condition. She would be exposed to every form of contempt and persecution, as well as obliged to suffer the bitter shame of her outraged feelings. The men, on their part, would declaim against the rule on the ground that it is contrary to nature, and to the practice of their fathers. It would be a deliberate attempt to frustrate the very purpose for which women are created. The primeval instinct to exercise and multiply is in overwhelming evidence amongst the Ibo people; it is really the controlling factor of their lives, the *motif* of their existence

One factor put forward in support of the multiplication of wives is rather ingenious. In theory women are regarded as inferior creatures, little better than other household property, but in daily life they hold a strongly entrenched position, the key of which is food. Every married woman holds the whip hand over her husband by means of this vital weapon. A crossed woman will torment her husband in galling manner by refusing to prepare food for him, He may resent the treatment by becoming furiously angry and by vigorous corporal punishment, but neither satisfies his appetite, and he feels keenly the insult of having to retire to bed supperless. To avoid these little domestic difficulties a man argues that it is diplomatic, if only for his stomach's sake, to have a second string to his bow. He can then have a more certain hope of getting his meals from at least one. If one be suffering from a fit of the sulks he can play off the other against her, or again, if one fall sick, there will be the other to minister to his necessities. On the food question the women are the acknowledged masters of the situation, and the men, in order to secure the daily meals, turn to polygamy as one of the means to that end. In the hands of the philistines the men are helpless, and the women can starve them into meekness unless they can successfully create a division in the camp, in which case the wives who rally round the husband will be disposed to minister with even greater care and indulgence than usual in attending to his physical requirements.

There is one particularly insidious evil in connection

with polygamy which is the root of much ill-feeling and jealousy, and is responsible for a tremendous amount of adultery. This is the inflation of dowries. In some parts the abuse is becoming notorious. Poor men cannot obtain wives, or can only marry them after years of toil and effort. The chiefs and rich men are practically creating corners in wives ; fathers are tempted to increase the amount of the dowry and, consequently, the rich men are accumulating wives oftentimes far in excess of their ability to control them. A custom exists whereby young girls are presented by their guardians to men who occupy positions of authority in order to win favour or assistance in some business—legal or otherwise. They are offered and accepted as gifts, the donors expecting to receive certain benefits in exchange in lieu of money. It is a pernicious state of affairs. It acts as a bar to the marriage of the young, virile men ; it creates dissatisfaction amongst the young wives as they are not prepared to endure married life simply as the appendages of one who, too often, is a more or less decrepit old man, and the result is an unprecedented increase in illicit intercourse. Sometimes this is merely tolerated ; at other times this promiscuous relationship between wives and outside men is systematised—certainly encouraged—for the sake of monetary gain.

In spite of the admitted evils of polygamy, yet, as matters stand, a general introduction of monogamy would, for a time, be attended with serious difficulties from political and social standpoints. It would lead to wholesale illegitimacy. One doubts whether a single case amongst the heathen can be quoted of an Ibo woman attempting—or even manifesting the slightest inclination—to live a celibate life. Her constant yearning is for a home and children of her own. She will strive for the latter though she be deprived of the former ; so long as polygamy exists she can have both. All elements of shame or dishonour, are, thereby, avoided, and she prefers the protection of a husband's name even though she be but a subsidiary wife. Hence proposals from any source to eradicate the system are bound to meet with strenuous opposition from both sexes. That so many are, at the present time, practising monogamy, is due solely to the revolutionising power of Christianity.

The Government recognises the custom of the country. Native marriage is valid and there are no restrictions as to the number of wives a man may own. Should a man, however, marry under Government regulations, whether in church or before a registrar, he places himself under the marriage ordinance of the Protectorate. In these circumstances if he marry another wife he lays himself open to prosecution for bigamy. This obstacle, however, is easily surmounted. When such a man desires a second wife he marries her native fashion. This time he ignores the registrar and skilfully contrives to evade the official regulations. He obstinately refuses to admit that she is his wife; she is his concubine—as flagrant an example of a distinction without a difference as could be invented.

Then no Ibo woman dares to charge her husband with bigamy be the case ever so scandalous. For one thing she does not seriously resent the introduction of another wife, but a more potent reason by far is that she is not prepared to risk losing home, *and*, in practice, though not legally, her children. She is fully aware that she would deprive herself of any further chance of marrying again. She might procure a divorce from her husband, and, if married under Government regulations he might be punished, but she, herself, must bear the consequences also. She is not prepared to sacrifice her all, and it is not difficult to understand her policy.

In itself there can be no question that polygamy is a deadly evil, blighting to the mind, degrading to the body, and a factor to be taken into serious consideration as regards population. The paucity of children in polygamous households is notorious—the theories being completely upset by the facts. The following are examples culled from amongst one's own acquaintances. A. has nine wives; from all of them but one daughter survives. B. has probably twenty (the Ibo has a rooted objection to stating exact numbers, all he will answer is "some," "few," "many"), wives; only one son bears his name and a few daughters. C. has several wives—no son at all, and only about as many daughters as there are wives. D. has more than three wives, but only one child. E. has five wives with three children between them. F. has as many wives as his compound can accommodate, but only three sons, and they are of a degenerate type—a type, indeed, which no form of imprisonment or flogging has been able to subjugate.

Of course, in some compounds the children are numerous, perhaps twenty or thirty, or even more, but, according to the number of wives, there should be a great many more, i.e. taking the average for each wife as four or five. Moreover in the majority of cases the polygamous husband is not the actual parent of many of the children who call him "father." The inevitable outcome of the system, as already stated, is practically unrestricted adultery; condemned unreservedly in theory, but condoned and often deliberately fostered in practice.

The custom is productive of bestiality, and the dulling effect on the mind is such that a polygamist is rarely capable of any real mental attainment, and certainly of none demanding strain for a lengthened period. Efforts to teach some of these men the elements of reading and writing have met with the poorest success. Frequently it leads to the spread of disease, and the children, who so often have to bear in their bodies the effects of the sins of their parents, demonstrate what a blot upon the community is the system of polygamy. One is bound to acknowledge that exceedingly unpleasant facts can be marshalled in connection with social evils in monogamous countries, but no one hesitates to denounce them as perilous and deadly in their effects. Witness also the earnest endeavours, parliamentary and otherwise, to check, and where possible, to eradicate from the community the root causes of these putrefying sores. In polygamous countries the dangers are wholesale and widespread, leading to the propagation of disease and the maintenance of a low standard of life.

There is another point which should not be overlooked in studying polygamy. Although the taking of additional wives may be a matter of mutual consent, yet, after a time, it is apt to lead to violent outbursts of jealousy involving not infrequently danger to life. So long as the husband assumes an impartial attitude to *all* the wives, or, if any special favour be shown, it be towards the head wife, then affairs run fairly smoothly. Domestic brawls among the women, however, will and do break out in a polygamous household, leading to fighting and general disturbance of the peace, but the husband leaves them to their own devices unless matters become serious, in which case he acts vigorously and some of them will quickly have cause to regret rousing the wrath of their lord and master. Every polygamist husband admits, without exception in my experience, that jealousy is a terrible curse to the system, and complains of the quarrels that arise amongst the wives and the children of the different mothers.

So great is the friction and suspicion that the common practice is for the mother of the heir to send her son to friends at a distance as the only way to ensure his safety till he can succeed to his inheritance. Every wife covets the heirship for her son and, should opportunity present itself, the temptation to remove a rival claimant is likely to prove too much for her, hence the necessity of sending the rightful heir away to a temporary home, where his life and interests will be safely guarded from the jealous machinations of the rival mothers.

Until the advent of the British, slavery was rampant amongst the Ibos. In earlier days great numbers of these people were transported to America, the West Indies, and to other places, and traces of their language and customs are said still to survive amongst the negroes in those countries. Many Sierra Leonians are descendants of Ibo stock. The first settled foreigner at Onitsha was a missionary, the son of Ibo parents, originally slaves, who after rescue were landed at Freetown. The suppression of the overseas traffic did not lead to prohibition in the interior, and slave dealing continued to exist until the operations became more and more restricted. Under the rigorous methods now in force the day cannot be far distant when slavery will be utterly abolished.

There are distinct differences between the customs of the Ibos proper and those of their neighbours in the Niger Delta. In the case of the latter slavery has led to the formation of what are termed "houses." A house may contain anything up to three hundred people or more, all rendering allegiance to the head (father). This form is not found amongst the Ibos.

Four principal methods prevailed for recruiting the supply of slaves, viz. capture in war, kidnapping, purchase and pawning. The first and second were the more lucrative but involved personal risk; the third was a purely business transaction. The slave was either bought outright, or he was made over to settle some financial claim, human beings being used as a medium of exchange whenever it appeared to be the most convenient method. The last was the custom in vogue as a debtor's last resource to meet his liabilities. In this case the "pawn's" position, and the length of his detention as a slave, were determined by the ability and willingness of his relatives to redeem him.

Internecine warfare was a regular part of life. On the slightest pretext one town would attack the next, regardless of the fact that the inhabitants were of kindred race. If they fought simply amongst themselves any captives taken were either killed and eaten, or sold as slaves, or set aside to serve as human sacrifices. It was not unusual, however, for the people of one town to hire mercenaries to assist them in their operations, and these mercenaries appropriated the major portion of the loot, including the captives, as part compensation for services rendered. Such were the dreaded Abams on the eastern side of the Niger and the Ekmu-meku on the western side.

A much more insidious method of obtaining slaves is that of kidnapping, a practice which at one time terrorised the whole country, and the fear of which is so ingrained that a long period will elapse before its effects are totally eradicated. Men lie in ambush and pounce upon any unwary individuals who happen to stray beyond the safety-limits of their own town. Formerly it was highly dangerous for folk to venture even as far as their farms, or for traders to travel from place to place, unless they journeyed in companies, were well-armed and kept diligent watch. In spite of all precautionary measures, great numbers of men and women were seized, and the possibility of being kidnapped practically prevented towns from enjoying peaceful intercourse one with another for any lengthened period.

Man-stealing was not limited to chance captures in farms or on the highway. It was carried to greater excesses by fearless and unscrupulous burglars whose speciality was the stealing of children. Observations were made to discover a hut wherein it was customary for children to sleep, and in the dead of night it would be raided. If an entrance were effected any elders present were in imminent danger of being ruthlessly murdered in order to prevent the town being aroused and, particularly, to ensure that none should be left to reveal the identity of the thieves.

The children were gagged and bound and carried off, rolled in cloth or slipped into a bag. The number of slaves originally procured by this process was extraordinary, and one is continually meeting with young fellows who have not the remotest idea of the identity of their parents or birthplace. All they know is that they were kidnapped in their infancy. The majority were sold as ordinary slaves, others were purchased specially for consecration to the alusi (town deities). Some of the latter were horribly mutilated. One has seen lads with mouths so distorted by gags that they were rendered permanently incapable of clear utterance; eyes injured until they were almost sightless, and legs broken and left to set in distorted positions, these atrocities having been inflicted to prevent escape. Slaves thus consecrated to the alusi are attached to no household; they must live within the precincts of the ju-ju house, and effective measures were, therefore, taken to ensure compliance with this rule.

The third method, viz. purchase, needs no explanation. In most towns of any importance and boasting a reputable market, slaves formed part of the regular merchandise.

A slave had no rights of person or property. He could be sold for cash, or given as payment of a debt, or simply handed over to a new master in order to procure a favour;

in fact he could be disposed of in any manner his owner chose. When slaves were required for sacrificial purposes, or burial ceremonies, they were usually purchased. Some of those dedicated to the alusi were also bought and they were considered as equivalent to a money gift to the deity. In certain districts they were not uncommonly acquired in order to furnish a supply of meat.

The system of pawning is based pretty much upon the idea conveyed by the literal meaning of that term, i.e. human beings are used as security for money owed. Parents pawn their children, or an elder brother will pawn his younger brothers or sisters, and he can even put himself in pawn. It is done always on account of debt. Borrowing is a pronounced habit amongst the Ibos, and usury, when imposed, is apt to be very excessive. But the debtor may defer repayment of the loan, if he prefers, until the lender himself stands in need of money. The result is that it sometimes falls out that a man is suddenly called upon to liquidate a debt contracted by a long-since-deceased grandfather. Then if he has not the wherewithal to pay he resorts to the system of pawning his children, relatives and finally himself. Such pawns are treated as, and remain virtually, slaves until their redemption, a method of relief acknowledged theoretically but scarcely ever put into operation. A child thus disposed of is, in fact, seldom redeemed. None of his kin would be sufficiently interested or unselfish to subscribe the money for such a purpose. It follows that a child so pawned remains a slave for life, and any offspring born to him are slaves from birth.

The owing of very trifling sums may lead to this catastrophe in a child's life. For a debt of a couple of pounds one has known a man forced to render as many years' service before being able to release himself. A typical instance was one met with in the hinterland west of Asaba. A lad was put in pawn by his father to meet a debt of £2 10s. When I met this lad he had already served ten years and was then full grown, but still a slave, his relatives having failed to redeem him. There is an ingenious method by which a man may raise the funds to purchase his freedom, provided he has one real friend and a big stock of patience. The friend must supply him with a she-goat, and by sales of the offspring he can, in time, accumulate sufficient money to pay the redemption price. Such a procedure is rare, the great difficulty being to find someone willing to supply the goat, and the longer a man remains in pawn the less his chances become of ever regaining his freedom.

One peculiar and apparently unjust feature of the system, entailing great hardships, should be noted. A debt is not cancelled by the death either of the contractor or the pawn who was given as pledge. When a pawn dies the original debt is revived, and the pawns, brother, or some other relative, must be handed over to the creditor as security in lieu of the deceased.

Although there is a recognised distinction between pawns and slaves proper, yet no actual difference is observed in their treatment or status, with the sole exception that pawns being members of the same community as their masters, would not be used as victims for human sacrifice nor to provide a feast; slaves from outside districts must be sought for these purposes.

As the very life of a slave depends upon the caprice of his owner, it is obvious that he can enjoy only such privileges as may be granted him. This does not mean that the slave must necessarily pass a hopelessly unhappy existence; on the contrary he may be quite cheerful and contented, and, in certain parts, may attain to a position of comfort and even affluence. As the "merciful man is merciful to his beast," so the wise master, to some extent, is watchful in his own interests over his slaves. It is to his advantage if his slaves dwell contentedly. For one thing the master's own life is too often in the hands of his slaves, and poisons are plentiful. With his manifold opportunities of handling food it would not be wise to rouse a slave to bitter resentment and keep him about the establishment.

In normal circumstances the owner gives facilities for the slave to build his own little hut, and to cultivate his own farm, and to make himself as satisfied as possible with his conditions. For these personal affairs he is granted the free use of one day in four (the Ibo week). When the question of marriage arises, several courses are open. The most desirable is for the master to hand over another slave to be his wife, the man of course paying nothing in the way of dowry. There is then no possibility of dispute as to the ownership of the children of the union ; they all belong to the master. The same result ensues when the master purchases a woman from an outside source as a wife for his slave. In certain cases two owners may enter into a compact, each retaining an interest in one party to the marriage, though of course the woman is passed on to live with her slave husband and comes under the general control of her husband's master. When this is done each owner takes a child alternately.

All slaves are called upon to contribute to the upkeep of the house and to subscribe their share towards maintaining or enhancing the dignity of their master. Extra levies are demanded of them on special occasions, i.e. when an owner is desirous of proceeding to a higher titular degree, or of erecting new buildings, or of making feasts. Discontent with their lot cannot be openly expressed, and any infringement of the established rules of the house will bring retribution of no uncertain character.

He is, indeed, a bold man who essays to run away, and woe be unto him if he be recaptured. He can be secured with chains, beaten, starved and ill-treated in the most horrible manner: mutilations and other barbarities that cannot be recorded may be inflicted. On the other hand it must be noticed that, in the majority of cases, masters and slaves remain in cordial relationship to one another. Where the slaves accept their lot, and settle down uncomplainingly, and are ready to fulfil the duties required of them, the masters in their turn usually treat them with consideration.

Not infrequently a slave becomes the companion and confidant of his master, and is put into a position demanding great trustworthiness. So much is this the case that I have never met a slave who hankered after or even expressed a desire for freedom. Indeed, in instances where the possibility of freedom has been suggested to young men they have indignantly refused to consider the proposal. On one occasion I talked at length on "liberty" and on all the advantages that liberty bestows upon a man, to a young fellow with whom I was closely acquainted. He listened attentively until I had finished and then quietly remarked, "What has N—— done to me that I should seek my liberty? I never knew my parents. I do not even know where I was born. All the love and affection that I have ever experienced have come from N——. He has been father and mother to me; he has clothed, fed and educated me. Why should I forsake my benefactor and by so acting repudiate all he has done for me? Why, he is my father!"

At present the majority of slaves would probably argue in a similar strain. As a matter of fact to emancipate a slave might be to confer on him a doubtful blessing. If he be old or uneducated he will simply become an outcast without home, farm, or any means of subsistence. He is not likely to meet with sympathy, for the natives would not recognise him as a freeman but would stigmatise him as a presumptuous renegade, flaunting a liberty which was not his by right.

In the end such a one would thankfully return to his former condition. Given a certain amount of education, or a knowledge of a trade, a man might take up his freedom and prosper. He could obtain employment from foreigners and soon attain to independent position. In any case the question resolves itself into "once a slave always a slave" in the eyes of the people. In the ordinary daily life the position of such an ex-slave would not be difficult, but immediately the question of marriage came up, or of the assumption of native titles, or of any advance in social rank, he would meet with insurmountable opposition. In these circumstances it would be forced upon him, without any possibility of doubt, that the stigma of slavery cannot be obliterated.

Domestic slavery has one very commendable feature in the political and social economy of the country. Every person is sure of a home and of food as long as a supply is forthcoming—this obviates all necessity for unions, casual wards, poor-law administration and its attendant taxes, and completely solves the problem of the unemployed. The whole system of domestic slavery, whilst being intensely repugnant in some of its aspects, yet has some features which are beneficial, and which bring the whole community into mutual relationship.[1]

[1] Cf. Chapter XIII, p. 153. The Repeal of the "House Ordinance" and the consequent abolition of all forms of slavery as from January 1st, 1915.

CHAPTER X

DEATH AND BURIAL RITES AND CEREMONIES

ONE of the particularly noticeable characteristics of the Ibos is the unsportsmanlike manner in which the majority give up the ghost. The simplest ailment is sufficient to produce collapse and the patient apparently loses all interest in life. A cough, a cold, a headache will render a man *hors de combat* and he at once considers himself incapable of exertion of any kind. He sits or lies down, a picture of abject misery, and receives, with fitting melancholy, the sympathetic condolences of his friends. Should he be attacked by serious illness he will stoically endure the treatment of the native dibias (medicine-men), however unpalatable and drastic it may be, but it is the hardest matter to induce him to exert any will power towards recovery. It is astonishing how many lie down and die for no adequate reason as far as one can judge. Life simply flickers out. One cannot help noticing how many of the younger men and women die in this manner.

Around the patient are collected the members of the family, and neighbours and visitors pass in and out unhindered, doing little more than excluding light and air. All are most persistent in addressing the patient, and with endless repetition utter the word "ndo," an expression which conveys a much deeper and more comprehensive meaning than the English word "sympathy." As long as breath remains in the body there is little excitement. Some sit or stand with sorrowful countenances, whilst others move about in a casual manner, seemingly but little affected by the scene. But immediately the patient dies there is a wild outburst of wailing. In the case of a near relative, as a wife for her husband, or a mother for

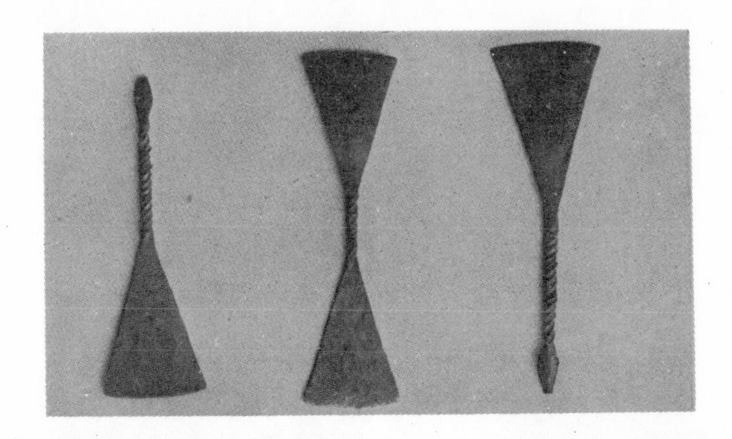

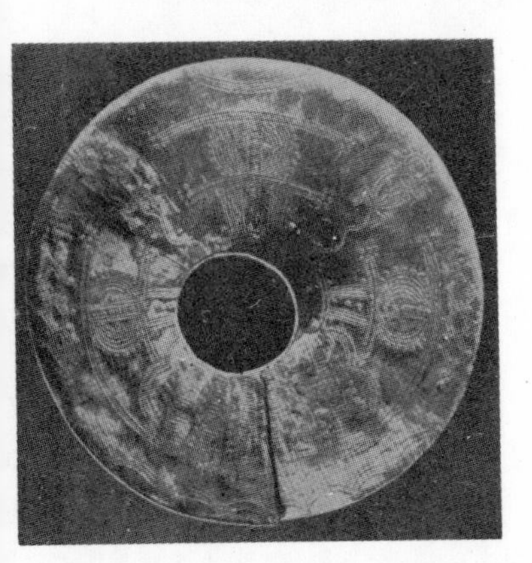

1. Surgical Knives
2. A Brass Anklet
3. A Copper Bracelet
4. Cast-brass Tobacco Pipes

her child, it speedily develops into a form of frenzy. The bereaved woman rushes forth from the death chamber, beating her breast, and runs through the village bewailing her loss at the top of her voice. She salutes none, but continues to cry out even when she has left the town behind her. A woman will thus pass the whole night in the bush pouring out her lamentations, and return next morning in an utterly exhausted condition.

Meanwhile other women attend to the corpse. It is washed and then stained all over with "ufie" (camwood). Wide lines are chalked round the closed eyes and all hair is shaved off the head. The body is clothed in the finest garments from the deceased's wardrobe, and, in the case of a man, the corpse is placed on a stool in a sitting posture, propped against the wall of the chamber.

For a woman the same procedure is followed but, except in very rare cases, she must be placed on the ground; occasionally a sitting posture is adopted, but usually she is simply laid flat—the idea being that as it is not customary for a woman to sit upon a chair in life, she should not be placed in a false position in death. In some districts, especially the river-side towns where gin is a regular article of commerce, the corpse is liberally sprinkled with the liquor. This is done solely for the sake of the odour of the spirit. Before the corpse, thus prepared, are placed the deceased's special treasures, also the implements of his trade, his hoe, his fishing gear, his blacksmith's tools, his gun and hunting outfit and so on. Should he be a rich man a bowl of cowries is added—a symbol to indicate that he was a man of means. This lying, or rather sitting in state, lasts for a few hours, and all old friends and relatives available will come and pay their last respects to the dead. When due time has elapsed for this sitting in state, young men wind the corpse in grass mats, carry it out to the burial ground and bury it in a shallow grave. The body is laid upon its back, and no thought is given as to the position or direction of the grave.

This is the customary course for a normal death and burial, but there are deviations from the rule.

The exceptions are governed chiefly by considerations of birth, rank and the cause of death. A slave receives but scant attention, and no unnecessary expense will be incurred in carrying out the last rites for him. Nor will any man be accused of neglect, or considered lacking in respect for the dead, for providing merely a pauper's burial. The deceased has simply passed from one existence as a slave to a similar position in the spirit world, and therefore is entitled to no more than a slave's portion—as much or as little in death as in life.

For a free-born man the best possible arrangements must be made—there must be no half-measures, and no stinginess on the part of the family. In the case of a chief or rich person the highest honours will be rendered and no expense spared to give their relative a worthy send-off. On the other hand, the bodies of lepers, and such as die from noxious diseases, and those whose death cannot be accounted for satisfactorily, are disposed of hurriedly. Lepers are wound in their sleeping mat. Those who die of smallpox are not buried; they are simply thrown out into the ajaw-awfia (bad bush) very often indeed before they are dead.

People dying as the result of accident; women dying in childbirth; lunatics, suicides and those who have been murdered, drowned or burned are considered as having come to their untimely ends by "awnwu ekwensu," i.e. by the instrumentality of the Devil. None of these may be rubbed with the ufie and they must be buried without delay.

When the head of a family dies, or a chief, he is buried in a deep grave beneath the floor of his private apartment. In the hinterland of Asaba the grave is marked by the figure of a man pricked out with cowrie shells. Ordinarily the heir succeeds to the property, and household affairs go on much as heretofore. In rare instances the whole compound is forsaken, but this is done, not out of respect for the dead, but because the surviving members of the family have come to the conclusion that it is located on an unlucky site. Deaths (or other calamities) have been rather too frequent, and it is deemed advisable to try another and healthier neighbourhood. Burial, as a general rule, follows within twenty-four hours of death. This rule, however, does not apply to men of very high rank. For these another course is adopted, viz. the body is preserved until suitable arrangements can be made for ensuring a funeral corresponding to the rank of the deceased. The most common plan is to lay the body on a couch of clay, hollowed out beneath in the form of an arch. Slow fire is placed under the arch and the corpse is gradually shrivelled dry.[1] When this procedure is followed it is not permissible to publish the death of the man; the fact must not even be mentioned in public. The announcement of the death of the late king of Onitsha was not made until a full year had elapsed after his decease. The fact that no one saw him during the interval signified nothing, as but few beyond his own personal attendants ever did see him, he being forbidden by royal custom from leaving his compound. To venture outside the gate would be to commit an act of grave sacrilege, except occasionally by night when he might surreptitiously slip out to visit some of his near relatives.

On the western side of the river the death of a king must not be proclaimed until the arrival on the scene of his eldest son, who naturally succeeds to the title. The underlying idea is that the throne is never vacant. "The king is dead; long live the king" is the maxim that applies in this case. The eldest son, up to the time of his recall, i.e. on the death of his father, lives away from his own town in the care of another king who undertakes to initiate and to train the young man in the mysteries and duties of the kingship.[2]

The desire of every Ibo man and woman is to die in their own town or, at least, to be buried within its precincts. For a long period it was very difficult to persuade a man to travel any distance from his native

[1] In the case of a king it is usual for the corpse to be decapitated before burial.

[2] See also Chapter IX, p. 104, for other reasons why the heir does not live at home.

place, and if he were in need of medical assistance an Ibo would seldom agree to go from home in spite of assurances that he would be able to have better treatment elsewhere. In case of death occurring at a distance, if it can be done at all, the brethren will bring the body home for burial. It may be that this cannot be done for several days, according to distance and other circumstances. I have often seen bearers conveying a corpse homewards in order to fulfil the last desire of their departed relative. That some time had elapsed since death had taken place was only too evident, the pungent reek of putrid flesh being almost overwhelming. This may account for the fact that the bearers of a corpse always travel at a jog-trot. One has even known cases where the body has been exhumed in order to convey it home instead of allowing it to remain in a restless and unhappy condition in a strange land.

The corpse is wrapped in a grass mat and pieces of cloth and is borne on a rough stretcher by two carriers. In times of peace, and where travelling is deemed safe, this duty is invariably performed by men. When hostilities are in progress, or there are other signs of danger, two women will act as bearers. In this case the bearers must belong to the same town as the deceased. Such a cortège would not be molested. In the same circumstances men would run the risk of capture or death, their errand not rendering them immune from attack.

An "ada," i.e. a daughter being a native of one town married to a man in another town, must be brought back to her original home for burial except she has grown-up sons, in which case these will bury their mother in her own house or compound.

The outward signs of mourning on the part of males are not extravagant. A sad demeanour is maintained, and a husband should restrict himself to the confines of his compound for seven Ibo weeks (28 days) when mourning the loss of his wife. A newly-made widow acts likewise, but in her case the wailings and other indications of mourning are profuse. At the conclusion of the lamentations—and after the burial ceremonies have been fulfilled—both widowers and widows shave their heads as

Visitors from the Spirit World

The ceremony of making "Maw" (ju-ju) prevails throughout the Ibo country. Men dress themselves in weird costumes covering every part of their body, and disguise their voices by means of a small instrument in the mouth (igwe). These represent re-embodied spirits.

a symbol of grief and bereavement. At intervals during the twenty-eight days of retreat crowds of friends and relatives visit the house and a general time of excitement prevails, with singing and dancing, drum-beating and other forms of music, and the inevitable consumption of palm wine and gin. Enormous quantities of food and liquor are consumed at some of these gatherings. This is all done with the sole idea of distracting the attention of the bereaved one from the thought of his great loss; he must not be allowed to brood over it.

As a general rule no signs are set up to indicate that death has visited a household, but in certain places—as at Awka—it is customary to hang strips of cloth, pennant-wise, on long poles, or to hang up a shirt or other garment belonging to the deceased to announce the fact that the owner thereof has passed away.

Holding the most profound belief in the supernatural, the Ibo is deeply conscious of his relationship to the unseen world, and every precaution must be observed in order to keep the spirit of the departed in a state of peaceful contentment. The Ibo will endure everything demanded of him in this life; will put up with hardships, the misbehaviour of his children, indeed anything, in order to insure that his burial will be properly performed. His whole future welfare depends upon this, and hence it takes, at all times, a most prominent place in a man's calculations.

In certain districts it was formerly by no means rare to find that a woman had made arrangements whereby she died before reaching the period of enforced inactivity. There was the perpetual dread lest she should be unable to secure a guarantee or leave sufficient property whereby she might be sure of a worthy burial. To relieve her mind she would strive to accumulate the necessary funds and then, divining that the days of her decline were near, she would enter into an agreement with her son, or some other young man, in which he undertook to fulfil all her wishes in connection with her burial, she, on her part, duly compensating him for all the expense and trouble involved. These preliminaries having been mutually settled, the woman either poisoned herself or the draught was administered to her, in order that the final rites in connection with the second burial might be fulfilled with as little delay as possible.

It was also a custom for poor relatives to sell old people, especially a woman decrepit and sick. She was bought by strangers to be converted into meat, and the money obtained by the sale was devoted to the expenses of the second burial, this being considered much more important than her latter end on earth, or the disposal of her actual remains.

Except in a few specific cases, as those mentioned above, the actual burial of a corpse takes place within a few hours of death. This of course allows very little time to make due preparation, and hence the spirit must, perforce, be content with a hurried despatch until adequate arrangements can be made for a fitting introduction to the spirit world.

There appears to be no distinction between soul and spirit; for all practical purposes they are held to be identical. Their belief in the "spirit-life" is exceedingly tenacious, and with it there is a profound conviction of the existence of a future state. This belief exercises an immense influence in creating fear and superstition, but in no way does it act as an incentive to regard the present life as a probationary one, preparatory to the life to come. When a man dies he is alluded to as having "gone home," or simply as having "gone to the spirit world," and the mourning of the survivors is that of those who have said "farewell" for the time being only. The underlying idea is that God sends men and women into the world for the purpose of fulfilling the functions of life, and thus maintaining a succession of mankind upon the earth. Each is sent endowed with the peculiar talents for his vocation in life, the farmer is fitted for his own work; the doctor for his profession, and so forth. In reply to the question as to what happens in the case of those who die in infancy one is informed that though the child does not, on this occasion, exercise its powers as a citizen, yet, in due course, it will be reborn into this world, and will then perform the duties to which it may be appointed. The term "going home" is never applied to the death of a child. On the other hand when more than two children of the same mother die consecutively, the first two will be given an ordinary burial, but the third and subsequent deaths will demonstrate the fact that it is an unlucky child and must not be reincarnated. The thought in the mind of the parents is that it is the same child reappearing time after time and as it will not live it is better to destroy it altogether. In some parts the father or the male relatives convey the corpse outside the town and there burn it. The ashes are ground to powder and scattered to the four winds.

When men have run their course in this world they return to their master—the Supreme Being—and live with him in the spirit world. In their spiritual state they are endowed with never-ending life, and, until the ceremony of second burial has been observed, they continue to haunt this world, wandering at will in the houses, compound and farms, invisible, yet ever present, and taking a distinct and unremitting interest in the affairs of the individual and the community with which they associated in life. After the rites of second burial have been completed the "spirits" depart to their appointed place and rest in peace until their reincarnation, i.e. as long as they behave themselves. Should they be so unfortunate as to rouse the ire of their master, they are in danger of being banished to "amanri maw na madu," an intermediate state between this material world and the spirit world. The term indicates that such spirits have no place of abode, they are thenceforth "wanderers," lost souls. There, for ever, they pass a miserable, restless existence, without hope for their spirit life, and prohibited from being reborn into this world.

There is no belief in transmigration into any but human bodies, but we find a strongly grounded belief in the perpetuation of individuals by the medium of repeated births. Provided a spirit conducts himself worthily, and so escapes relegation to amanri maw na madu, he will be reborn at the appointed season and he will resume his life in this world. In due time he will be called "home" once more and so the process will be repeated for all eternity.

Mention has been made of the term second burial. This needs brief explanation and any account of the Ibo belief in the "spirit" would be incomplete without it. Second burial is the name adopted by Europeans and arises from the fact that, to all intents and purposes, there are two burials—the first real, the second by proxy. Amongst the natives the custom is known by two names, Those on the west side of the Niger speak of it as "inu-ozu" (to bury the dead) whilst those on the eastern side term it "ikwa-ozu" (to mourn, cry, for the dead). The deceased has already been buried amidst much lamentation but with little ceremony. In the meanwhile all preparations have been completed to enable his friends to introduce him with due honours to those with whom he must henceforth associate in the spirit world.

A day is fixed for the festival, usually "oye day" for a man and "nkwaw day" for a woman (the second and fourth days of the Ibo week). The articles required are meal, palm wine, coco-nut (to be eaten as a special token of grief) and as big a supply of gin as circumstances permit. In the case of a man renowned in warfare a ram is slaughtered as a mark of honour; it must be killed by a brother warrior, and only warriors may partake of its flesh. These old comrades of war and the chase are expected to organise a great hunt in honour of their deceased brother. Whatsoever is killed—whether man or beast—is then consecrated and partaken of in pious memory of their late companion in arms.

On the evening prior to ikwa-ozu guns are fired to intimate to the friends and neighbours that the ceremonies will be duly observed on the morrow. By the same means the spirit of the dead man is also notified of the coming proceedings, in order that he may rejoice simultaneously with his relatives, and that he may be fully cognisant of his dispatch to join his brother spirits. A sort of wicker-work coffin ("ibwudu") is constructed of a size corresponding to that of the deceased, the corpse having

1. SKENGAS

The one on the right is covered with the remains of blood from sacrifices. The one on the left is a new Skenga, as yet uninhabited by a spirit.

2. THE "MAW-AFIA"

The spirit of a dead man appearing to his friends.

been measured with a line immediately after death. This is covered with a grass mat and then with white cloth, and, thus enshrouded, serves as the substitute for the body. The ibwudu is placed in the man's house or compound, in a position where it can be viewed by the assembled folk. Two alusi (idols), viz. the ikenqa and the afaw are set up before the "ibwudu" and these are sprinkled with the blood of the sacrifices. The flesh of the animals thus offered to the spirits is then consumed by those participating in the ceremonies. The night following, the ibwudu is buried in the same grave as the actual corpse. This last act is performed by the same company of the "umu-ilo" (children of the street) who buried the real corpse. Having now been accorded an honourable burial, the spirit of the dead will, henceforth, rest in peace. Neglect to fulfil the rites of second burial leads to disastrous consequences. The "spirit" itself is unhappy, a homeless wanderer, and finding no rest, will not cease to haunt its former dwelling-place, and will assuredly wreak fitting vengeance on the relatives for their unfeeling and unwarrantable negligence. According to custom a widow (or widows) may not leave the compound without liability to incur disgrace or reproach for disrespectful conduct towards the dead, nor can any of them re-marry as long as the rites of second burial remain unfulfilled.

These second burials are costly affairs. The very poorest will spend their all, and often heavy debts are incurred in the desire to give the best possible "send-off" to a relative. Some idea of this lavish expenditure may be gathered from an instance of which I made some notes. I was passing through Awka one day and came across a display of funeral trophies. There were 21 skulls of cows, 11 of pigs, and 10 of goats. The price of cows is £5 apiece, pigs £2, and goats 10s. In addition to these animals provided for sacrificial feasting, many cases of gin (then 15s. per case) and an unlimited supply of palm wine, yams and other provisions were consumed. That funeral must have cost at the lowest estimate £150, and it would probably be nearer the mark to fix the figure at £200. Of course such expenses could be incurred only by a rich family, but every family will spend to its utmost capacity when fulfilling the rites of second burial.

One of the functions allotted to women in the solemnising of the rites of second burial is that known as "itu-uni." It is performed on the day of the ceremony and must be done whilst the ibwudu is still in position, i.e. prior to its burial. Beneath the ibwudu is the deceased's idol called "chi" (God) and alongside this are placed the special offerings brought for the occasion by the women of the house. The first-born son then places a piece of white cloth upon the chi. The cloth having been consecrated, it is removed by the ada (chief woman) of the clan or village, who proceeds to tear it into strips for equal division among the dead man's daughters. The strips are girded round the waist of these daughters, and they indicate to the public that the final ceremonies for the glorification of their father's spirit have been duly performed.

For the actual burial of a king or for the second burial of a chief it was customary to put to death one or more slaves (ndi iji kwa ozu). As already noticed the death of a king is not noticed officially until all adequate preparations are made for a burial commensurate with his dignity, and hence there is no need for second burial in his case.

It is essential to distinguish between mere execution in the course of funeral rites and the custom of human sacrifice. The latter appears to be always of an atoning character, whilst the victims at a burial are put to death solely to provide attendant spirits to accompany the chief into the great beyond. A king or chief must not enter the spirit world unaccompanied by a retinue. He must have his messenger and personal servant and slaves to attend to his needs, sentinels and so forth. The presence of these slaves will demonstrate his rank and dignity to those with whom he will associate in the spirit world, and he will thus be accorded every mark of dignity and respect. The number of slaves (one or more) who accompanied a chief through the gates of death was determined by the resources of the deceased's estate. The initial stage of the proceedings was common to both a king and a chief, and was as follows: A strong lad of fifteen or sixteen years was selected to act as the messenger and personal servant. Over his shoulder was placed the private bag—a receptacle made from the complete skin of a goat or, more usually, from that of a small animal akin to a leopard. The head is severed and the skin flayed off without further cutting. Into this bag the personal treasures of the deceased were placed, such as his own cup (calabash) and snuff-box, together with kola nuts and certain eatables. As soon as the lad was thus prepared two young men were seized, half killed, and then laid in the grave. The lad with the bag was forced to lie between them. The corpse of the king, or the ibwudu in the case of the second burial of a chief, was laid lengthwise on the lad in such a way that it rested partly on all the three victims and, thus arranged, the grave was immediately filled in.

In the case of a king more attendants joined him in his journey to the unseen world. The public executioner was employed for the purpose. One man was bound hand and foot and placed beside the door of the house, and he was despatched by his throat being cut. Another was killed at the outer gate of the compound at the spot known as the "obubus madu" (place of execution). He was likewise bound hand and foot, but the method employed in bringing about his death was different. He was laid upon his back with his neck across a piece of timber, a second piece was then fixed above the neck, and when in position men stood on the two ends till the unfortunate wretch was suffocated. This was known as "nfi-bu" (lit. killing by tying). A third man was led to the sacred grove of ebwo trees in the compound and there beheaded. More were killed at other spots, e.g. upon certain alusi (idols) fixed beneath the ebwo trees. The corpses of all these victims were not buried; they had to be cast away in the ajaw-awfia (bush devoted to receive corpses of outcasts) where the remains of human sacrifices were deposited.

In the Asaba hinterland the custom for the burial of leading men was to place them in a huge coffin constructed of roughly hewn planks. The grave was deep and wide, and the bottom was lined with from one to three, or even more, human victims. The cumbersome coffin was raised as high as the bearers could lift it over the open grave, and then allowed to drop with a sickening thud upon the wretched creatures below.

At Onitsha, Asaba and other riverside towns, some later customs have been introduced from the Igarra people. Under this heading comes the "ozu-alu," a ceremony which is performed only in connection with the second burial of those who are of the rank of a chief. For a man of first rank the second burial rites are prolonged for several days. On the day following the burial of the ibwudu the ceremony of ozu-olu begins. The signal for this is the appearance twice a day (morning and evening) of the maw-afia (spirits of the Olu people).[1] There is a terrific din from the beating of tom-toms (egwu-olu), and the shouts of the assembled company, and the whole proceeding grows into a noisy drinking carousal. The number of the maw-afia is determined by the number of "umunna," i.e. the heads of the different families constituting the clan—each head being required to provide one maw-afia. These quaint apparitions, needless to say, are men disguised in grotesque fashion, with their bodies completely enveloped in cloth, and uttering peculiar sounds by means of air instruments fixed between their teeth. To the excited audience these are verily believed to be figures animated by spirits from the underworld. For four consecutive days the programme varies little, and then comes the formal visit to the grave of the deceased chief. The noise and excitement reaches the utmost pitch, all the relatives crying out "Welcome, welcome to our father," until, suddenly, firearms are discharged, and the maw-afia appear escorting the "spirit" of the dead man from his house, beneath the floor of which his body lies buried. On his return to this world the "spirit" walks slowly, with tottering, uncertain steps, and muttering words with a feeble voice—his speech being disguised similarly to that of the maw-afia. The poor "spirit" is as yet weak from its enforced imprisonment in the grave, it needs time

[1] All spirits (maws) are supposed to rise out of the ground.

and food to recover its lost strength. Meanwhile the escorting maw-afia are busily engaged in dusting down the " spirit " to remove the earth stains of the grave. Amidst profound expressions of joy on the part of the assembled relatives and friends the " spirit " meanders round; on this first day for a short time only. His strength is soon exhausted and he returns to the house and disappears.

On the fifth day the " spirit " comes forth again but without the attendant maw-afia. They are no longer needed as the " spirit " has fully recovered his powers. He can walk faster, and speak loudly and clearly. He goes in and out amongst his kinsfolk comforting and exhorting his wives and children. After this tour he returns to his house and assumes his former position on the " ukpo " (seat of honour), his attendants all the time vigorously fanning him. His daughters bring presents of gin and cowries, and to manifest his gratitude for the gifts a day is appointed by the men present, acting on behalf of the " spirit," on which he will make a special visit to the women-folk of that particular village. The " spirit " then retires to his own place once more.

On the appointed day he tours the whole town speaking words of comfort and counsel, and in return receives abundant presents, and thus having fulfilled every duty of a good, kind-hearted and contented " spirit " he disappears finally. For men of secondary rank the ceremony of ozu-olu extends over but two or three days.

After second burial the departed spirit finds a home at Ezira. This is a town lying some twenty-five to thirty miles south of Awka, and it is considered the gate of heaven by the people of all the surrounding country. If anyone wishes to know the opinion of a deceased relative upon any matter he may be put into communication with the spirit of the departed. It can all be arranged for him, at Ezira, for a consideration, which varies in amount according to circumstances, £12 being the price paid on some occasions. But direct communication is not advisable; there must be a medium, otherwise the spirit from the other world may exercise such a powerful influence over the inquirer that ere long he himself will be a permanent dweller at Ezira. Hence all conversations with departed friends are carried on indirectly, i.e. through a third person.

After a visit to Ezira I was asked eagerly to describe what the place was like. Was it very beautiful? Did it appear to be like heaven? and many similar questions. So long as inquirers are content to employ mediums to carry on conversations between themselves and the departed, so long will Ezira continue to be regarded as the gate of heaven by the people dwelling thereabout.

CHAPTER XI

SPORTS AND PASTIMES

ORDINARILY the Ibo is a very serious person. At the same time he has a well-developed humorous side to his nature and he can, on occasion, give play to his emotions with complete abandon; so much so that he becomes totally oblivious of things around him.

The games commonly played by the boys and girls have been described in Chap. V. In the case of adults it is not always easy to distinguish between recreation and serious occupation; sometimes the two are combined, as in shooting. In the case of dancing it is often difficult to differentiate between that which is simply recreative and that which is the physical expression of religious enthusiasm. Shooting, wrestling, dancing and swimming are the sports of men; comparatively few of the women swim, but all indulge freely in dancing. The national game of okwe is common to both sexes.

Every Ibo man is familiar with the use of a gun. Prowess in the art of shooting is acquired, in the first instance, by practice with bows and arrows, but a young man will never rest until he becomes the owner of a firearm of some sort. Archery has practically degenerated into a haphazard pastime, however, and is but rarely relied upon in hunting or war. It provides recreation and amusement to the young men, especially during the slack seasons of the year. As a rule the bows do not measure more than three feet from point to point and are usually less. The bow-string is a finely cut strip from the tough outside of a creeper cane; the arrows are proportionate in size and notched, not barbed. Competitions are held for small stakes of cowrie shells; sometimes each man puts a certain number into the pool and the winner of the shoot takes the lot. At other times the successful man takes all the arrows of the bout, the eventual winner being the one who at the finish is the possessor of the most arrows. The target is a piece of the pithy stem of a koko leaf or banana tree. The winner of a set throws the target to a distance of some ten paces, and shooting follows immediately it touches the ground, the first man to pierce it becoming the winner in his turn, and so the competition repeats itself. I received great applause one afternoon on piercing the target at the first attempt, but was not to be persuaded to try again, otherwise the fluke would have been too obvious. The first time that I handled a bow, before I realised what had happened, my host's dog was yelping furiously and running around with the arrow sticking in its ribs. It was more frightened than hurt, but I lost no time in extracting the arrow all the same, and I was thankful my host had not been an eye-witness of the catastrophe.

Arrows can be shot with tremendous force and will carry up to seventy or eighty yards. If feathered for the purpose, they can be made to drop and strike perpendicularly. But whilst this pastime affords some amusement, the Ibo man must have a gun to be really happy; in this he is the unconscious imitator of almost every white man he has ever seen.

When I first came to the country there was an abundance of firearms of many patterns, from old tower guns to Snider rifles and American pistols. Arms of precision, i.e. any other than flintlock guns, are now prohibited, and great numbers have been called in and destroyed since British rule was established, and now the Ibo man must, perforce, be content with what he can get. He wanders through the "bush" with his fearsome weapon, a real source of danger to the owner himself. I have seen some ghastly accidents, the result of barrels bursting. Here I speak of men who are not professional hunters, but who habitually use their guns for protection or other purposes. Occasionally these men shoot small game, but they use their guns more frequently during festivities and especially for second burials.

Guinea-fowl Dancers

These are professional dancers. Round their ankles are clusters of shells.

Wrestling is universal amongst boys and young men and it is a very popular sport. Every youth physically capable practises it and continues to do so up to the time of marriage. There are great yearly contests; it is a purely amateur sport and there are no prizes. Each bout is complete in itself, the successful competitor being fully content merely to receive the plaudits of the crowd as an acknowledgment of his skill and strength. Yet it must be confessed, that though many of the "ikolobia" (athletes) are adept in the art, they manifest but little sporting instinct. They cannot take defeat with good grace. If a man has but an idea that he is likely to be worsted he refuses to wrestle. He will not engage in the sport after marriage on the ground that it is considered *infra dig.* to do so, but this is simply an excuse to cover up the fear of possible defeat; the Ibo man has a wholesome dread of being taunted and ridiculed by his women-folk. He cannot endure disgrace and, therefore, after marriage, he becomes a sturdy advocate of the doctrine that "discretion is the better part of valour."

The lack of sportsmanship is noticeable also in the actual contests. A man may apparently be putting up a sound fight, when suddenly he releases his grip and retires. On asking the reason for his action he explains that he seemed to be making no headway and what purpose could there be in continuing the struggle? In spite of these shortcomings, however, some exciting wrestling may be seen and there are exhibitions of rare skill and endurance. Every part of the body is brought into play; hands, legs and head. I am not sufficiently acquainted with the various schools of wrestling to be able to pronounce definitely what styles chiefly prevail amongst the Ibos, but should be inclined to class them generally as "Catch-as-catch-can." These styles are not all uniform, and the most thrilling bouts are those in which the competitors are from different localities, when the particular tricks and twists of each school have full scope.

Prior to a contest the athletes go through a course of preparation, quite distinct, however, from training. Charms are purchased to aid them in the struggle, and "medicine" is applied externally and internally, the latter to endow them with extraordinary strength, the former to nullify the power of the adversary and render him incapable of retaining his grip. The charm must be secreted in the "awgawdaw" (the rolled cloth girdle adopted by athletes), the sole article of clothing worn by the wrestlers. In the actual contest the rivals advance towards each other, smack their right hands together, and then retreat to the outskirts of the ring. From these points they begin to manœuvre around each other, crouching down until the hands touch the ground, but with heads well up and eyes fixed. These preliminary tactics remind one of leopards rather than men. Gradually the combatants warm up to the fray and very soon they are dodging and feinting, twisting and turning at great speed, and some vigorous slapping of face and body is given and received. The main object, of course, is to gain a favourable opening and secure the advantage of first grip. Some are extremely agile and clever and their tactics are thrilling to witness. Often the opening stages are quite protracted and then, with dramatic suddenness, one man is lying on his back. His opponent has seized a favourable opportunity, rushed in, and with lightning speed has grasped leg or ankle and upset his opponent's equilibrium. When they come to grips the struggle is a severe test of strength and staying power. With arms interlocked, legs rigid, and head pushing hard, they pull and twist and strain and pant. And oh! the dust, the sweat, and the noise! The onlookers shout their loudest to encourage their particular favourite, and it is intensely exciting until, at length, one competitor is pinned on his back to the ground, or, as often happens, the men separate, utterly exhausted, and the battle is a drawn one.

There are no fancy rules regulating the contests—no limitations to the size of the ring—the spectators must move if necessary. Every kind of grip or hug or trick is admissible. The business is for one man to throw the other, and the lack of restrictions is equally fair to both men. The only stipulation is that they must wrestle, not fight or bite or scratch.

Dancing is the great national pastime, and it is practised by everybody capable of movement. There are many forms—for boys, for girls, for men, for women and for mixed companies, the last being more especially associated with religious observances and festivals. It is the religious element which distinguishes the set forms of dancing from those which are the outcome of the emotions.

The stereotyped set dances are all performed by professional men, and they are very elaborate and extraordinarily difficult and exhausting. The movements are perfectly rhythmic, and the time is set by music. The instruments are crude but effective. One youth grips in each hand a carafe-shaped calabash (awyaw) surrounded by flounces of cowrie shells, and these are rattled with methodical vigour, producing a sound not unlike the backwash of waves on a shingly beach. Another youth hugs closely under his left arm a clay pot from ten to twelve inches in diameter. It has two holes, one at the top of the neck, the other in the side. To make music the performer beats sharply upon the mouth with the open palm of his right hand, the left hand, meanwhile, being passed backwards and forwards over the side-hole. The effect is not unpleasant; it is a sort of mellow booming sound which rises and falls as the side-hole is covered or left open. There may be wind instruments also, short reeds pierced with three holes for fingering; these give highly pitched notes more like those of a piccolo. In addition there are drums—small and great—which are also capable of variation in note by pressure of the left hand over different parts of the surface.

The instrumentalists squat on the ground in no prescribed order, with neither programme nor conductor. Presently one of the musicians sounds a few desultory notes, which gradually evolve into a recognised melody, the others join in, and time and tune are thus established. The dancers range themselves and begin slow rhythmic movements, unconsciously swaying their heads in time with the music. As the dance proceeds they appear intoxicated with the motion and the music, the speed increases, and the movements become more and more intricate and bewildering. The dancers work themselves into a veritable frenzy and the spectators keep silence from sheer excitement. The twistings, turnings, contortions and springing movements, executed in perfect time, are wonderful to behold. Movement succeeds movement in rapid succession, speed and force increasing, until the grand finale is reached. By this time the onlookers, as well as the dancers, are almost breathless. Then, in a flash, music and dance cease abruptly, the performers remaining rigid in their last pose. For a second absolute silence prevails, followed by an outburst of applause. The effect of the sudden arrest of music and motion cannot be described; it breaks upon one with such an unexpected shock. The dancers are streaming with perspiration and quite exhausted with their efforts. The sign for the dance to end is given by the chief drummer, the dancers themselves, naturally, having a pretty clear idea when to expect it. For these set dances, e.g. those executed by the "Guinea-fowl dancers," the physical strength required is tremendous. The body movements are extremely difficult and would probably kill a European. The whole anatomy of the performer appears to be in serious danger, and it is a marvel that his internal machinery is not completely thrown out of gear. The practice of such dancing leads to a wonderful development of the back and abdominal muscles. Moreover the movements are free, there is nothing rigid about them, and they produce no sign of "physical exerciser" stiffness. Every movement is clean, sure and decided, showing absolute control of the muscles. For some of the dances the performers wear clusters of shells around one or both ankles, and these are shaken simultaneously by all the members of the party. The precision with which this is done, and the execution of the many intricate figures, are marvellous.

The professional dancers are very well paid for their services, and when fulfilling an engagement are liberally entertained. The dances are not all uniform; usually the displays of one town differ in character and movement from those of its neighbours.

Of quite another type is the dancing connected with religious festivities, and particularly that in which women take a leading part. Such dancing is always the physical expression of joy and thanksgiving. It consists almost entirely of strange sinuous movements of the limbs and body. If these movements are the expressions of the primeval idea of dancing, then, to judge by the illustrated papers, a great deal of so-called dancing in England and America is merely a reversion to type. It would appear that the exponents of twentieth century dancing are engaged in a feeble imitation of the first.

In all native dances each man (and woman) acts independently of his fellows and yet fits into his proper place in the general scheme. When men and women are dancing in company they do not even touch hands. It is contrary to etiquette for a man to touch a woman, and any infringement of the rule may meet with stern rebuke. As a matter of fact each person becomes so completely absorbed in the dance that any interference would give rise to emphatic protest and annoyance. I have watched such dances and can testify to the extraordinary manner in which the dancers, for the time being, lose consciousness of their surroundings. One stands before them, and they give no sign of recognition; one speaks, but there is no response other than a fixed stare. Only gradually do they become normal again.

The dances are always held in the open air, but not always in a public place. Frequently they are held in the compound of a chief or other prominent man. In either case it is a hot and dusty pastime, and hence is invariably associated with heavy drinking. After joining in a few short figures at the beginning of the festival many of the old men find it difficult to rise from their seats of honour with any degree of steadiness.

Some of the movements are peculiar, as when the lower limbs are kept perfectly rigid the feet are not lifted from the ground, but all progression is made by swaying the body only, and by sinuous movements.

The pastime has a fascination of its own, and even the spectator finds it difficult to keep his feet and body from moving in sympathy with the dancers. As one watches the swaying figures, and listens to the rhythm of the music, one naturally responds. It is doubtful whether any native could resist the spell inwardly, whatever outward aspect he might assume—and this is no matter for surprise to those who have been present at such a dance.

Swimming is one of the ordinary accomplishments of people living near the great waters ; many are very proficient in the art, and are as happy in the water as out of it. The natives of some of the riverside towns seem perfectly fearless and plunge into the stream regardless of its state, whether in flood or otherwise. The greatest excitement prevails when a steamer passes a village. The little "dug-outs" are instantly manned by boys and girls, untrammelled by garments, and they approach as near as they dare, on the look-out for empty tins and bottles. When any article is thrown from the steamer, the little canoers at once plunge into the water and race madly for it. Meantime the empty canoes drift down-stream until the steamer is out of reach, when with lusty trudgeon strokes the owners overtake them. A youngster grasps by the stern and, by a series of vigorous fore and aft movements, swishes out the water and tumbles in once more. One has seen boys in their eagerness to pick up treasures swim right into the steamer's line of progress, and then, as the vessel appears to overwhelm them, laughingly fend themselves off along the vessel's side and disappear in the swirl and foam set up by the revolutions of the stern wheel. One naturally thinks that that must be the end of them, but presently their heads pop up again twenty or thirty yards astern, the black water-babies having apparently quite enjoyed the extra excitement created by the steamer's wash.

No account of the pastimes of the Ibos would be complete without a description of the game of okwe.[1] Probably this remark applies to the whole of West Africa, as the game is almost, if not quite, universal. It

[1] The word "okwe" is derived from the name of the tree, the fruit of which supplies the seeds used as counters in the game. They resemble black marbles in size and appearance.

is a recreation more in favour with the elder folk, the old men being particularly partial to it.

In order to play the game counters and a properly prepared board are necessary. The board (ubaw-okwe) has two parallel rows of holes. The number of holes varies from ten to twenty per side and the boards are often nicely carved. Some of them are black and polished with long usage and are treasured as heirlooms. The players may be two, three or four, the opponents facing each other on opposite sides of the board. It is impossible, without taking up a huge amount of space, to write full directions for playing the game. Briefly, the procedure is as follows:

Working always from left to right on the board the counters are distributed thus :—

5 counters in each of the first 7 holes, on both sides.

1 counter in each of the next 2 holes, on both sides.

5 counters in the tenth hole on both sides.

1 counter in the eleventh hole on both sides.

The challenger always concedes first move.

Player No. 1 immediately appropriates (lit: "eats") all the counters in holes 8, 9, 10 and 11, as a sort of nucleus for his working capital.

No 2 likewise appropriates a number, but in his case leaves the single counter in hole eleven, i.e. No. 1 is one counter to the good from the start.

Players can begin where they like on the board but must take all—save one—of the counters from the hole selected, and these must be distributed singly along the row of holes until they are exhausted. The object is so to place the counters that the last one drops opposite a hole in which the opponent has one or three counters. If a player can do this he "eats" the one or three, i.e. he appropriates them. The object is to force one's opponent to move out his counters in such a way that he cannot save himself from the one and three traps. As soon as a player wishes he can replace his playing counters by redistributing his own working capital, but to do this he must drop in the counters singly, one for each hole, and if a surplus remains after passing down all the holes of the board then the process is repeated until all the "eaten" counters are once more in the game. It is astonishing how quickly a capable player can force his opponent into distributing his counters so as to bring about the existence of holes containing one or three. A clever player will calculate numbers and spaces at an extremely rapid rate ; a weak opponent is apt to lose his original thirty-five counters in an incredibly short time, which is either very humbling or exasperating, according to temperament. A white man usually has no chance against a good native player. The game often leads to excessive gambling, some men accumulating large debts in this way. Resort is had to theft and other undesirable methods of raising funds to clear the debts. Some cases come into special prominence ; there may be quarrels and other disturbances arising out of the incident and then the chiefs have recourse to prohibition and so put an end to the evil—at least for a time. In the majority of the Mission Stations hockey and football have been introduced and bid fair to meet with success. The games are being taken up with enthusiasm and provide strenuous exercise for all who take part in them. Instead of spasmodic bursts of recreation the habit of regular exercise is being inculcated, and there is no doubt that it has proved beneficial to the health of those who play. It is also a useful agency for developing energy, self-control, independence and all those virtues which we English ascribe to the practice of athletics, and which, therefore, need no mention here. A boy is a boy whether in England or West Africa, and what applies to one nationality applies very much to the other in the sphere of sports and pastimes.

CHAPTER XII

THE IBO AT WORK

Of the capacity of the Ibo for work there can be no doubt. He has sufficient latent ability and physical strength to undertake any task allotted to him. On the other hand, he is of an impatient temperament, lacks determination and perseverance, and is more or less untrustworthy. As in games so in work, unless matters proceed entirely to his satisfaction, the Ibo man becomes hopelessly depressed and quickly gives up in despair. Trying until success rewards persistency is not an inherited trait.

In his old natural state no serious demand was ever made upon his strength of purpose whether in work, recreation or war. The ordinary avocations of both men and women demand little energy and force of character. Their requirements were few and easily supplied without undue strain upon time or powers. Food and a hut for shelter are the only necessaries in this country; all other things must be classed as luxuries to the native in his normal state. Whether any, or many such luxuries are accumulated depends chiefly on the man himself. Some remain content with bare necessities, others strive for the outward signs of affluence, and acquire various quaint and curious treasures. The number of such articles which the ordinary man acquires and the value he attaches to them is in proportion to the amount of EXTRA work he is prepared to perform beyond that which is essential for the maintenance of himself and his dependents.

The first necessity of man being food, the Ibo seeks in a perfunctory manner to secure what may be required, and hence we meet with the three primitive occupations of farming, fishing and hunting. Though the soil is very poor in places, nature is fairly bountiful on the whole, and the only cultivation seriously undertaken is that of yams. Whilst preparing to set seed yams the opportunity is seized to sow maize in between them. The women cultivate quantities of edde (koko) together with cassava, beans and gourds; in some parts millet and ground nuts are grown also. Deep-water fishing by line or net and hunting are the work of men; fish trapping is practised by both sexes.

The staple food of the country is yam, and to the cultivation of this vegetable every man must apply himself either in person or by employing others. This is what is commonly called "farming" in the Ibo country, but the term is liable to misinterpretation as it does not correspond to the orthodox meaning of the word; the term ought not to be employed to designate the primitive hoe-work of the Ibo. It is true there are a few cattle of a pygmy breed but they are in no sense "farmed"—nor even milked. They have a certain property value and are guarded for that reason only. Goats and fowls and the few sheep fend for themselves; they likewise are not farmed and the stocks remain as they have been for generations.

The native, then, is an agriculturist and that of the simplest type. His solitary implement is the hoe, and this is the universal tool for work on the land. It varies in size according to district, that on the western side of the river being much smaller than the pattern in use on the eastern side. The blade is wrought from bar iron, and is fixed into a stout elbow-shaped handle and manipulated similarly to an adze. The ground is prepared with the hoe which, for its purpose, is superior to the spade, both as regards the quality of the work done, and the speed with which the soil is turned. Give a native a spade and he instinctively grips the stem of the handle with both hands and drives it hoe-fashion. The farm is usually situated outside the town, and not infrequently lies at a considerable distance away. In this case the men usually build little booths at the beginning of the season wherein to camp and thus save the long tramp to and fro daily. The yam and the yam supply being so important, more particular attention is given to the subject in the succeeding chapter.

Wherever the fish of a stream are not under taboo as sacred objects, men living in the vicinity follow the profession of fishermen. Many methods are in use for netting and trapping fish, and there is an enormous demand for smoke-cured fish as a relish for palm oil soup. This article of diet practically serves in lieu of flesh-food, the meat supply of the country being totally inadequate to meet the demand ; it is forthcoming only for occasional feasts.

In the Niger and its larger tributaries netting is largely employed for catching fish. The nets are worked from canoes, or from towers, or by wading. The first and second are novel methods, whilst the third is a primitive use of the seine. For canoe work quiet water must be sought, i.e. out of the direct flow of the current, and two men are essential. A shallow net of woven cane (ekwe), in length corresponding to the straight part of the canoe side, and in width from six to nine feet, is lashed to the upper edge of the canoe in such a manner that its outer beam is just awash when the canoe is balanced by the men to an even keel. When travelling it is hoisted just clear of the water.

A likely spot having been selected the two men stand in the canoe, one at either end, release the net and allow it to sink to the requisite depth, the balance of the canoe being controlled by the distribution of their own weight. To haul the net the men stand on the opposite gunwale and throw their weight back, at the same time hauling on the beam, thus bringing the net to the surface, the process being repeated at the fishermen's pleasure. The chief purpose for which this method is employed is to catch a fish called ellem which resembles whitebait. Occasionally larger fish are caught, but not often, as the net is too shallow and the raising is much too slow to catch larger fish.

Fishing from a tower is another familiar method. Towards the close of the hot season a row of stout stakes are driven into the dry river-bed—the row being at right angles to the bank and extending from thirty to forty feet. To these stakes a net is lashed very similar in construction to, but deeper and more commodious altogether than, the one used with canoes as described above. On the actual bank of the river a tower is built of rough timber, running up to a height of from twenty to thirty feet. At the top is a tiny platform which is protected with a roof of thatch. As soon as the waters rise sufficiently to cover the net, the fisherman takes up his position on the platform; it is somewhat cramped but he manages to contrive a small fire and endeavours to make himself as cosy as circumstances permit. A long rope of twisted creeper stretches from his lofty perch to the net and with this, at regular intervals, he hoists the net to the surface. His companion, who is encamped at the base of the tower, answers to his call, and should fish appear in the net, it is the business of this co-worker to scramble along the stakes and bring in the catch. Between the haulings he can find occupation in smoke-curing the fish.

The seine method scarcely needs description other than to mention that it is very primitive, except in those localities where foreign nets have made their appearance. The native production is worked from sandbanks, aided by canoes. The net is taken out by the canoes, sunk, and then hauled ashore by the ends. Owing to its great weight, it being also woven from cane, it is never very long and is a very crude affair in comparison with an English-made cotton net.

Women weave large ball-like contrivances of yarn tendrils, which resemble huge bird nests, and fix them in the banks of streams. They are baited and lure many prawns to destruction.

In some of the lakes fish-traps are built stretching out from the banks. They are constructed of stakes driven in close together with an opening left for prowling fish to enter. Fish swim in when the water is high and then, as the water recedes later, are easily secured.

Neat little snares called "iko" are made of light wicker-work and placed in fish runs. All other ways being blocked the fish swim through the mouth of the trap and find that they can neither go forward nor return; they simply wait till the owner of the snare comes along and bags them.

They are extracted by releasing the draw-string at the pointed head of the trap, this action permitting the head to expand to the full circumference of the body of the trap.

Hook-and-line fishing is practised in most waters, more especially in neighbourhoods where foreign hooks can be purchased. The hooks of native manufacture are too crude to catch anything but the most guileless of fish. The line may be attached to a rod, or tied to a stump, or a calabash may be used as a buoy. A baited hook, with a length of line, is attached to a calabash, and this is thrown into the water and allowed to drift, the fisherman meanwhile paddling his canoe at leisure. The sinking of the calabash indicates the hooking of a fish, and all the fisherman has to do is to hover round until the calabash reappears. By that time the fish is probably dead from exhaustion or nearly so. In land-locked waters the calabash system can be practised with little trouble. Night-lines are also regularly set for fish.

In back waters particularly, though the practice is often employed in running streams, poisoning is freely resorted to in order to obtain fish. The flowers and leaves of the iwelli plant are bruised and scattered upon the surface of the water; they have an anæsthetic effect upon the fish, and after a short interval all those in the poisoned area will float belly upwards, at first only stupefied, but very soon quite dead.

By the end of the rains great tracts of country are under water, and fish naturally retreat into the quieter waters away from the swirling currents. Moreover. as the waters spread over ground covered with trees and dense undergrowth, the fish have a royal time, feeding on grubs and other forms of insect life. But when the waters recede great numbers are cut off from the stream, and are trapped in land-locked pools. The natives know these spots; further, they block the mouths of small streams by barricades of stakes, and thus prevent fish from returning to the rivers. In due season fish drives are organised or recourse is had to poisoning; in any case great quantities of fish are taken annually in this manner.

The European fisherman will, of course, attempt to follow his own methods, or adapt them to local conditions. For big fish, spinning is a recognised style of angling, but I have found it so troublesome that, except in certain waters, it is wiser to leave this method alone. In lakes and in cleared rivers it may meet with success but the waters are so full of trees and other debris, that it is practically impossible to spin. The same may be said of fly-fishing. One cannot wade, and the bush is so dense about the banks that there is scarcely room to raise the rod, certainly not enough elbow-room to cast. Better work can be done if a canoe is available with a paddler endowed with sense—it is very difficult to convince a native that one is sane and sober when one tries fly-fishing. The special difficulty is with the line; dressed lines become very sticky, whereas undressed lines absorb water so freely that they soon get too heavy for casting properly. Sole-skin minnows thrown as flies, and budding cassava leaves have proved the best attractions in my experiences of this mode of fishing. As far as my experience proves the best sport is obtained from simple bottom fishing—or ledgering, using as bait the gut of fowls or lob-worms dug out from near the water's edge. The common worm (idide) is an extraordinary freak. It cannot be used for fishing, inasmuch as directly it is handled it has a tantalising habit of falling into tiny sections and even if, after considerable trouble, you succeed in threading one, either the water will wash it off, or small fry nibbling around will speedily leave the hook clean. Some fish give a fair amount of play and are very good eating; some are hard pullers, especially the scaleless kind, that lie in the deeps; these have tapering bodies, large flat heads, and most ugly mouths furnished with two or more whiskers.

The manatee [1] flourishes in certain waters and its

[1] *Manatus senegalensis*, or sea-cow, of the Sirenian family, an ar-breathing and vegetarian animal. It has no teeth in the front of the jaws but has a good set of grinders. It is a slow, sluggish creature and quite unhappy out of water. It prefers quiet, shallow water. It has but one calf at a time, and this the mother is said to hold under her fore-flipper, the teats being situated just behind the arm-pits.—*The Wild Beasts of the World*, Frank Finn.

capture might reasonably be included under fishing. This quaint dark-skinned animal attains to a length of five feet and more. It lows like a cow and gambols in the water. In the district with which I am most acquainted, it is usually trapped. The traps (nkwu) consist of stout stakes placed near the bank, or in a patch of weed favoured by the beast as food. Immediately it has passed through the entrance, it displaces a catch and the door of the trap falls ; the animal is thus imprisoned and is dispatched with spears. No woman may look upon the carcase until the tail and flappers have been removed. The flesh is highly prized, and the thick leathery hide off the back is cut into tapering square strips, which are then twisted into spiral form and allowed to harden. When hard-set the strips are used as canes; they are of dull-amber colour but are greatly improved by polishing. Sometimes they are split up for two-thirds of their length and made into switches, which, in capable hands, can be used with most enlivening effect. The underpart of the animal is not skinned; the skin of this part is eaten with the flesh. It is soft and the natives liken it to the creamy contents of a young coco-nut.

There are several legends connected with the manatee. One is to the effect that when a man gets into difficulties in deep water, the beast tickles him under the arm, thus causing him to laugh; the result is that he opens his mouth and is drowned.

Hunting proper is confined to comparatively few men, and except in special circumstances the hunter's equipment is limited to trap and flint-lock. For some years past a man here and there, at certain riverside stations, has wrought great execution amongst hippopotami, buffalo and buck, with a modern rifle. Egrets and marabouts have also been ruthlessly slaughtered for their feathers; but in the hinterland the native hunter must depend upon his old flintlock and his stalking powers. Such a hunter is easily recognised by his gun and bag. The former is long in barrel, of the pattern seen in museums and military tournament pageants. Over the flint and striker is a cowl of untanned skin—on the western side of the Niger a piece of chimpanzee skin is preferred to all other kinds.

Encircling the stock is a daubed mass resembling pitch; really it consists of cords bound round the stock which have been so frequently smeared with the blood of victims that they have become a congealed mass—black with exposure, and polished by continual handling. As each bird or animal is slain, the blood is offered to the gun in token of success. A hunter's prowess can be calculated by the amount of congealed blood deposited on the stock of his gun. Common black powder is used, and the slugs are manufactured by local smiths from bar iron; or what is termed "pot-leg" is used, i.e. old cast-iron cooking pots broken into pieces. The flint comes from the old-world village of Brandon, on the borders of Norfolk and Suffolk, where the knappers ply their ancient trade, some of their handiwork finding a ready sale at the "kwulu awtaw" market at Ubulu, a large centre of trade with a flourishing market held every sixteenth day.

The hunter wears nothing but the scantiest of girdles. He needs to be untrammelled in his movements in order to wriggle his way through jungle, grass and scrub. Nor must he grudge a lavish expenditure of time and strength. He must not be particularly fastidious about weather nor indeed allow any circumstance, however uncomfortable, to interfere with his profession. Scratches must be treated with indifference as he traverses the hunting ground, and clothes are impossible in his work. His knowledge of woodcraft generally develops into a sort of instinct, and he hears and sees game long before the European is aware of its vicinity. Good hunters imitate the calls of birds and beasts, and by this means are often successful in attracting game within reach of their gun. Unfortunately they have wrought great execution amongst the animals and birds, and their efforts have been so persistent that game is exceedingly scarce. The native hunter being able to adapt himself to the conditions of the country enjoys better sport than the white man. Buck, large monkeys, and occasionally a bush cow or leopard are brought in. For the last, traps are preferred to a gun, the hunter being in dangerous plight if he does not kill with his one shot. Traps are built with logs; some are oblong in shape with

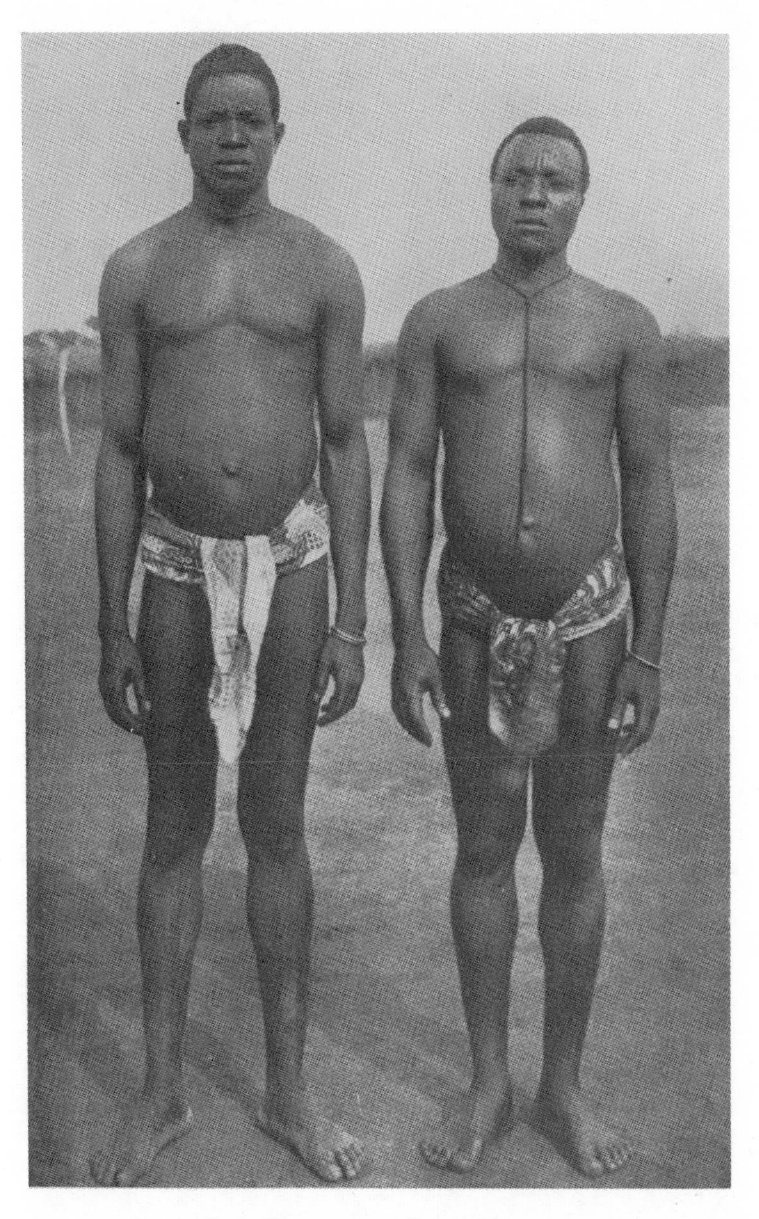

FINE SPECIMENS OF YOUNG MANHOOD

The Ibos are capable of great endurance, but quickly lose heart.

a falling door, others with simply a falling log heavy enough to pin down, if not break the back of the unfortunate brute. The customary bait is a dog or young kid. The flesh of every species of animal and bird is stock for the pot, but the skins of the buck and leopard family are the only pelts preserved.

The killing of a leopard is a red-letter day in a hunter's life. On accomplishing the deed, he cuts off the tail and feet as trophies. The carcase is taken to the house of the chief, who formally waves it as a thankoffering before his alusi (idols). The chief presents a fowl to the hunter as a token of congratulation. These ceremonies over, the town is paraded, the carcase being carried round in procession, the slayer bearing the tail in his hand amidst the plaudits of the crowd, and being greeted with the salutation of "leopard-slayer." When these perambulations cease the beast is skinned, and the chief receives his portion, viz. one leg; the remainder is disposed of at the hunter's pleasure. The teeth and claws always fetch a good price for ornamenting necklaces.

Elephants are now rarely killed in the Ibo country, though the older men can remember the days when they were fairly numerous. Whilst travelling in the Asaba hinterland in 1900, one of the leaders of our party carried an elephant's ear, chiefly as a symbol of his profession and prowess. When convenient he used it as a fan or seat cover.

The hunter has his own particular fetishes, whose aid is invoked prior to undertaking any trip, and due acknowledgment is made to them for a safe return, and especially if the expedition has been successful. The skulls of the animals slain are preserved and hung in the hut of the hunter. Here we see primitive instinct manifesting itself in a desire to display trophies of the chase; the same passion for the evidence of man's slaying propensities which dominates the owner of the manor house and baronial hall, the only difference being that whereas the native hangs up the crude skull, undressed by any process of taxidermy, the civilized hunter has his specimens embellished—each according to the resources at his command.

The native hunter can also relate stories of the chase, and dilate upon adventures in the recesses of the forest; of monsters encountered and hair-breadth escapes, especially from gigantic buffaloes and pythons.

Man-hunting had its recognised place in the Ibo hunter's profession, and a stranger encountered during the hunter's travels was stalked and shot as a wild animal would be. Indeed, regular expeditions used to be organised for this purpose, and the man-killer was duly proclaimed a hero similarly to the leopard-slayer. In this case, a limb of the victim was carried in procession round the town and the hunter received congratulations from cheering crowds. An instance of this barbarous custom occurred within a few miles of Onitsha as recently as 1906.

CHAPTER XIII

THE YAM—THE IBO STAFF OF LIFE

The cultivation of yams absorbs such a great proportion of time and energy that it deserves appropriate attention when writing about the occupations of the Ibos. To be deprived of yam creates a condition of acute distress. Whatever substitute may be offered it cannot satisfy the native's desire for his favourite food. Yam is not indigenous to the country—tradition says it was introduced by the Portuguese. There are many varieties, which differ greatly in size, appearance and flavour, also as regards the soil they require for successful growth ; but the method of cultivation is practically the same for all. Any native can reel off a list of from ten to twenty varieties, and can dilate upon the soil suitable for the production of each. The yam is a tuber ; as a foodstuff, and as an agricultural product, it is equivalent to the potato in Ireland. To ensure good crops the location of the " farm " must be changed at frequent intervals—generally after two or three successive plantings. The necessity for such changes arises chiefly from the fact that no dressing for the soil is procurable, other than a poor supply of leaves and grass, hence the soil must be allowed to lie fallow in order to recover its fertility. In most parts of the country fresh ground can be arranged for without difficulty as the area at the disposal of the people is ample for the purpose.

The site of the farm having been chosen it receives a rough clearing. The smaller trees are cut down to the stumps, and the larger ones lopped unmercifully, and the whole of the debris is burnt, but no roots are grubbed up. The soil is earthed up into circular mounds on the higher levels, but into large oblong beds in swampy districts.

The depth is regulated according to the size of yam under cultivation. A foot high is sufficient for certain varieties, whereas others require twice that depth and a full square yard is worked up to form each mound. One seed-yam is set in each mound, the best crops being raised from whole seed, but where economy has to be studied the tuber may be cut into sections.

The planting of the yam is a serious and important business to the native, and under the old system of government any infringement of the farming etiquette led to grave consequences. Yam stealing—whether of freshly planted seed or the mature root—was punishable by death. In spite of the extreme risk farms were sometimes raided. Since the introduction of English criminal law this sort of robbery has increased greatly, as the penalties now do not inspire sufficient fear. The risk comes, of course, when the thief is discovered red-handed at his nefarious work on the farm. In such circumstances it may result in tragedy, for the thief, or the detector may be rendered *hors de combat.* The thief will fight for life, and one has seen cases where most desperate consequences have followed the surprising of a thief in a yam farm. On one occasion a woman was brought to the Mission House in a horribly mutilated condition after an encounter with a thief in her farm. At the time of the setting of the seed it is no uncommon incident to be aroused in the early morning by the wails of some unfortunate person whose farm has been raided during the night. I have seen a man labour diligently for weeks preparing a farm, and then every seed yam was stolen in a single night, the thief though unaided by light having done his work extremely neatly, unearthing each buried yam with unerring precision. To prevent their seed from being stolen in this manner some men sleep on their farms during the early part of the season, and again as harvest time approaches.

I remember one case in which a boy planted a farm. Shortly afterwards he had to go away on a short visit. During his absence a woman came in with a basket of seed-yams; she poured out a long story to the effect that her farm had been raided, and that she had traced the footprints of the thief, and found that they led to the lad's farm; she had, therefore, dug up the seed planted there declaring that they were the identical yams stolen from her own farm. I kept the basket until the lad's return and then conducted an investigation. The case was decided by examination of the seed yams; without hesitation the witnesses declared the yams had been cut by a man: a woman would have cut them differently. It was a mystery how this fact could be discerned with such indubitable precision. Then a man stepped forward and picked out certain yams from the basket and said, "I gave the lad these yams." How he recognised the yams again is a further matter of wonder, except it be on the analogy of the huntsman distinguishing his hounds, a feat which invariably astonishes the casual spectator. The evidence being overwhelming, the woman was declared guilty of yam stealing. She ought, by native law, to have suffered the extreme penalty, but that did not commend itself; instead she was let off on agreeing to replant the lad's farm, and on her husband paying him ten shillings compensation for the attempt to defame his character.

A flourishing yam farm bears a strong resemblance to a Kentish hopfield. The vines need support, and for this purpose sticks are provided. The tendency, in the early stages of growth, is for the tendrils to run up the supports too rapidly, and they must frequently be unwound and set back to a lower level. Certain kinds, grown more for specimen roots and ornamental foliage than for use, need poles from twelve to fifteen feet long, or strings stretched from the ground to branches of tall trees. Up these the yams climb, and when in full leaf present a very pleasing and picturesque aspect.

The largest and earliest variety (ji abi) is grown either actually in the bed of a stream or on the lowest part of the banks in the rich vegetable deposits left by the floods of the previous wet season. Here the growth is extremely rapid and progress can be fostered by regular watering from the neighbouring stream. The yams need to be ready for lifting by the time the waters begin to rise; they cannot, however, be left to ripen. These yams grow to an immense size; often they measure two feet or more in length by from five to seven inches in diameter. They are always the first in the market and meet with a ready sale. They are unsuitable for storage, as they have to be dug up before they have the chance to dry, and they correspond to the early potatoes in England. In substance they are of softer consistency and more watery, and also whiter than yams grown on drier ground.

Though there is a great rush to buy these early yams, the native greatly prefers the more substantial varieties gathered in at the close of the season. Moreover, a too free use of ji abi is liable to lead to stomach troubles. The main crop is not dug up till the middle of October or later, i.e. when they have completely dried and are fully ripe.

After sticking the young yam plants the soil around the roots must be earthed up, and during the early torrential downpours this work is frequently necessary. Weeds flourish in most extraordinary fashion and constant labour is required to keep them under. This is mostly done by the women, who use small semi-circular hoes—a simple bow-shaped piece of iron with a handle at each end worked in the same way as a spokeshave.

. . . . .

The place of the yam in the political economy of the country presents a study of no little interest. Land needs to be fairly rich and extensive in area for the raising of large crops. Where the soil is poor, as in parts of the Awka district, it is a moot question whether sufficient yams could be raised locally to supply the needs of the population. Of agricultural products, serving as the staple food of a people, the yam must be classed as one of the most extravagant. In comparison with the yield, the production of yam entails a large acreage, strenuous labour and constant attention during some seven or eight months of the year. Were it not for intermediate crops of maize and beans, and a subsequent catch-crop of cassava, it is doubtful whether yam would repay cultivation.

Each seed yam planted produces two of its kind—one

fit for food, the second, a tiny one which is the seed for the ensuing year. Seed yams are also specially raised by two methods. When the yams are at all fit for food, i.e. before they are ripe, they may be dug up as required. The sap being still fresh in the foliage the bulbs of the tendrils are replanted, and by the end of the season a small seed yam is formed. The second method is to cut up larger yams into small sections and plant them ; in this way good stock seed yam may be raised in readiness for the following season. The occupation of the country by the British, and the extraordinarily rapid opening up and development of hitherto closed districts, have brought about changes which have quite upset the equilibrium of the yam market. Prior to the influx into the country of a multitude of non-farming aliens, the yam supply, eked out by the use of cassava, maize and koko (edde), was equal to the needs of the natives. Each household raised its own crops by its own labour, and could, should circumstances be adverse, make itself completely independent of outside sources of food supply. There were a few exceptions to this general rule, the town of Awka furnishing one such instance. Here the men are all blacksmiths, and agriculture is considered *infra dig.* Their business is moreover, a lucrative one, and the Awka men rely upon their ability to purchase food for their households, which, hitherto, they have found little difficulty in doing.

But with the ever-spreading development of the country this primitive state of things is being upset and the problem of a native food supply is becoming acute in centres like Onitsha, where the population is steadily increasing. The native agriculturist, with the conservative instincts of his forefathers, continues to cultivate solely for the needs of his dependents, and only here and there are to be found men who realise that there is a ready market for yams under the new conditions. The number of Europeans has grown tremendously during the last decade, and behind them comes a host of coast-born native immigrants who flock into the country and take up positions as clerks and traders. In addition there are hundreds of local natives who are employed by these foreigners as servants, labourers and artizans—all of whom have practically forsaken agriculture as a means of livelihood, and who now rely upon being able to purchase their food supply. The consequence is that the quantity of yams available is quite inadequate and recourse must be had to imported provisions.

There is another aspect to the study of yam cultivation. Not only does it make exorbitant claims on land, labour and time, but, when brought to perfection, the yam appears to be singularly deficient in nutritive properties. A man expects to eat from four to ten yams per diem, and thus even a small household will consume an enormous number in a week. In the case of ji abi the number is much less, of course, as they are of great size, but, on the other hand, they are only in season for a very brief period. If the supply be less, a man speaks of himself as being in a state of hunger, and he invariably answers any enquiry concerning his health by, "Very well, only for hunger." Pounded yam disappears at an astonishing rate, it being swallowed wholesale, without mastication, and a person must needs eat a very generous allowance to sustain his physical powers. To retain his strength a man has to make up in quantity for what is lacking in quality, and an Ibo vegetarian diet is the reverse of attractive.

With the suppression of inter-tribal warfare, slave raiding, infanticide and other depopulating customs, the establishment of pacific government and the introduction of sanitary laws, the indigenous natives will increase much more rapidly than heretofore. With the improvements in the state of the country resulting from these measures, the expansion of trade, and the widening of Government control, more and more foreigners will enter the country. The consequent increase in the population will necessitate a corresponding increase in the food supply. The immediate effect has been to create a demand which cannot be met from the existing local resources, and prices have advanced in ratio at least 100% since the Government assumed direct administration of the country in 1900. Were it not for the importation of rice,

CLIMBING A PALM-TREE FOR NUTS AND WINE

A rope composed of twisted creepers encircles the trunk and the body of the climber, and by a series of jerks it is raised a foot or more at a time, the weight of the man's body preventing it from slipping. The rapidity with which these climbers literally "walk" up a palm-tree is marvellous. The large knife is for the purpose of severing the bunches of nuts.

biscuits, dried fish and preserved provisions generally, famine and distress would have been sorely felt by many, especially during the last few years. It goes without saying, that this introduction of foreign food is another of the host of sins laid to the missionaries' charge; one more denationalising factor for which, no doubt, they will be accounted responsible.

For augmenting the supply of both food and drink, the natives living in important centres are beginning to rely very largely upon the trading canteens. This is inevitable, partly because of the scarcity of native grown products, but quite as much for economic reasons, the foreign commodities often being cheaper than the local supplies, particularly so at certain seasons of the year, when yam is at a prohibitive price, a single root fetching as much as sixpence or more in the open market. On the eastern side of the Niger, the conditions are much worse than on the western, the soil being less fertile while the demand is greater.

The repeal of the "Native House Ordinance" (as from January 1st, 1915), magnificent in its conception, and in true accord with British principles of liberty, and ultimately tending to the uplifting of the Ibo nation, will, nevertheless, raise further complications in the matter of the yam supply. Hitherto chiefs and other wealthy men have relied solely upon their slaves to till the ground. No wages were paid, but the slaves were granted every fourth day for their own affairs. It follows that a man's agricultural operations need only be limited by the acreage and the number of labourers at his disposal, and some rich men planted huge tracts of land. Even in these circumstances, with unpaid labour, we have seen that yams have appreciated in value to an extraordinary degree during recent years. What is the situation likely to be with the introduction of paid labour? As soon as there is an exodus from the "Houses" many chiefs will cease to farm on a large scale, and probably, in many cases, will themselves be reduced to straitened circumstances. The introduction of such a sweeping reform cannot be accomplished without creating difficulties, entailing, in some cases, heavy financial loss. There is every hope, however, that in the course of a few years, when the liberated slaves find their feet, many will become agriculturists and relieve the pressure, but meanwhile the economic problems are going to be more pronounced as a result of the repeal of the ordinance.

Successful yam cultivation requires a distinctive method of earthing up the soil, and this fact rather points to the improbability of any great agricultural reforms being introduced into the country so long as yam growing is the paramount industry. Ploughing would not answer, even were it possible. With no draught animals available the plough could not be adopted for general use ; it might find its place in maize growing if motor-driven ? As a matter of fact it seems highly probable that the primitive hoe will never be displaced for yam-farming purposes, and there is no doubt that the implement is peculiarly suitable and very effective in the hands of the native.

The future of agriculture in the section of Southern Nigeria under review provides scope for thought. It may follow a line of development in which certain crops will gain favour at the expense of others. Produce for which there is a good foreign market, such as palm oil, copra, maize, cocoa and cotton, may prove more profitable to the agriculturist than yam growing. In the place of yam the natives will purchase rice, biscuits, fish and other commodities. By these means the prosperity of both the import and export departments of commercial activity will be increased.

CHAPTER XIV

PALMS—FOR USE AND PROFIT

The palm trees indigenous to the Ibo country are blessings of inestimable value. Every part of them can be used—timber, leaves, sap and fruit. From the trunk the favourite timber for building is obtained, the leaves are used for thatching, the stem yields copious supplies of palm wine, and the fruit is not only good for food but it is also a very profitable source of income.

No attempt is here made to write scientifically upon the subject of palms, and nothing will be stated beyond what any ordinary man might observe.

There are many species of palms, but we shall confine our remarks to the more common and important varieties which figure so largely in the daily life of the people. By far the most abundant, and withal, the most valuable, is the oil-palm (*Elœis guineensis*), which flourishes over almost the whole of the Ibo country in greater or less degree according to locality. In certain parts palms rear their lofty heads in the richest profusion, whereas in other districts they are comparatively few and are limited to such as are grown within the precincts of the villages.

One cannot describe the Ibo's method of cultivating the oil-palm, because he has none. All that can be said is that no native will deliberately destroy a palm, except where thinning out is essential for the good of the trees. At the same time he will not exert himself, or put himself to any inconvenience, in order to save a palm tree from destruction. All the oil palms spring from self-sown seed. Thousands of seedlings shoot forth their upright spikes of leaves, and great numbers are trampled underfoot or destroyed in the furious bush fires which rage towards the close of the dry season. This, of course, accounts for the fact that the choicest trees are in the vicinity of the houses, where they escape burnings, and also receive the benefit of the compound sweepings. The kernels from which the seedlings spring have fallen from over-ripe bunches of nuts, or have been cast out as refuse. Those found in the bush grow mostly from the seed scattered by parrots and other birds. No attention is bestowed upon the tree until it begins to bear fruit. This occurs as soon as the crown of the palm is matured, beginning when it is about a foot above ground level. The nuts grow in dense clusters close to the stem of the tree, at the base of the fronds, and are like bunches of jet until they ripen, when they gradually change to yellow and bright red, leaving only a small part black at the top of the nut.

Every oil-palm is owned by somebody; the trees can be sold as they stand, but when land is transferred by purchase all oil-palms go with it, they are accounted as part and parcel with the plot; but coco-nut palms are not included in the transaction; these remain the property of the man who planted them, and they cannot be interfered with without the sanction of the original owner or his successors. A man may be merely farming a piece of land, or he may actually be dwelling upon it and working portions of it, but such occupation does not necessarily imply rights of ownership over any coco-nut palms standing upon it.

From the time that the crown of the oil-palm reaches maturity the fronds (ìgù) are regularly lopped off, usually in most ruthless fashion, leaving but two or three undeveloped fronds standing upright out of the crown of the tree. The welfare of the palm is not considered by the native when lopping it; he wants the fronds for various purposes and he takes them. In the farming season the goats must be kept in the compound, and immense quantities of palm leaves are then consumed by the animals.

The trunks of the trees are grey and black in colour, and extremely rough through regular lopping and continuous tapping for palm wine. At intervals up the trunk, ferns and parasitic plants find root-hold and flourish luxuriantly, adding much to the picturesqueness of the tree. The crown of the palm, whence the fronds spring, is a large bowl-shaped growth, out of which, between the stumps of the fronds, the fruit forms.

The trunk of the tree is composed wholly of fibre and can scarcely be described as timber. At the root the fibres are separate and distinct, and they spread out into a stringy mass some two or three feet above the surface of the ground. The trees are not firmly rooted and, but for the springiness of the trunk tissue, would be easily uprooted. As it is the tornadoes often wreak considerable havoc amongst them and not infrequently the crowns are snapped off by the sudden gusts of wind. When once the trees are established, the bush fires appear to inflict no permanent or serious damage ; indeed, the natives maintain that they derive benefit from the ordeal. The dry refuse collected in the crown of the palm is ignited by tufts of wind-driven burning grass, and this continues to burn until it is all consumed. For the time being the tree is black and blasted, but in a very short time it puts forth fresh green shoots.

When the nuts are ripe the bunch is sometimes allowed to fall, but it is preferable to cut it whilst the nuts are still attached. For this purpose professional climbers are employed. There are two common methods followed by these men, one requiring a single climbing rope, the other two ; for the former method some stout live creeper-canes are selected and these are plaited into a rope from eight to ten feet in length. The central part is heavily sheathed with grass carefully bound on, thus increasing the diameter to three or four inches. This precaution is taken to prevent chafing the rope itself, and further, which is equally important, the extra size enables the craftsman to slide the rope more readily up and down the rough surface of the trunk ; the larger it is the less liable it is to jam in a notch. When about to climb, the man encircles himself and the trunk with his rope and firmly knots the two ends. Slipping his matchet into his girdle, or carrying it between his chin and shoulder, he grasps the rope firmly with both hands, throwing his whole weight back upon it. Then, assuming an angle of about 45° he proceeds to walk up the trunk, throwing his rope higher as he ascends by jerking it upward about two feet at a time. To execute the movement he must press his feet firmly against the tree and keep his legs rigid. He then pulls himself forward with his hands and, for a second, takes the strain off the rope, at the same time sliding it up the trunk before he drops back into the reclining position. Although each act is separate and distinct, yet so rapidly is the whole carried out that it appears to be one movement. The top of the tree is reached in a very short time, and there the climber maintains his position by stiffening his legs and pressing backwards on the rope. He thus has the free use of his hands and he proceeds to cut nuts or branches as required, working round and round the crown of the palm until his task is accomplished.

The double rope method is quite different. It is more intricate and it looks more dangerous also. The two ropes are about five feet in length with looped ends. The climber casts one rope round the tree, threads one loop through the other and pulls it just taut enough to prevent it from slipping. He then passes his left leg through the dangling loop as far as the middle of the thigh. The second rope is treated likewise, but is placed some eighteen inches lower down the trunk than the first, and instead of the right leg being passed through, the sole of the foot presses upon the loop. Whilst climbing up and down the weight is changed alternately from one rope to the other, each being slipped higher or lower in turn. It is obvious that greater balancing power is demanded for this second method. The man must assume a more or less upright position, always pressing backward with his foot and leg to keep the loops from slipping. He is necessarily brought closer to the trunk of the tree, and consequently the scope for arm play is much more restricted.

Occasionally the rope breaks or slips, or the climber misses his grip, and the result is always horribly painful, if not fatal. The man makes a desperate effort to throw his arms round the tree; he may save himself from an actual fall and yet be unable to check his descent before he has slipped a considerable way down the trunk. The rough sharp projections tear the climber's flesh in a particularly agonising manner. He may, of course, lose his hold altogether and fall to the ground, which is still more disastrous; one has had to practise rough surgery in order to alleviate suffering, and generally to patch up some who have been unfortunate enough to meet with mishaps of this kind. I was once converting an ancient and rusty fangbolt into a woodscrew, and, thinking that it had reversed clear of the die, I grasped the screw to release it from the revolving head of the machine, a simple operation. But it had not passed clear, and the rough edges carved spirals in the flesh of my hand. When a man slips down a palm tree he receives a series of gashes of a somewhat similar type, only in a greatly magnified degree and, moreover, the whole front of his legs, body, hands and arms suffer. One's whole sympathy naturally is aroused for the victim of such a merciless "screwing" process.

The oil-palm is put to many uses by the native, of which only the principal need be mentioned. For house-building purposes the trunks of the trees are split and the parts serve for rafters, cross-beams and wall-plates, but only as a last resort for posts. The wood rots quickly and also suffers greatly from the depredations of those unmitigated pests—the termites, more commonly known as white ants. The fibres of the trunk are woven into fish traps; when finely drawn they are manufactured into very good substitutes for banjo strings; they are also plaited into cord. The leaves (fronds) are in great demand for protecting the clay compound walls; they are laid lengthwise, between supporting pegs, on the top, and are excellent for throwing off the heavy downpours of rain. They are also used as fodder for goats.

After the green parts are removed the bones (as one of the boys aptly described them) of the leaves are converted into very efficient little brooms. These uses are common to all the oil-palms, but for wine and fruit the value of the different species varies greatly. Of these the natives have distinguishing names for three, viz. awsukwa, okpoloko and ojukwu. If a tree be exceptionally prolific in nuts, yielding good oil, it receives a courtesy title such as nne-nkwu (mother of palms) in acknowledgment. Some trees produce nuts of magnificent appearance but which are mostly kernel and hence of little profit; such are the ok-poloko. Others yield oil in abundance irrespective of size and appearance, and these are styled awsukwu. The ojukwu is not a large producer, but its oil is bright red in colour and is highly valued by the people.

There is one other palm which it is of interest to note, viz. the one called oke-nkwu (the male palm). No fruit is ever found upon it; it merely produces a cluster of flowers which dry up and remain on the tree for a considerable time. From these particular trees, tapped immediately beneath the bunch of flowers, is extracted the most powerful palm wine, known as "up-wine." It is "up" in two respects: it comes from the top part of the tree and it is more liable to get "up" into the consumer's head!

It is the men's business to cut down the nuts and the women's duty to extract the oil. The bunches are deposited in a corner and left for a few days, after which they are readily stripped from the large pear-shaped stalk (obwe-akwu) upon which they cluster in a compact mass. The nuts are thereupon placed in a mortar for pounding. This implement is made from a section of hardwood tree, hollowed out, and fixed vertically in the ground. The leading man only of the clan owns a mortar, and it is usually fixed just outside the front door of his compound, convenient for the use of the villagers. The nuts are vigorously pounded, an operation in which the young men will often render assistance, until the kernel has been entirely stripped of its fleshly covering. The whole mass is then carried down to the stream; a hole is scooped out in the bank and filled with water, into which the pounded nuts are cast. The women keep the water on the stir and gradually the kernels and fibrous matter are disintegrated; the oil rises to the surface and is skimmed off. It is a smelly, unattractive process, but to fishermen the vicinity of a palm oil wash-hole is always worth giving a trial.

This is the method adopted by the folk eastward of Onitsha, but it is not favoured by the people of that town nor on the western side of the Niger. In these districts,

1. Town Deities, Adonta, near Awgwash
2. A Medicine Man, with his Stock-in-Trade

after stripping, the nuts are first boiled in large iron pots. Then they are pounded and the oil is squeezed out by hand pressure. The refuse may be reboiled and the final drops of oil skimmed off. This strict economy is rarely practised, however, as the refuse is utilised as fuel. The ashes (ngu) from this fuel are used in the manufacture of native soap; they are dissolved in water for medicinal purposes, or again, they are especially prized for boiling with breadfruit or beans.

As an article of diet the oil is preferred in its liquid state. If it has not been boiled, it sets as hard as butter in a few days. Many traders will accept, nowadays, liquid oil only, i.e. boiled oil. This is a precaution against adulteration. The West African needs no instruction in that art; he was not incapable of mixing a good proportion of sand with the oil so long as the trader would buy it in solidified form; the native is an expert in the subtleties of trade.

The natives retain as much oil as they need for household use as food, lamp oil and for the manufacture of soap and other purposes, and, where there is a market for it, dispose of the rest. In the districts tapped by the trading companies immense quantities are brought in by the people, and exchanged for cash, trade goods, or the inevitable gin.

The nuts (commonly termed kernels) are dried and sold separately, a few only being retained by the women. Those that are kept are cracked and the kernels fried for a considerable time, in order to extract the oil. This particular oil is in demand for anointing the body, and hairdressing; it has a certain brilliance which is much appreciated by the natives. They are also partial to chewing the kernels as a relish with corn and dried cassava. In normal nuts there is one kernel only, but occasionally one will be found which divides into two or three sections. In such cases one person must eat all; should they be shared those guilty of the foolish act will later become the parents of twins, a most undesirable issue. Double kernels are, in consequence, usually preserved and used as "medicine."

Palm wine is drawn from the palms and varies in sweetness and strength according to the species of tree selected.

The most common method for extracting the sap is by tapping the standing tree near the crown, but at one time many trees were felled solely to provide wine quickly. This custom was much more prevalent on the western than on the eastern side of the Niger, where the palms are not in such abundance as to permit of this wanton destruction. By far the greatest proportion of the wine supply comes from the ngwaw palms ; these flourish in marshy localities only. The fruit is of no use except for providing seed, but the leaves are valuable for the manufacture of "bamboo mats"—an excellent thatching material. The "bamboo" poles serve as rafters and laths to which the thatching mats are tied. The ngwaw plantations furnish huge quantities of wine. In appearance, and in taste, it resembles the old-fashioned stone bottle ginger-beer ; it is pleasant to drink and very refreshing. The strictest teetotaller may drink freely of this without experiencing undue excitement. There are natives who will not touch this ngwaw wine. In some cases an embargo against its use is laid upon a man by the dibia who, after consultation, declares this to be the will of the ju-ju. Such a person will never attempt to drink palm wine, nor will he even be tempted to break the solemn injunction laid upon him ; the consequence of trifling with the commands of the ju-ju is far too serious. Old men frankly despise ngwaw wine as being too weak and fit only for women and children ; they have to continue drinking so long before they feel that they are making any headway.

The wine procured from the oil-palm is much stronger ; it is likewise extracted by tapping. This is classed as nkwu-enu (up-wine). It is quite different in taste from the ngwaw and has a more powerful effect upon the drinker, especially if he be at no pains to restrain his appetite. It quickly ferments and becomes more vinegary than ever, and is then extremely unpleasant to Europeans. It is never wasted, however, by the old men ; if it gets beyond even their powers, it is mixed with the new supply. One is bound to admit that there is, on the whole, very little drunkenness from palm wine drinking. This is probably accounted for by the fact that the suppliers do not hesitate to dilute their stocks very liberally with water. This again applies more particularly to the eastern side of the Niger. On the western side where the trees are in greater abundance, there is not the same inducement to, or necessity for, adulteration.

In many parts, notably in towns like Onitsha, palm wine is being rapidly superseded by foreign drinks. One is almost invariably offered whisky, gin or some other imported liquor nowadays.

The trees are tapped by driving in a sharp chisel. Beneath the hole thus pierced a calabash is hung, the wine being conducted into it by means of a funnel made with a leaf or a reed (ami). The collector visits his trees night and morning, emptying the calabashes and retrapping as he considers advisable.

There is another species of palm which flourishes freely in certain localities, generally where the soil is inclined to be poor and stony. The native name is "ubili." The foliage is extremely graceful, each frond springing up on a long stem and then opening out fanwise. The divisions of the leaves are webbed for about half their length and then separate into individual spikes. The fruit is not unlike a large orange in appearance and has a very hard kernel. It is consumed by the natives, but it is by no means a popular article of diet. The chief value of this tree lies in the wood, which is eagerly sought after for house-building purposes, the posts, wall-plates, and any part coming in contact with the clay walls, being of ubili whenever possible. The leaves are cleverly plaited into fans, baskets, mats and the like.

Finally there is the coco-nut, which, though not indigenous, is widely distributed over the country. We have already noted that every coco-nut palm is the property of the man who planted it, wherever it may stand. The slender, graceful trunk often develops a leaning tendency, in contrast with the more stocky oil-palm. It grows to a great height, and the blossom, springing from the crown, is a pronounced feature. The fruit is in season all the year round; the timber of this palm also is in great request for building purposes. A great many nuts are cut down whilst the kernel is in the creamy stage ; they are gathered solely for the sake of the refreshing liquid they contain. The quantity of milk yielded by some of the fresh green nuts is extraordinary. It must be used without long delay as the unripe nuts spoil quickly. The ordinary nuts are eaten, not exactly as a recognised foodstuff, but rather chewed as something pleasant to the palate. In famine time they are eaten as a relish with dry corn. The eating of coco-nut is also one of the signs of mourning. In one town I visit from time to time, the coco-nut is taboo in every farm, and no native will touch it. I had the greatest difficulty in purchasing one or two when travelling in that neighbourhood. It is the more remarkable inasmuch as there are no water-springs thereabouts, and the natives are forced to rely for water largely on the impure and limited supplies stored in catchpits. The natives extract oil from the ripe nuts chiefly for the purpose of anointing their bodies. The copra industry, I understand, does not pay around Onitsha, though it has better prospects in other neighbourhoods.

When nuts are required the boys readily climb the trees, clasping the trunk with their hands, doubling their bodies and then walking up on their feet. The tallest trees are climbed in this manner without the slightest hesitation or fear. It will now be obvious that no trees could be more generally useful to the native than the various species of palms which grow, more or less abundantly, throughout the length and breadth of the Ibo country.

CHAPTER XV

SOME ARTS AND CRAFTS

THE arts and crafts of the Ibo manifest themselves first in his home. The ideas and tastes of both husband and wife are indicated by the care bestowed in the building and decoration of the house. The styles are many; the materials are practically alike for all. Every man can be (and usually is) his own architect and builder, and, with the aid of relatives and friends, constructs such a house as he considers suitable or as circumstances permit. The walls are always composed of clay of terra-cotta colour. About the middle of the wet season clay puddling begins, an occupation which though simple is strenuous, and demands care to ensure the best results. Somewhere on the building site a hole is dug, all the loamy top soil being thrown aside, and the red clay subsoil exposed. This clay is broken up into clods with hoes and left in readiness until the next fall of rain, which is conducted into the pit through channels cut for the purpose. After a shower young men go down into the hole and puddle the loosened clay with their feet, more and more being added, or more water being thrown into the mixture as required, to bring it to a proper consistency. This is tiring work as the clay pulls heavily on the feet. When prepared the clay is thrown out, and at the close of the day's work the heap is well covered with banana leaves or grass to protect it from rain and sun. The task is repeated at intervals throughout the wet season, or until a sufficient quantity of clay is ready for the proposed building. Meantime the superfluous water drains away from the heap of clay, and the mass is greatly improved by this mellowing process.

With the advent of the dry season the builders bestir themselves, and on working days the site is alive with a company of busy men and boys. The native seldom troubles to peg out the lines of his house; he opens out foundations simply by rule-of-thumb methods. He makes no calculations either as to materials or finances; he simply starts, and then proceeds as long as the wherewithal is forthcoming. Should plans fail he waits for better times, and then continues the work.

The footings are from six to twelve inches in depth and about a foot in width, and upon these he raises the clay walls, but these do not carry the roof; that is always independent of the walls.

The now stiffened clay is pulled off in lumps, the size of a football, kneaded together, and carried by the boys to the builder, who flops them into position and rams them with his fist, at the same time roughly trimming the sides with his hands. A complete course all round is laid, some eighteen inches in height, and work ceases for the day. In a few days the sun has hardened the clay sufficiently for a second course to be added, and so it goes on until the walls are of the required height. Before the clay is quite hard, and when it is in sound condition for trimming, the walls are straightened with a sharp matchet. They are much benefited if well rubbed with water at this time, and all interstices plugged; the best clay (upa) opens out in large cracks as it is drained of liquid.

It sometimes happens that a man is not prepared to go to the expense and trouble of such sound walls; he also wants them erected quickly, and he then has recourse to the Ibo jerry-builder, but a clever man for all that. There are experts in dry-wall building. These men use hoes and matchets and a sprinkling of water only. The soil is loosened in a straight line and this is piled, rammed first with a foot, and finally trimmed and beaten hard with wooden beaters, the face of the wall being occasionally moistened with water sprayed on with the mouth. It is surprising what a quantity of water some of these ekwe builders can hold in the mouth and how clever they are at spraying it. Frequently good builders will erect quite a long wall in the course of a day. After wet rubbing it is sufficiently substantial for ordinary buildings and, up to six feet in height, if protected from the most severe of the torrential downpours, will be serviceable for many years. Such a building must always be tapered in structure, the base being much wider than the top.

For the roof, centre and side posts are fixed, either in the ground clear of the walls, or more usually buried in the walls. A very common course is to erect the framework of the roof first and then make the walls fit it. The rafters are of offolaw (palm-fronds stripped of their leaves); the laths are of the same material but smaller in size. When these have been lashed into position the roof is ready for the thatch. This may be of palm leaf, termed "bamboo mats," (akanya or atani) tied on in regular courses like slates, or a grass thatch made somewhat roughly in sections on the ground, and then fastened on in overlapping rows, as seen at Onitsha; or it may be a really superior style of thatch, as adopted in the eastern districts. In the last case great pains are taken and a very thick and heavy covering of grass is bound on, necessitating an enormous number of rafters and laths, placed almost side by side, and stout timbers to carry the excessive weight. For these roofs the underside is finished off in a special manner with cleverly plaited string work (palm fibre). Such a roof will last a generation and corresponds very closely with the old English style of straw thatching. On the western side of the Niger huge leaves are used as substitutes for grass; the leaves of the ume being most in evidence. Those obtained from the ibwodo are preferred by the people but they are not so easily procured, this tree being rather scarce. The leaves are simply fastened on the roof-frame by their stalks.

The thatching is finished off with a thick layer of grass bound across the ridge, and over the corner angles should the roof be hipped.

A house constructed in this manner, if due care be taken, may be a veritable work of art. Not a nail is driven, the lighter framework being maintained in position solely by lashings of "tie-tie (ekwe)." This building material comes from certain climbing plants, and is used whole for parts subject to heavy strain, and split for the lighter work. When bamboo mats are chosen for thatching they are tied with fine tie-tie or young palm leaves (awmu) prepared for the purpose by being passed rapidly through fire. Such a roof is peculiarly suitable to the country. The non-rigidity of the structure and the springiness of the materials employed secure for it great wind-resisting qualities. There is no restriction as to length for a house built on native principles, but the width is arbitrarily limited, and the rafters must be steeply pitched to ensure the roof being watertight. To extend beyond a given width leads to sagging of the thatch, a fatal weakness which quickly renders the roof non-weatherproof.

The great drawback to houses thatched with palm leaf mats is the unceasing need of repairs, due to the extraordinary rapidity with which the materials perish. Where fires are continually burning the resinous smoke from the wood fuel proves a very serviceable preservative of the bamboo mats which then remain in a sound condition for a comparatively lengthened period.

Houses built by natives of local materials for occupation by Europeans are not to be despised, and those who have had experience of them often prefer them to the corrugated-iron roofed type. But in the European's house the volumes of smoke ascending from the fire on the floor are absent, and hence the thatch soon shows the devastating effects of boring insects and dry rot, or, what is infinitely worse, of white ants. Thus Europeans are wont, upon closer acquaintance, to lose their first affection for native-built houses, as for many other picturesque things. The roofs harbour mosquitoes and unnumbered insects of all sorts and sizes ; they also shed dust and bits of broken thatch. They are always low, in order to resist wind pressure, and the rooms are consequently dark and depressing. The constant repairs become wearisome, and especially in these latter days when there is increasing difficulty in purchasing bamboo mats and other materials. These bamboo mats are manufactured from the leaves of the ngwaw palm. Two long narrow strips, pulled off the out-

Thatching with Palm-leaf (Bamboo) Mats

side of the midrib of a palm branch, are laid upon the ground parallel to one another some six inches apart. A single leaf, so held that the stalk end projects a couple of inches beyond the lower strip, is then folded over the upper strip and pressed down flat, the glossy top side of the leaf being kept uppermost. Each leaf is pinned in three places with splinters of wood, one immediately below the upper strip, and the other two above and below the lower strip. Each leaf must be attached separately and must be fixed parallel with its fellows. When complete the mats may be from two to four feet in length. On casual inspection they appear to have a covering capacity of one foot in depth, multiplied by the length, but when actually used the width is limited to from four to six inches—the more they overlap the better if a thoroughly sound thatch is desired.

Allied to the builder's craft is the art of the decorator, and in this there is distinct scope for the expression of individual taste. It assumes the forms of modelling in relief on prominent parts of the clay walls, and working out flat designs in colours. Some of the clay mouldings are quite clever both in design and execution. The patterns are roughed out with a knife and smoothed off with the fingers, followed by a course of wet rubbing and polishing. A well-modelled wall is very effective; this work is allotted to the men. Designing in colours belongs to the women's department, being included in the domestic occupation of rubbing the house. (*Vide* Chap. VIII.)

The next big effect is concentrated upon the entrance to the compound. Chiefs and rich men like to fill in a long section of the front wall with a door and panels of uroko-wood, decorated with chip carving. The panels and the doors are literally chopped out of solid logs of timber. Butt ends are left projecting at the top and bottom of one side of the doors, and these fit into holes, one in the threshold and one in the lintel and serve as hinges.

On the face of the front wall rude drawings of fantastic figures may sometimes be observed; perhaps simply a series of strokes, or possibly rough outlines representing crocodiles and other strange creatures. I have questioned many natives about these in order to find out whether such marks possess any significance, but my inquiries have, without a single exception, met with a negative answer. The only wall marks to which any meaning is attached are the splashes of " medicine " sprinkled on with the native equivalent of the " bunch of hyssop."

The medicine itself is contained in a pot standing just inside the doorway, and the proper procedure for each visitor is to lift out the bunch of twigs and sprinkle the liquid (generally an evil-smelling concoction) across his feet. The sprinkling of the medicine upon the wall is part of the ceremony of protecting the house and its inmates from disease and the attentions of malignant spirits. The plain drawings, whether mere strokes or more defined outlines, are, as a rule, the productions of boys who exercise their propensity for such amusements exactly as children in England find pleasure in chalking figures on a wall.

Carving is a skilled occupation and is confined to professional men. Their tools are crudeness itself, and yet they turn out some neat handiwork, by no means lacking in artistic merit. Besides the chip-carved doors and panels already noticed, these men manufacture stools, ju-jus, dancing masks, and kola and snuff-boxes. The stools, upon which a real value is set, are carved out of solid blocks of uroko-wood and may be round or oblong. Some very good ones are produced solely for the use of chiefs, and no ordinary native will offend by attempting to sit upon one. The seat is supported on a single pillar which divides at the base into three or four curved feet. Other stools have fancy patterns worked out beneath the seat. The ju-jus consist mostly of the god " ikenga," the chief idol in every house. There are also town idols, and every Government Court House is furnished with a special ju-ju for swearing purposes, of hideous and revolting aspect; fearsome objects to behold but as ineffective as they are ugly; subjects of amused contempt to the native. No oath taken on or before such monstrosities is considered binding, nor do they serve in any way to elicit the truth and nothing but the truth. The native never accepts the invocation rites for such a ju-ju as genuine and binding, but, more important still, the oath of a native is never really effectual unless he swears on his own fetish. Their main interest is to demonstrate the ability of natives in carving figures in wood, many of them being nearly life size. The Court ju-jus usually represent a man sitting upon a stool: in his right hand he holds a drawn sword, and in the left a victim's head.[1] When the figure is new it is embellished richly with yellow, black, white and purple stains; these however quickly fade, or are hidden under an accumulation of dust. A large ju-ju is a conspicuous object of native art in a Government Court House. It scarcely merits commendation as an ornament, but it excels as a dust trap.

The dancing or "devil" masks are also carved from a single piece of wood, including all the wonderful decorations which adorn them. The wood used, aron or ebwu, is very soft and breaks easily. They are made in many styles, some are faces only, others are complete heads, but quite plain, whilst others again are covered with a gorgeous array of carved birds and animals, and many tower up in a series of tiers to a height of three or four feet. Although crude, and usually horribly ugly, they display considerable skill, and the carving is a long and tedious business. One feature is noticeable, viz. that the artist paints all these carved faces white—never black.[2] The nose is represented as being long, straight, and very narrow; the mouth is small, with thin lips, and the teeth are also small. The masks bear a striking resemblance to the cast of features noticeable in ancient Egyptian sculpture.

Tom-toms, or drums (ekwe) are the work of specialists. Some of these are monumental examples of patience and industry. More will be said of these in another chapter.

Probably the craft which is the most useful and valuable is that of the blacksmith. It is very remunerative, the more so because it is practised by natives of certain towns only, and these are able to control affairs almost as effectively as a Trade Union, and yet leave every man independent. The Awka smiths practically dominate the

[1] Really a magnified "ikenga."

[2] White, because all ghosts or spirits are supposed to be that colour.

situation, and they hold the leading place in the profession throughout the Ibo country and in many places beyond. They travel to such distant parts as Bonny, Calabar, Warri and even Lagos, plying their craft. About two-thirds of the year are spent away from their homes. In this work also, great skill is often displayed, especially when the tools used are taken into consideration. The outfit is primeval; it consists of a block of wood, fixed in the ground, into which is driven a round iron head, about one and a half inches in diameter, which serves as anvil; the hammer is simply

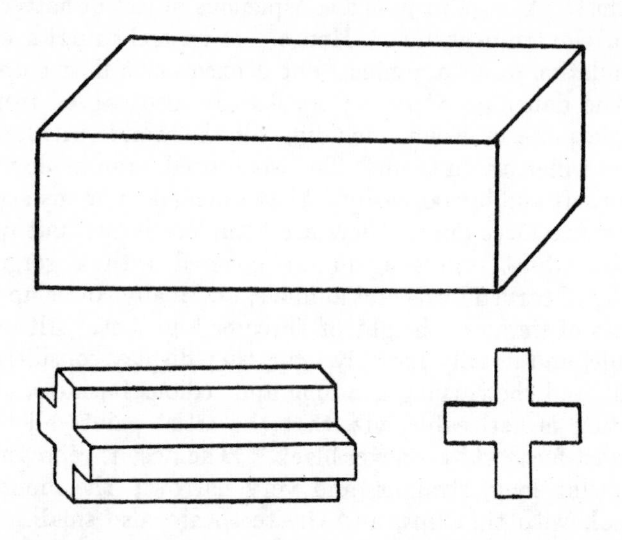

a piece of iron from twelve to fifteen inches in length and about the same diameter as the anvil. One or two pairs of tongs complete the outfit. The bellows consist of a goat-skin fitted into a clay continuation long enough to reach the centre of the fire. They are manipulated by a boy pumping up and down with two sticks which he works alternately; the fuel used is charcoal prepared from the roots of the iceku (araba) shrub.

An apprentice serves as a blower for a certain period, and after watching his master at his trade, usually begins to practise by making small chains. For this, odd bits of brass can be used up; they are beaten out into fine wire and then fashioned into links. These chains are much in demand amongst the young bloods of some towns; they are bound tightly round the legs from the ankle upwards, the length varying according to the purse of the wearer. The chains are bound very tightly upon the leg, which must be harmful, and they are certainly not ornamental. The art of welding must be mastered in order to join up brass rods into the spiral leg ornaments (nza) worn by unmarried girls. For the massive brass anklets ordinary bar brass is used and each anklet is beaten out of a single piece. The metal is softened by being treated until it is red-hot and it is then laid aside to cool gradually, the process being repeated several times. When sufficiently tractable it is again made red-hot and the smith begins to beat out the edges until he has brought the metal down to the proper thinness, i.e. about one-eighth of an inch. By that time it is a four-angled shape thus:—

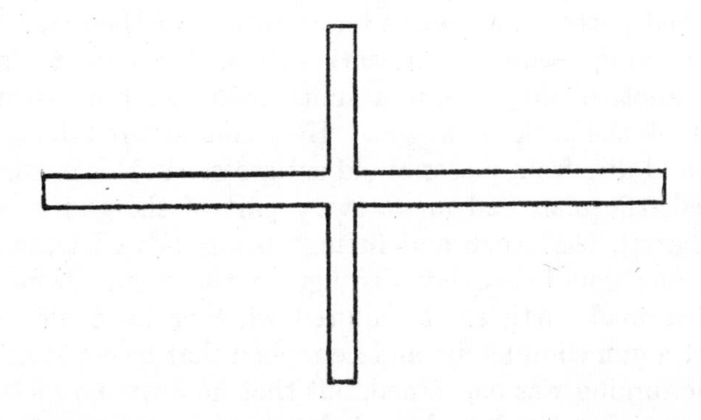

It is now ready for the final bending and the ends are brought round until they overlap, and a complete circle is formed. Upon the upper side patterns of flying frogs, and other creatures are pricked out with a punch and the anklets finished off by being highly burnished. Much technical ability is required in forging these anklets, and a well-made pair will always command a good price. In my early days a pair could be purchased for 15s. With the influx of Europeans the price (to them only) was inflated to £3, but latterly the tendency has been towards a fall in prices and they may now be obtained at from 25s. per pair. (*Vide* Chap. VIII.)

At one time I followed a regular practice of visiting some of the tiny blacksmiths' shops and saw some clever work done. On one occasion my visit turned out to be one of those apparently unimportant events which often turn the tide of affairs. I was able to show the smith a simple device whereby he was relieved of the task of gripping his tongs throughout the time his metal was heating. We were in a town never previously visited by Europeans and this little incident did much to establish friendly relations with the people. I had strayed from the party and, seeing the smith's shop, I entered and sat down to watch. A crowd gathered round and were greatly interested when we started working together, and the confidence of the folk was won. In return for the professional hint received, the blacksmith there and then took a piece of an old cutlass and forged it into an armlet. He duly chased it with a punched pattern and presented it to me. I then watched him making needles; fine work with such clumsy tools.

In another shop I saw a smith make all the essential parts of the lock of a gun. He manufactured his own taps and dies from pieces of old cutlasses. In this instance, indeed, the man had made every part of the gun except the barrel, the stock and fittings being so well executed that one could scarcely distinguish the result from an English-made article. I inquired whether he could construct a gun completely, and he replied that he could as far as the forging was concerned, but that he knew no method for tempering the barrel, and therefore it was no use his making that part. In any case it could never be anything but a failure, as the only material at his disposal was the ordinary trade bar-iron.

It is for their skill in repairing guns that the smiths are welcomed in all parts of the country. They are quite capable of converting old flintlocks into cap-guns, and, as long as caps are procurable, men were constantly purchasing the old flintlocks at the factories, and then getting them converted. This work was a source of great profit to the smiths, and they stand to lose considerably under the changed condition of affairs brought about by the restrictions placed upon the importation of ammunition.

The smith referred to made me a pair of brass tobacco pipes. The bowls were moulded to represent the faces of men, and were furnished, one with a wood, the other with an iron mouthpiece. Whether a native could venture to smoke a pipe which had an iron mouthpiece I have never ascertained; up to the present these particular pipes retain their original virginity.

Chiefs, as they attain to the higher degrees, receive the right to carry the insignia of their rank. This takes the form of an iron staff, ornamented with wrought and brass bindings; occasionally the whole staff is of brass. These are also the outcome of the blacksmiths' craft.

The smiths forge door furniture, chains, hair ornaments for women, brass and copper bracelets and anklets. A copper bracelet in my possession is the sole remaining relic of one who prepared many meals for us, but who, alas, shortly after passing on the ornament to me, mysteriously disappeared, and was generally reckoned to have been himself cooked and eaten.

In the early days of European occupation, bronze money was not acceptable to the natives, and they were ready to exchange four pennies for a threepenny piece. Copper pennies in Nigeria are undoubtedly "filthy lucre," with an emphasis on the adjective; they are soon coated with palm oil, vegetarian and other objectionable substances. The only men who wanted pennies were smiths, and these came occasionally to exchange silver for coppers; these were afterwards converted into ornaments.

In addition to objects of personal adornment, purchasable only by people of means, the smiths manufacture great quantities of hoes and axes. Practically every person is supplied with the former and most households possess one at least of the latter. The axes are wedge-shaped, the top passing through the head of a wooden club-shaped handle; with it and a cutlass most of the native woodcraft is executed. The blacksmiths also make bullets from bar-iron, pot-leg, or from remnants of brass of different shapes, square, oblong and round.

In the blacksmiths' profession there is an intensely rigid system of "Trade Unionism," and any attempt to usurp the privileges of the Awka men was obstinately resisted, even unto war. Our early days at Awka were spent amidst scenes of constant strife, and numbers lost their lives in the struggle to maintain the supremacy of the Union. This was especially the case when certain other tribesmen began to engage in the work; they were regarded as interlopers who were attempting to wrest the trade from the regular craftsmen, and the ensuing conflict was only brought to a conclusion by the intervention of the Government.

Smiths' work in the old days was undoubtedly the premier industry in the country, and it is not surprising that its interests were so jealously guarded. However, denationalisation in this respect must inevitably follow the introduction of Birmingham and other hardware goods. Hinges, locks, tools, and all sorts of useful articles are now sold at the factories at prices which must compete seriously with locally produced articles; also with the widening of civilising influences, the old cumbersome and unwieldly brass anklets must be abandoned. English saws are rapidly displacing the wasteful native axe for cutting planks and joists, and the same principle of change is operating in almost every craft.

Puddling Clay preparatory to House Building

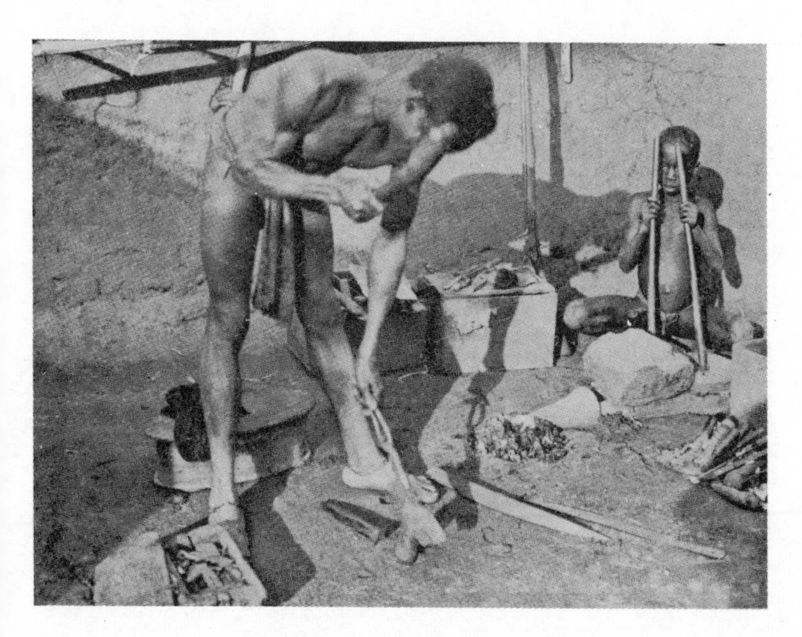

A Blacksmith at Work

CHAPTER XVI

ARTS AND CRAFTS FOR WOMEN

CERTAIN of the arts and crafts are in the hands of the women. The chief of these are pottery making, spinning, weaving, basket work and grass plaiting and, specially, freehand drawing on the person by means of stains. Earthen pottery is manufactured by women skilled in the art, dwelling here and there throughout the country. The pottery is limited to vessels designed for utilitarian purposes. Some of it indicates a faculty for decoration, but it is not developed to any great extent. The clay is dug, puddled, and is then ready for the potter. The greatest demand is naturally for water-pots ; these may be of any size, but those in common use are from fifteen to eighteen inches in height and about the same in diameter. The ware is rubbed down until it is less than one quarter of an inch in thickness. The pots are used exclusively almost for fetching water, and, on the eastern side of the Niger, for steeping raw cassava roots. There is also a fair demand for pots of decanter shape for the collection and storing of palm wine. These may bc plain or decorated, all black or of terra-cotta colour, relieved with white. The white markings soon perish as they are applied after baking. Other vessels are manufactured, such as bowls and cooking pots, the former being, perhaps, the best finished of all the pottery, and the latter the most primitive and inartistic. Some of the bowls are of good workmanship, being moulded in relief and finished outside with black polish and inside with beautifully rubbed terra-cotta.

All the pottery is burnt directly by fire ; it is not baked in ovens or kilns. The process is a very simple one, the women burning the pots at any spot convenient to themselves, sometimes right in the middle of the footway. A quantity of dry grass and sticks is spread on the ground and a layer of pots placed upon it ; more fuel is added and then more pots, until the whole collection is in position. The grass is then fired and burns fiercely at the outset ; the residue retains great heat for some time so that when the ashes have begun to cool the pots are ready. They are as brittle as eggshells and require but a tap to break them, yet though often handled with apparently little care, they may remain in service for a very long time. The marvel is that they do not burst with the water pressure. The breaking of a water-pot at the spring, or when passing to and fro, is the signal for a fearful outburst of weeping and wailing. Sometimes in the early morning one is suddenly aroused by most piercing shrieks and, at first, one is ready to think that nothing short of murder is being committed. Experience, however, soon teaches one to realise that nothing worse has happened than the breaking of a water-pot. The young people take the calamity very seriously, for what particular reason I do not know.

Clay pots are being displaced wherever possible, kerosene tins being adopted for water and iron negro pots taking the place of the earthen vessels for cooking.

In most parts of the Ibo country native cotton is cultivated, or rather gathered in, as the effort expended is almost negligible. The fluffy raw cotton is cleansed by fingering and by threshing with a bow string. It is then spun by means of a bobbin which revolves by its own weight after being started with a sharp twist between thumb and finger. By constant practice the women are able to impart so great an impetus to the bobbin that it spins at such a rate as to appear stationary. Spinning is done whenever the operator finds herself free from domestic affairs, much in the same way as the Cornish and Scotch women ply their knitting needles. The business requires but little effort either of mind or body, and can be practised anywhere in the street whilst gossiping or in the market when trade is slack.

The cotton thread thus spun is coarse, but very durable. It is woven on hand looms into strips of cloth from twelve to fifteen inches in width. The finished article is used for caps and loin cloths, and on the western side of the Niger shawls are made by sewing strips with blue or brown. The colours are fast and do not fade easily, either by washing or by the action of the sun. In this respect they surpass English dyes, particularly the blue.

Like other primitive industries, however, native spinning and weaving are doomed. Foreign cloth, especially certain German lines, has captured the native market, and in a comparatively short time the local article will be quite discarded. It cannot compete with European cloth, either as regards price or attractiveness. Here occurs another instance of the inevitable disintegration of native trade, the denationalising of the people. Again, the missionary is held to be the culprit, as he is generally accused of introducing clothing for his converts. But the missionaries have no interest in canteens! The stocks of cloth cleared annually by the trading firms are enormous. On the one hand the wearing of clothes is condemned in emphatic language, but on the other the enterprise of merchants in selling cloth is commended. We do not find that European directors are prepared to place sentiment before dividend! Why should they? The only trouble is that there are critics who are hard to please and who, if taken seriously, are hopelessly inconsistent. In large towns like Onitsha the market is ever growing for foreign cloth, and, except amongst the Hausas and other up-river natives, native cloth is scarcely ever seen nowadays.

Some of the women are adepts in mat weaving and grass plaiting and, as in so many other directions, the work of each district is marked by its own peculiar characteristics. On the western side of the river we have the "Asaba" mat. This is from five to seven feet in length and from thirty to forty inches in width. It is made from the pith of bamboo palm fronds cut into long thin strips whilst green, and then laid out in the sun to dry. The strips are placed on the ground in parallel lines and then lightly stitched across, at intervals of two inches, with dyed fibre. They are stiff and useless as body coverings, but are in great demand as bed mats by the natives and by Europeans as a serviceable material for ceilings and screens. Another form of ute (mat) is plaited from the leaves of water flags (akamala) and, as these are from one half to a full inch in width, it is not a difficult process. This is the simplest of all forms of weaving and is equivalent to that done by children in the first stages of kindergarten education.

But work of a higher order follows when, with upili (palm leaves), baskets of different designs are made. For these the plaiting demands close attention, particularly in the case of baskets provided with a detachable cover. Best of all is the plaiting of the ata (spear grass) into baskets and trays; likewise the weaving of the midribs of ngwaw palm leaves into bags. The ata work is very durable, consisting as it does of a number of strands of grass securely whipped together like a wire-protected hose-pipe. The bags are delightful examples of fibre weaving and invariably meet with a ready sale. They are also highly appreciated by English ladies and are quickly bought up when offered for sale at bazaars. The best specimens are made attractive with brown and blue dyes, by fancy edging and other little embellishments.

A very fine fibre is drawn from the fresh green leaf of the bamboo palm. The leaf is bent and gently broken, and the glossy side is pulled back evenly. The silky stands are pulled out and it is then woven into strips about a yard in length and half a yard in width and finished with fringed ends. It may be left natural colour or dyed. It is designated as ukaw. It is woven on the western side of the Niger and worn by none but chiefs, and by these only on certain days, as a sort of sacrificial vestment. Two or three strips are joined, and the ukaw is then thrown over the shoulders toga fashion. Women extract the fibre and weave it, but they may not wear the cloth except when one is mourning for her husband. It is more costly than the ordinary cotton cloth.

The more expensive cloth is that known as ufa, again a production of the western side. The thread for this is spun from the downy substance found under the bark of the young branches of the ufa tree. It is collected by the women, spun and woven similarly to cotton, and corresponds to the European "fine linen." It is highly prized and very strong, but its price is prohibitive to any but well-to-do folk.

There is no greater opportunity for the women to display their artistic abilities than in the adornment of their persons by means of stains. The practice is met with in all its stages, from the crudest daubing with yellow and red (camwood dye), to the beautifully executed patterns traced with uli (indigo). The camwood stain (ufie) is used almost exclusively by girls who are passing through the nkpu ceremonies preparatory to marriage; the uli is common to all—men and women. It is a quaint spectacle to see a party of women and girls assisting each other in this part of their toilet. The custom of "painting" as an essential element in a lady's make-up is practised quite openly. It is not limited to the face—the whole body is treated from head to foot. When passing through the town of Nibo one Sunday morning we came to a charming shady glade, and there met a group of women and girls engaged in beautifying each other. They were quite engrossed in their art. The stain was pressed out from the fruit into a wooden bowl and applied with a small curved iron tool, which followed the line naturally and enabled the artist to draw clean strokes in the same way as a sign-writer does with his long-haired brush. Where iron instruments are not procurable recourse is had to pointed pieces of stick. The freehand designs are usually cleverly drawn, and the pattern is different for each woman. In the process the one undergoing it is very often soothed to sleep, and the whole work may be completed whilst she is blissfully unconscious. When first applied the stain is of a greenish tint which changes to a deep black after a few hours. The patterns remain clearly visible for about a week and then gradually wear off. The art in itself has distinct merit, and shows originality in design and treatment, but the beautifying effect is open to question. Sometimes the result is rather startling and it is always weird, judged by

European ideas. In the past men were given to the habit quite as much as women, but latterly they have begun to discard it. When men are thus painted they always submit to its being done by women. It has one feature which makes it superior to rouge and such-like preparations —it does not rub off nor cause annoyance when the atmosphere is slightly heated!

Cicatrisation is *à la mode* for great numbers of the Ibo people, either as an aid to beauty or as tribal markings (ichi). Both sexes submit to the operation, but it takes different forms for men and women. In the case of the latter it is performed chiefly as a preliminary to marriage. Men are not so keen on the marking of the body by mbubu, but are decidedly partial to the ichi form. To produce the mbubu the body is first smeared with chalk and upon this the lines are sketched out with charcoal, the most common figures being a reversed cross on a star; I never remember noting patterns containing curved lines. The artist then cuts a series of small slits in the flesh with a pointed triangular-shaped razor (ugelle, or uche). The skin is forthwith raised and a pellet of tightly compressed cotton-wool or palm leaf is inserted under it. When all the slits have been thus padded a preparation of charcoal is smeared over the whole. The charcoal treatment is repeated on several successive days until the desired result is attained, this being a regular pattern of black oval blobs which stand out conspicuously upon the skin. In some cases the slits are not plugged, and then, of course, the mbubu are less pronounced, but nevertheless are plainly visible.

By a somewhat similar process men are provided with permanent, unbreakable, and thief-resisting necklaces. No plugging is done for this, but the wounds are repeatedly irritated and prevented from healing until scars are developed of the size and style desired.

The ichi (tribal marking) is a much more elaborate and serious affair, and where the custom prevails no freeborn male would dream of forgoing his inherited right to display the marks of his town and family. The operation is a very painful one, but is stoically, and even cheerfully endured. In no case is it conducive to beauty; usually, indeed, it leads to gross disfigurement.

The styles are wonderfully diverse, sometimes consisting of but a few crude cuts, as practised on the western side of the Niger. These are designated ebwuba, and they are inflicted upon the face of the baby at the age of one month. The marking of the body is deferred until the initiation ceremony by which citizenship is conferred. This work is done by women; the flesh is cut in a series of lines, and soot (lamp black), straight from the nearest cooking pot, is rubbed in thoroughly to produce the intensely black effect.

In other cases the whole of the upper half of the face is cut and scarred, and this is what is termed ichi. For this operation the services of men from the town of Umu-di-awka are in great demand; in fact, these men hold a sort of monopoly of the profession, and travel all over the country for the purpose; and, judging by the number of those bearing the ichi marks, it must be a prosperous business.

The same instrument is used as for cutting mbubu, but the method is somewhat different. The flesh is cut to the standard tribal marking. Each slit in turn is then opened out and the flesh pressed back with the thumb-nail, and the cavity is filled in with lamp-black procured from the roof of the kitchen. Boys submit to the custom between the ages of eight and fourteen, according to their social position and zeal for the prerogatives of the tribe.

It should be observed here that the ichi operation is performed by men, but it seemed convenient to touch upon the subject in this place. The same remark applies to a simple form of tattooing, for which lamp-black, usually from a kerosene lamp, is the medium used. The drawing is made upon the skin of the person and it is then pricked out with a pin. The design is sometimes a rough drawing, such as a spread-eagled crocodile, often it is simply plain lines and crosses, whilst of late years it has become the fashion for a man's name to be tattooed on his forearm. Cases are also reported where a man has had the brand of his favourite "gin" indelibly inscribed upon his person!

Finally there are the medical and dental professions. Doctoring is inextricably bound up with the native religion, and comments on it must be reserved for the chapters dealing with the religious customs of the people. The business of the Ibo dentist is not to cure toothache nor to improve the patient's masticating powers. His work is to extract, chip, or file the teeth, according to the owner's taste. In order to conform to the fashions of some localities it is incumbent to have all the single teeth chipped so as to give them sharp, saw-like points. Others leave the cutting edges of the teeth intact, but widen out the interstices between them, leaving the part of the teeth near the gums sometimes less than half their original width. The chipping is performed with a chisel and mallet and is a very painful operation—the tap, tap, tap being exceedingly irritating to the nerves.

Many of the rising generation, now coming under the influence of education and some degree of civilisation, are discarding these primitive customs which entail mutilation. The Onitsha women regard the ichi marks as alo (an abominable thing), and usually refuse to sit upon the same seat with a man so marked. Many even go so far in expressing their disapproval as to refuse to shake hands with such a man. Men from the interior feel this treatment keenly, and the fact that they are thus put to open shame is likely to prove a strong incentive to abolishing such customs. The professional cicatrisers and the dentists will soon have to seek some other means of livelihood. Their occupation, which has been practised for generations, and the rights of which have been so jealously guarded, must inevitably cease to be—the old must, once more, give place to the new.

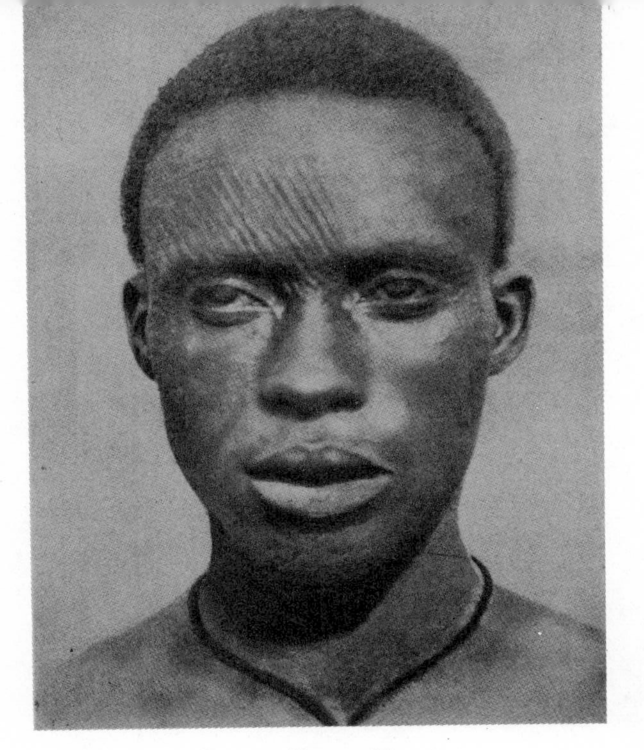

ICHI OR TRIBAL MARKS

AN OLD IBO WOMAN

With aggry beads and elephant hair necklaces.

CHAPTER XVII

MUSIC

WHETHER the Ibo people trace their ancestry back to Jubal-Cain it is not my purpose to discuss, but they certainly have inherited a fair share of the art originated by the "Father of Music." How long they have been performers upon the instruments now in use, and who invented them, are questions to which answers are not forthcoming. As the people of the interior have never, until very recent times, had any intercourse with the civilised world, we conclude that their musical proclivities, their instruments and their songs, remain practically as they existed in primitive times, or at any rate that they have developed spontaneously.

On investigation we find a small number of wind and string instruments. These are all crude in form, but constant practice is demanded to master them. To compensate for the lack of mechanical contrivances greater skill is needed.

The simplest and most primitive instrument is the "ugene"—a kind of whistle. It is made of baked clay, in shape round, and about the size of a billiard ball. A substitute is occasionally used, cut from a piece of ukpadi wood. It has two holes, one at the top which serves as the mouthpiece; the other at the front for measuring and varying the piped notes. I first met with it during the war between the Nkpaw and Ogiddi peoples, where it was used for signalling purposes. The notes, which are produced by blowing through the upper hole, piccolo fashion, are shrill and piercing. The men on outpost duty, perched in trees, sounded the alarm and communicated messages by means of these little instruments.

The custom of transmitting signals by sounds is a common one, and is not confined to these whistles. The chiefs entitled to carry ivory horns send out messages by powerful blasts of dot-and-dash (Morse) notes. The horns are blown flute-wise, and the note can be varied in length, but not in tone. The chiefs are adepts in the art of trumpeting on the horns and use them for communicating quite long messages. More often they perform upon them purely for display, especially in assemblies, and the din created by half a dozen chiefs in full blast is deafening. A big supply of breath is required, but a satisfactory result depends entirely on the proper use of the lips.

Other methods of spreading information are practised, notably by the beating of tom-toms, of which more will be said later, and by simply whistling with the lips. Men can communicate with one another quite freely by this method when completely out of speaking range. Boys early find out how to prepare whistles from grass stems, and some of the youths can imitate bugle calls in a very clever manner by blowing down the hollow stalks of a freshly cut pawpaw leaf.

Besides these I know of but one other wind instrument—the "awja," a reed some six inches in length furnished with three holes for fingering—one in front, one at the back for the thumb, and the bottom outlet. It is always used in assemblies of men, especially when a big piece of work is in progress. The instrumentalist sits down on one side and blows vigorously through the pipe; the tones are shrill and piercing, and at times peculiarly trying to the nerves.

It is supposed to instil energy into the labourers and help them to forget the burden of their task, and the effect is similar to that of bagpipes. It undoubtedly does make a difference, and natives work much better when inspired by its sounds. Europeans soon develop murderous tendencies if forced to stay long in the neighbourhood of an awja enthusiast. The native, of course, recognises the air, but the foreigner would be equally pleased, and driven to desperation, were he condemned to a steam syren in charge of a mad locomotive driver.

The mention of tom-toms at once conjures up the picture of the savage in all his war-paint, but this is a false impresssion, They are not exactly brain-soothing instruments, any more than drums would be were they the only instruments composing a military band. Yet the Ibo tom-tom is not such an ear-splitting contrivance as the drums of an Orange lodge. So far as my experience goes County Armagh still retains the leading place in drum-beating. For one thing the tom-toms are mostly nothing but hollow blocks of wood; the sound carries a long distance in a country where there is no vehicular traffic and no roar of industry to deaden it. The big tom-toms (ekwe) are not intended to be instruments of music, but are used chiefly for spreading information for certain ceremonial purposes, and at sacrificial festivals; meetings are called by their use, and various announcements proclaimed. An ekwe is in great request when a man proceeds to the highest titular degree. On completion of all the business connected with the taking of the Awzaw title, the fact is communicated by beating the tom-tom. The smaller tom-toms may be of similar pattern, or they may be wooden cylinders with skin stretched over one end, the most prized—and now rather rare—being those covered with human skin. In the old days it was not uncommon for human victims to be flayed alive and their skins converted into drum-heads.

Some of the drums are of smaller pattern. They are distinguished from the ekwe and are technically known as ufie. Steady application for a long period is necessary in order to become a qualified performer on these. The performer must know his instrument thoroughly, and be able to gauge the differences in sound to be extracted from the whole top surface of the drum. Each square inch around the slotted opening in the cylinder has its own peculiar note, and these notes are further supplemented by fingering. Often two drums are used simultaneously and the hands cross and recross like those of a cavalry drummer; hence, although to the European tom-toms are apt to become monotonous and wearisome, yet it must be allowed that the native exponent exhibits great skill in beating his tattoo upon it. To him, indeed, the beating of the instrument is always significant; something is conveyed to the native mind which is utterly incomprehensible to the European, and our inability to grasp that meaning in no way detracts from the importance of the drum in every Ibo function.

Many of the ekwe are of huge size, particularly those which form part of the municipal regalia, and some have romantic histories attached to them. There is such a one at a town called Umu-Nze. On one of our journeys we had trekked across country and passed through the outlying parts of the town until we reached the market-place. In the centre there is what, at first sight, appears to be a house, but on closer examination we found it was a shelter built over an immense tom-tom. It was sufficiently interesting to induce me to measure it. The dimensions are as follows: length of actual drum cylinder, 5 ft. 8 in.; extended ornamental ends, each 2 ft. 3 in.; length over all 10 ft. 2 in.; height, 8 ft. 5 in.; width, 7 ft. 10 in.

It is hewn from a single block of uroko wood, but it now shows distinct signs of age and use. Local tradition affirms that this tom-tom was the work of a man from the town of Amawbia. He had earned a great reputation by drum-making, and his services were therefore sought by the Umu-Nze people. He was promised a very large fee on condition that he produced a larger drum than any possessed by other towns in the district. He undertook the task and the tom-tom duly appeared, and was at once the object of intense pride to the people of Umu-Nze.

Then arose the disturbing thought, "What if a rival town contracted with the maker for a yet bigger drum?" Horrors! In such case the glory of Umu-Nze would speedily depart and the pride of the people be humbled to the dust. This was altogether too serious a prospect to contemplate, and drastic steps had to be taken to prevent such a catastrophe. Hence it came about that the maker of the wonderful tom-tom was paid his price and allowed to leave for home well satisfied with his handiwork and its reward. His satisfaction was short-lived, for he had hardly got clear of the town when he was waylaid, led back to the market-place and then and there sacrificed, his own blood being shed to dedicate that which his hand had wrought. All town tom-toms are consecrated, and consequently regarded as sacred things, and it was customary to sprinkle the blood of a human sacrifice upon them before they were ceremonially beaten.

The " ubaw " is an instrument which cannot be compared with any foreign one with which I am acquainted. It is composed of thin pieces of a very soft wood (okwe) and in shape resembles an oblong box. It is from five to fifteen inches long, from four to six inches wide, and from one to two inches deep; thus far it is similar in principle to a violin, but in lieu of strings thin strips of offolaw [1] are used. These are fixed at the tail-end and then pass over a low bridge to which they are also bound. The loose ends are cut to different lengths and separated widely enough to permit freedom in fingering. The instrument is held in both hands, with the tail piece pointing away from the person, and the thumbs are used for manipulating the strips of bamboo. The thumbs press cleanly on the strips and are then slipped sharply backwards, and a twanging sound results, the notes varying according to the different lengths of the six or eight keys of the instrument. Occasionally loosely threaded cowrie shells are attached to the tail end of the ubaw, which are shaken to make an accompaniment. The music is not unpleasant, but there is little life in it, the bamboo strips producing a dull note. One notices young men leisurely parading the streets strumming these instruments, but they are not in demand at assemblies; indeed they could not be heard; the ubaw is eminently a solo instrument.

Probably the most interesting of the Ibo instruments is the "ubaw-akwala," a sort of primitive guitar—or is it the original of the nigger banjo? It has a triangular-shaped body formed by sewing together three pieces of soft wood with fibre. To the under part from four to eight pliable canes of different lengths are securely laced, all of them extending well beyond the head of the instrument. They

[1] "Offolaw," as used here, means the hard outer skin of the frond of the bamboo palm.

are then bent upwards and the strings are tied to the ends, crossed over the bridge, and finally fastened to the tail-piece. The strings (awmi) are pieces of fibre taken from the base of the palm tree and carefully rubbed down to the required fineness. The instrument is held like the ubaw, but the method of playing is different, the thumbs lightly twanging the strings, the left and right working an equal number of them. It has rather a sweet sound, not unlike light staccato notes from a violin. The instrument is tuned by bending the canes and passing the strings one or more times round them until the desired pitch is secured. The musician must learn all tunes by ear, or compose his own, which he frequently does.

The ubaw-akwala is the favourite instrument for accompanying songs and chants, and is particularly favoured by strolling singers at night. One is often awakened by the pleasant strains of a party of musicians on their rounds.

Instrumental soloists of any reputation, especially performers on the awja and ekwe, are treated with great respect, their services are in demand and their reward is generally liberal. Talent is recognised and many artistes become very popular. From a musical point of view one is inclined to think that the native singing is more fascinating than the instrumental music. It is doubtful whether there are any proper songs, but there are a great number of established refrains and recitatives. The leader of a chorus is accorded much the same honour amongst the Ibos as that granted to the minstrel in ancient days in England. He must possess not only the musical gift but the poetical instinct also. He creates his theme as the song proceeds, and great ingenuity is displayed in fitting words to time and tune on the spur of the moment. Any unusual incident is seized upon and utilized as material by the leader, and when this fails he has recourse to the retelling, in song, the exploits of old.

Couplets appear to be most in favour with the Ibos, the leader chanting two lines as a solo, and the full company joining in with a double-lined chorus. Occasionally one hears a four-lined song without solo or chorus, and there are a number of songs intended to be sung as solos. The last mentioned are the only ones for which the natural voice is used; for all chorus work a falsetto voice is assumed. So accustomed do men become to the practice of using their voices in this manner that with many it develops into a confirmed habit, and they adopt this artificial high-pitched key in conversation. This is very objectionable, but the singing, in contrast, is at times very fine. The best entertainments take place on the darkest nights, on moonlight nights dancing usually supersedes all other forms of amusement. In the darkness, when none of the party can see the leader, the most perfect time and tune are maintained; the members of the party may be few or many, but the voices of all rise and fall as of one man; no individual voice can be distinguished above the rest; there is not a fraction of time lost at the beginning of a passage, nor is there the slightest sign of dragging at its close. It is fascinating listening to such a party, and the foreigner is astonished at the precision with which the men sing. They never need speeding up or slowing down, but render the whole selection perfectly, each man familiar with his part and able to perform it independently of a conductor.

To be able to start a native chant is a most useful accomplishment, and if an opportune moment be seized when some irksome labour is in progress it will lead to more than ordinary effort on the part of workmen. When canoeing it is extremely helpful, and paddles which have been inclined to lag quickly liven up to the strains of music. It is amusing to watch the effect of a song upon a crew. At first it makes no apparent change in the situation, then gradually chatting ceases, and one here and there begins to hum the tune. Within a short time the song grips the men, and at once the paddles begin to strike in tune with the rhythm, and a good stretch of water will be covered without conscious effort on the part of the men.

The only attempts to introduce European ideas of music amongst the Ibos have been made by missionaries—with what success is mainly a matter of opinion. That there is an inherent love and instinct for music there can be no question. The native boy will quickly pick out tunes by ear on any instrument, and there is no doubt that some would well repay proper instruction, as in the case of other West Africans. Up to the present English hymn tunes and chants, set to Ibo translations, are apt to be treated mechanically. The singing is not lacking in volume—far from it—but the living and soul-stirring effect engendered by the native songs is practically lacking in the translated productions. There is never the same spirit of abandonment in the foreign article as in the native one. European music, as they interpret it, has not yet succeeded in gaining access to the inner being of the Ibo; it may have the form of music, but it lacks the essence. He will sing hymns as continuously as formerly he chanted native lyrics, but he is never carried away by them, however much he may enjoy singing. With English music volume is the one object in view, and congregational singing in the larger churches in the Ibo country is like the thunder of many waters.

The more one listens to native music, the more one is conscious of its vital power. It touches the chords of man's inmost being, and stirs his primal instincts. It demands the performer's whole attention and so sways the individual as almost to divide asunder, for the time being, mind and body. It is intensely passionate, and no great effort of the imagination is required to realise that such music could only have originated with the son of Cain! Under its influence, and that of the accompanying dance, one has seen men and women pass into a completely dazed condition, oblivious and apparently unconscious of the world around them. Both sexes are drawn under its spell and lose themselves in it. It is savage; the instruments are barbaric; but it pulsates with the spirit of the thing in its most potent forms. It lifts men and women out of themselves; it may leave them almost prostrated with exhaustion; it may bring into activity all the baser instincts. The outcome of a full programme of song and dance frequently ends in voluptuous debauchery. Even the European, if he has within him the feeblest susceptibility to music, is liable to find the elemental forces of his nature strangely stirred by the passionate fervour of the "possessed" musicians. What the bagpipes are to the typical Highlander and the drums to an Ulster Orangeman, that, and more, is native music to the Ibo. In each case the emotions are roused and the pulses quickened; but the native yields himself to its influence with absolute abandon.

CHAPTER XVIII

TRADE AND CURRENCY

By "Trade" we mean everything that is connected directly with buying and selling, and more especially the functions of marketing. The term does not include industries. Trading is a distinct profession and as such practically fills up the lives of many Ibos. It might almost be affirmed that the whole of the native trade is in the hands of the women and by them largely the markets are controlled. In former times the women had direct transactions with the trading factories, and hosts of them still pursue this course, but there is springing up a class of middlemen who work on commission.

Ordinarily no Ibo man takes any part in the actual buying and selling; he may have some share in preparing the goods for the market and may, occasionally, assist in carrying to and fro, but there his activities usually cease. If an Ibo man be seen buying in the market, it is almost a certain indication that he is either a stranger or a man with no womenfolk to act for him.

As previously observed (Chap. VIII) marketing is the central feature in the life of every Ibo woman, and to be successful in trade is the signal for generous congratulation. By this a woman's value is calculated; it affects her own position and comfort; a man considers it in the choice of a wife, and a husband's favour is bestowed or withheld largely according to the degree of his wife's success in the market.

Even if she have not the wherewithal to buy and sell, yet a woman inevitably gravitates to the market for its own attractions. It is the hub of the universe and the centre of all news and gossip. To deprive a woman of the privilege of visiting the market would be to cut off one, and, perhaps, the greatest pleasure of her life.

Markets are held in every town and village. They are named after the days on which they are held, according to the four days of the Ibo week, viz. Ekke, Afaw, Oye (Olie) and Nkwaw. Occasionally for Ekke and Nkwaw, instead of every fourth day, the market is held every eighth day, and they are then designated as Ekke Uku and Nkwaw Uku. In very rare instances, as at Upulu, the great market is held every sixteenth day.

So it falls out that women may spend some part of every day in one or other of the markets, and many do this. In the interior parts it is customary for the middle of the day to be occupied in this fashion. The women have time to fulfil their domestic duties before starting and, if the market be within easy distance, need not leave home till 10 a.m. Often, however, they have to tramp a long way, and this means an early start and a correspondingly late return.

The markets are controlled by the influential old women, and they frame and administer the rules and regulations and settle all questions as they arise. Each market is presided over by its "queen" (Amwu), assisted by the women's council, of which she is the head. This council often fixes prices, the rate of cowrie exchange, what markets shall be visited, and with what towns commercial relations shall be established or maintained. It decrees what articles are to be admitted into the market and what is taboo; this latter being also greatly influenced by the patron alusi (idol-fetish) of each market.

The first queen of the market to whom I was presented was presiding over a busy market scene at Akwukwu (some 18 miles N.W. of Asaba). She was installed in the appointed place apart from the other women. She was one of the senior women, but by no means ancient. Across the bridge of her nose and around her eyes were prominent chalk lines, giving her the appearance of wearing a monstrous pair of white spectacles. At close quarters these rings give a peculiar effect to the eyes and they are accentuated out of all proportion to the face—exceptionally so on a black one. About her body was a white cloth—native woven—and on her head a quaint brown billy-cock hat, pulled well down and resembling a candle extinguisher. A single feather, the sole ornament, reared itself in a rakish manner at the side. The hat and throne indicated her rank and position, no other women in the market being allowed such prerogatives, except such as happened to be queens, belonging to other towns.

In former times there were no booths or stalls or any equivalent to them; the only semblance of a building was the small, ill-kept hut of the patron-deity of the market, and possibly the rude shelter covering the town ekwe (tom-tom). Sometimes, also, on one side are the tiny dwelling places of the Osu people, i.e. those who are devoted to the alusi or ju-ju of that particular place. With the peaceful settlement of the country it is becoming more and more common for rows of booths to be erected in the markets.

The first comers to the market squat down where they please; those who arrive later squeeze in somehow, for an incredibly small space is considered to constitute an excuse for thrusting in themselves and their wares. The ground is literally covered, and one must walk carefully. The articles are laid on the bare ground, or spread on a banana leaf, or arranged in wicker trays and baskets. There is no hawking and no crying of wares; the goods are left to advertise themselves, the women, meanwhile, sitting mute before them, or holding friendly converse with their neighbours. If a woman wishes to make a purchase she leaves her pitch in charge of a daughter or friend, and proceeds to tour the market in search of the desired object.

As the market fills, it becomes a veritable pandemonium. It gives the impression that no business could possibly be conducted in the midst of such chaotic confusion. The haggling over prices, the shouting, the hurling of epithets, the incessant clatter of tongues create a din that can often be heard a mile away.

All goods are sold in the terms of the local currency; there is no bartering of commodities in exchange for other commodities. It is true that in disposing of produce to the factories the women bring away cloth, gin, and other wares, but the produce is usually paid for with a cheque equivalent in value to the goods brought. The cheque is afterwards presented at the retail selling store and goods are handed out according to the face value of the cheque, i.e. the value of the produce is reckoned in cash and the value of the goods on requisition is based upon cash. The same procedure is in force in the markets. Each transaction is an entirely separate and distinct affair. A buys B's yams for cowries and B buys A's oil for cowries also; they make no attempt at direct exchange.

In the open market there are no fixed quotations for goods; on the one hand the seller strives to make the highest price, and on the other the buyer is just as keen to drive the closest bargain for herself, hence the outrageous haggling over prices.

The goods are handled and re-handled, commented upon and rejected by a critical crowd, before an actual buyer appears. Then ensues a wordy contest, both buyer and seller exerting themselves to the uttermost and hurling personal epithets at one another in no uncertain fashion. When the bout has run its course the goods change hands, and the parties are immediately on amicable terms once more.

Everything that is at all saleable finds its way to the market, irrespective of quantity or quality. Food-stuff naturally takes precedence of all other goods, yam, dried fish, palm oil, ground nuts, beans, and so on. One can buy single bananas at six cowries each, or tiny slices of paw-paw for two cowries. As an instance of taboo on certain articles, no coco-nuts may be brought into the market at Adazzi, nor indeed may they be eaten by any of the folk there.

For some articles the prices fluctuate tremendously at different times of the year. From September to December yams are at the lowest price, i.e. immediately after the harvest and before they have been stored on the awba frames. From December the price steadily rises, until from May onwards the cost becomes prohibitive to many people, and substitutes are sought. Taking the country as a whole, since 1900, when the Colonial Office took over the administration of the country, prices have advanced greatly. Fowls, and in many districts yams, are double the price they used to be. Roofing mats used to be bought at the rate of one hundred for three heads of tobacco (9d.); now they are sold at forty for a shilling, and inferior mats at that. Every commodity has increased in price in like proportion, and the whole political economy of the country is passing through a great transition stage.

Before the introduction of English coinage a local currency was in use. In the more southern and eastern districts there was a strong demand for manillas and brass rods; in the northern and western parts cowries were, and still are, the most popular form of currency. In all the country south of the prohibition line, trade gin is a recognised medium of exchange. In the northern parts the manilla is not current, and the brass rods are wanted solely for the sake of being converted into "nza" (leg-rings for girls). At Onitsha, and on the western side of the river, the large cowrie shells are used, whereas in the eastern hinterland the small type only are acceptable, these smaller being reckoned at double the value of the larger. In cowries the table of value is:—

6 Nkpulu (= single shells)	=	1 Ekpetti
10 Ekpetti	=	1 Ukwu
20 Ukwu	=	1 Akpa. (i.e. bag).

An akpa is calculated as a man's load. In the counting of cowries the number six is the standard. The one counting squats on the ground before a heap of shells and starts by separating groups of six, and then sweeps ten such piles into one heap to form an ukwu.

As in goods, so also in cowries, the price in English currency fluctuates with the market, and again it is notable that since 1900 the cowrie has appreciated in value to an extraordinary degree. For one thing they are no longer imported, and hence, with no means of increasing, or even maintaining the supply, they are liable to appreciate. They certainly have not yet declined in favour with the natives, especially in interior towns, and they always ensure preferential treatment to the customer able to tender them. Many natives refuse to sell at all except for cowries, and it will be a long time before they are finally displaced by a metal coinage unless forcible measures be taken.

In spite of the fact that the importation of cowries ceased some years back, immense quantities are still in circulation, and the tendency to hoard them is as strong as ever. But the fact that the supply has been cut off has led to their appreciating fully 100%. Whereas one remembers when the exchange was calculated as 25 ukwu to the shilling, it has gradually changed to 16, 15 until now 12 and 13 ukwu are often quoted in the markets for the English shilling. Moreover, the purchasing power of the cowrie is greater than that of metal coinage. Whatever may be the market exchange value, a buyer is able to purchase more with cowries than with their equivalent in cash, and, in addition, be saved much inconvenience, since the shells are much more readily accepted.

I can offer no suggestion as to how and why the cowries gained their position and popularity as a medium of exchange. They have all been imported, chiefly from the islands of the Indian Archipelago, I believe, and the number must be literally as the sand on the seashore. I have been in some treasure houses where the store of cowries has reminded me of heaps of newly threshed corn. The shell when clean—a rare condition—is of light colour and has a corrugated top and edges; very often the top is chipped off to make a hole so that it can be threaded on string. It is amusing to see the neat way a spurious shell is flicked out from the heap by the counter. A native may have a false shell passed upon him if he accepts a quantity as counted, i.e. without checking the amount on the spot, but no native would pass such a shell when actually counting, even if he were blindfolded. A cowrie shell, even though its value is only one ninetieth part of a penny (or, of the larger sort, the one hundred and eightieth part of a penny), is seldom wasted. One may fall into the road; the next woman passing that way, should she notice it, deftly picks up the stray shell with her toes, thence transfers it to her fingers and puts it in her bag.

The introduction of a metal coinage is really a great boon. It has brought much relief in many directions, not the least being in the matter of domestic economy. The ordinary silver, and the nickel subsidiary coinage, enable one to calculate prices and make purchases with ease. Prior to this use of metal one was constantly being confronted with bewildering problems in arithmetic when marketing, e.g. a fowl might be quoted as 1s. 4d. To pay for it sixteen multiples of ninety cowrie shells had to be counted and handed over.

The lowest value of the subsidiary nickel coinage is the tenth of a penny, equivalent to 9 or 18 shells according to the cowrie in use. This is a low value, but an enormous number of purchases are made at prices much less than a tenth; moreover the tenth is so small and light that it has a pernicious habit of losing itself. A number may be strung together, but native string breaks easily and the tenths shew a lively aptitude for disappearing.

Silver coinage must win its way, and the men in many places are cute enough to realise that it offers greater facilities for banking than the old cowrie shells. It is a commonly accepted theory that money is hoarded, and this is indeed a fact. In evidence given before the Liquor Traffic Commission mention was made of the practice of purchasing gin to hold as a treasure. This may be the case in some parts, but it most certainly is not so in the districts with which I am acquainted. There are huge stacks of gin bottles—sometimes hundreds together—but they do not contain liquor; they are merely records of what once existed. But money—either in cowries or silver coins—is banked extensively, native fashion. I have seen hundreds of pounds in silver and immense stores of cowries in a man's possession. Then how is it banked? Some say it is buried; if so, how and where? These questions I leave others to answer; it would not be cricket to reveal what one has learned in confidence. It was a matter of many years before I was let into the

NATIVE MARKET. A BUSY SCENE

secret, and then I made the discovery more by accident than design.

In one particular district to the north-east of Awka, we met with a currency which appeared to be quite unique. What was stranger was the fact that the natives would not accept cowries; apparently they did not consider them as currency at all. The currency in use consisted of tiny pieces of iron resembling small squashed tin-tacks, half an inch in length with arrow-shaped heads and the stem about the thickness of a large pin. The exchange value was roughly 45 to the penny, at Awka these umumu are reckoned as equal to two cowries each. In former days the Awka men used this currency for acquiring slaves from the people of Umu-mba. How many thousands had to be counted when making such a purchase baffles one's imagination. In the same parts the higher currency consisted of brass rods, based on a cash value of sixpence each.

Certain of the chiefs of Awka carry numbers of these tiny tack-like pieces of iron in their wallets; a man holding an Awzaw title will never be without a small supply. They are used in a sacrificial way whenever the chief takes food in another man's house. They form part of the special offering for the purification of a house, or of anything that needs ceremonial cleansing, those that are used for this purpose being eventually bound up in leaves and cast away.

CHAPTER XIX

WAR AND WEAPONS

In common, I suppose, with all savage peoples, the Ibos, prior to the British occupation of the country, occupied their spare time with fighting, generally town against town. The evil of this was not so much the blood shed, but rather the paralysing of trade and intercourse. It led to the isolation and independence of each town through the perpetual state of fear which existed. It was never safe to venture far beyond the confines of the town, nor was this done except by bands of men armed ready to defend themselves. It was a rare thing for towns to remain at peace for very long, and when quietness did happen to prevail for a time, the spell was broken on the slightest pretext and hostilities began again forthwith.

During the dry season fighting was a sort of pastime, either between different quarters of the same town or between neighbouring towns. In the former case, i.e. civil war, firearms were not always used, but recourse was had to knives and staves. Helmets woven from the dried stems of the largest koko leaves (akasi oyibo) were worn, which gave fair protection to the head, but left the face exposed. Some men wore doublets made from the same material, others had chest and back protectors fastened over the shoulders. The majority carried shields composed of plaited palm stems (igu). The knives were the ordinary trade matchets, and these, when well sharpened on a stone, and in the hands of a hefty warrior, were dangerous weapons. On the days of battle the noise and excitement made up for that which was lacking in blows, and frequently the preliminaries were prolonged beyond all apparent necessity. As a rule fighting ceased for the day when a warrior was killed; the parties straightway drew off, the one side to rejoice and make merry with feasting, the other to mourn the loss of a comrade.

On occasion the outbursts were more serious, and during our first months at Awka the town was engaged in a civil war in which a number of lives were lost. Several sections of the town attacked a single quarter, and placed it in a state of siege. Skirmishes between outposts were frequent with no particular advantage to either side, and all assaults in force were beaten back. It was extremely difficult to locate the enemy by sight as every advantage was taken of the cover of the dense bush. Sharpshooters were posted on platforms hidden high up in the large trees, who sniped any member of the attacking force who happened to expose himself within range of their guns. Immense quantities of powder and ball were used—most of it wasted—but such men as were hit suffered rather badly, the slugs causing large gaping wounds.

An interesting feature of the war was the preliminary preparation for a general attack. The day having been fixed, a medicine-man of repute was imported, whose business it was to concoct medicine, to provide charms, and offer sacrifices to ensure success, these to avail for all such as could and would pay the price. For three days the ceremonies, with much chanting and excitement, were observed without ceasing, and in due course the head and body of each warrior was smeared with the medicine, which, though of various ingredients no doubt, at sight appeared to be nothing more than chalk and water laid on in streaks. Anointed with this solution the fighter would be immune against flying bullets; either they would not touch him at all, or, should they do so, they would simply flatten against his body and fall harmlessly to the ground. Some of the warriors were surprised at a later stage to find that the medicine did not act in accordance with the guarantee, but the blame did not fall upon the medicine-man. The accident was due to the fact that the marksman had managed to secure a medicine of superior power to that used by the unfortunate victim, or else the stricken man had not fulfilled some necessary condition, and thus the medicine had failed to act. Had he been willing to give a higher price and fulfilled the conditions (to be evolved from his own inner consciousness !) he would not have suffered ! In their predicament some of the men sought our aid, and begged for that English medicine which was a sure remedy against bullets. They asked for the kind that, when a man was shot, caused the bullet simply to pass through the outer shell of the body and then to fall into the stomach leaving no serious result nor any more internal inconvenience than his breakfast might have caused !

Men wounded in any part of the body suffer greatly, and especially such as are shot in the chest or abdomen. Their native friends can do little or nothing for them, and many bleed to death. Others die of exhaustion, but we saw no case of septic poisoning, although theoretically all ought to have died from it, considering the filth and lack of proper treatment. The wounds are dressed in a very primitive way ; they are bound up with leaves and fibre, or covered with clay. In some cases attempts were made to extract the slug. In one case the operator cut into the back of a man to provide an outlet for a bullet which had entered his chest ; this patient eventually bled to death. In other cases the bullets are left, and I have seen men walking about for a long time with large pieces of iron embedded in their flesh. During the disturbances at Awka we were able to render assistance to some of the wounded ; indeed by the practice of a little amateur surgery we won the confidence of our neighbours, and were thus able to establish ourselves in a place where, up to that date, our tenure had been more precarious than we comprehended at the time. From being merely tolerated we were accepted as friends, and the relationship thus established has remained a cordial one ever since.

Battles are fought in a haphazard manner ; there is little attempt at leadership or organisation. Each unit follows his own devices, advancing, firing or turning tail exactly as he feels inclined. Those whom one would naturally expect to lead their soldiers in battle, i.e. the chiefs, are never present. It is convenient for them to retire to a remote spot in the bush, well away from the fray, where they can in quietness (and security) invoke the help of the gods. When there is no further need to pray they return home.

Warriors of renown are respected and honoured, and happy is the man entitled to don the eagle's plumes and the red tail-feathers of the parrot, in token of his prowess in battle. In life he enjoys special privileges, and in death is granted the dignity of a warrior's funeral.

The native guns and ammunition have been noticed in an earlier chapter (p. 128). The former consisted of flint-locks, cap guns and Snider rifles, but cartridges for these last, though always purchasable at certain markets, were not so easy to obtain as the ordinary trade powder and caps. The black powder is packed in barrels, and a dozen of these were sometimes stored in the houses of leading men. A good supply is still available, but nowadays it is used by hunters, and, even more extensively, for ceremonial cannon-firing at second burials.

The chief disturbers of the peace were certain bands of raiders who either acted on their own account or, more frequently, were hired by the men of one town to help them fight against another. Such were the dreaded Abams on the eastern side of the river, and the Ndi-Ekumeku on the western. Both these societies had a large membership and were responsible for a vast amount of havoc in the districts where they operated.

The Ekumeku was, and is still, the most formidable confederation in the country lying between Asaba and Benin. Some account of the society may be given here, inasmuch as war was one of its principal functions, otherwise it would be more rightly described as a secret society. It is rather difficult to decide what the precise meaning of the word Ekumeku is. During the last rising (1904) the members of the confederacy were named the "Silent Ones"; but that rendering assumed that the word was a corruption of Ekwumekwu, i.e. "Don't speak." It has also been interpreted as meaning a "breathing" or "blowing." Probably the idea is based upon that of the wind which "bloweth where it listeth; thou canst not tell whence it cometh nor whither it goeth." So it is with the Ekumeku; they went here, there and everywhere, swiftly and silently. Their gatherings took place, and their exploits were always carried out on dark nights. No country could be better adapted for their operations than the forest districts of the Asaba hinterland.

The king of Iselle-Ukwu was the accredited head of the whole society, but members could and did act independently of him. A description of him by an actual member of the Ekumeku reads rather quaintly, but it clearly illustrates the awe he instilled into the minds of the rank and file. "He is the greatest man ever seen in the world and second only to the king of Benin! (What superlative should be attached to the king of Benin is not stated!) And his wives will be more than fifty." When I called upon his majesty in 1900 it was maintained that the harem contained some two hundred wives; it required a good-sized village to house them and their children. A report was circulated later to the effect that, having wearied of some of them, and become impatient owing to their constant quarrels, he had divorced over fifty of them; "and he died in his bed," i.e. a natural death, which, apparently, was quite contrary to expectation. For a period the society was wont to remain quiescent; its members disbanded and pursued the ordinary avocations of normal citizens. The oath of allegiance was not necessarily life-long, but was repeated with every revival of activity. These outbreaks of violence were not governed by any fixed rule, but were quite spontaneous; when the spirit moved any one member, in any district, he would communicate with eight or ten other members, and they met together and conferred in some secluded spot in the forest. They laid their guns crosswise in a pile on the ground and over these the men clasped hands and took a solemn oath of loyalty and secrecy. The oath stipulated that any member revealing the watchwords or plans of the society should be shot, the executioner to be chosen by the leader of the particular band of which the traitor was a member. After the first meeting the members separated and forthwith took steps to augment their forces. They knew, of course, all their old comrades and every likely freshman, and gradually the band increased in numbers until there were sufficient to begin operations. The whole of these preliminaries were carried through with the utmost secrecy under cover of darkness ; nothing whatever could be done by daylight. A sufficient number having been recruited they proceeded to waylay travellers and market women, and entered upon a course of systematic pillage, inspiring such fear that none dared report his losses openly.

It was a safe and quick method of acquiring property, and hence, within three months of the original gathering practically every able-bodied man in the locality was an active member of the society. Their main movements were still carried on during the hours of darkness, wild, wet and intensely dark nights being usually chosen for their nefarious purposes. Should the men of any town refuse to join in the movement the members made it their special business to persecute the inhabitants of it.

Before any really serious expedition was undertaken the raiders had recourse to the inevitable medicine in order to safeguard themselves against the bullets of those whom they attacked. The men whitened their bodies with chalk and thus were able to recognise fellow-members in the darkness and avoid fighting with their confederates. When on the war-path the company marched in procession, the leader bearing the calabash containing the medicine which was to protect the party from the guns of the enemy. In the centre were the buglers, i.e. those who sounded the calls on the "akpelle." This is a long cucumber-shaped calabash with both ends cut off and a blow-hole provided in the middle. With it a series of notes or calls were blown, as with a bugle.

The force worked its way towards the town selected for attack and fell upon it suddenly, driving out the inhabitants and taking full possession of the place. The invaders quickly made their position secure and laid hands on all the foodstuff they could discover, cows, goats, yams and other possessions ; following this up by a systematic looting of the town at their leisure. They manifested no inclination to depart until supplies showed signs of running out; sometimes they settled down and their occupation extended over a month.

The wives of the members of the Ekumeku society enjoyed certain privileges; they came under the protection of the society and were free from molestation when passing to and from market. When the time was considered opportune the Ndi-Ekumeku abandoned all pretence of concealment and proceeded to rob and plunder in open daylight. Each member provided his own equipment, which consisted of two bottles (calabashes) of powder, his gun and cutlass, and they foregathered at an appointed town. The king of the town sat in the place of honour, supported on each side by the chiefs from all the towns represented, sitting on their stools. Together they acted as a council and drew up the programme for future operations. At the close of the deliberations the young braves (ikolobia) had their turn and rushed about, firing off guns, whilst the buglers surpassed themselves; in fact, the whole assembly resolved itself into a general display before the natives of the town. The men yelled out challenges, and by gesture demonstrated the kind of treatment that awaited any who should dare to defy them. After these manœuvres the king presented two slaves, one of each sex, to those who had condescended to honour his town with their company. The rendezvous was regularly changed, but the general programme was followed with but little variation.

It is not so easy to give a detailed account of the Abams on the eastern side of the Niger. Their expeditions were not spontaneous affairs as with the Ekumeku; they were in a state of perpetual readiness for war whenever it was made worth their while, and, consequently, the whole country was terrorised, inasmuch as the people were in a continual state of nervousness, not knowing when a raiding party might suddenly burst upon them. They were the dreaded enemies of the adults and bogies to the young, naughty children being silenced by their elders under the threat that the Abams would come and eat them up.

The Abams were controlled by the Aros, and all transactions had to be negotiated through them. Any town having a dispute with another, and wishing to wreak summary vengeance upon it, applied through the Aro agents for a force of these mercenaries. Prior to operations being undertaken a sum of money had to be paid in advance to the Abams, and, in addition, the lands of all captives became their property. These warriors used no firearms whatever; they depended on their cutlasses, their reputation, and their sudden onslaughts. Actually they themselves were out for heads, and they were intensely insistent on the fulfilment of this part of the contract. The bands were always ready to ravage a town, and the Aros, with their aid, gained complete control over the country. They moved up from the south, established large setttlements amongst the Ibos, and became virtual owners of large areas of land. They prospered in their enterprises and added to their incomes by wholesale and retail dealing in slaves. As long as they were able to retain and control these bands of mercenaries the Aros remained all-powerful, particularly in the country lying between Akwa in the north, and Aro-Chuku in the south. Their agents were also in touch with the coast, and were in a position to purchase firearms and ammunition such as no ordinary native could procure, and hence they were well equipped for the task of maintaining their superiority over the Ibos. The firearms were for their own use, not for the Abams.

With the advent of the British Government the Aros have received a knock-out blow, from which their chances of recovery appear to be rather remote. It remains to be seen whether they will succeed as legitimate traders. Certainly a large number have come down in the world during the last few years, having been deprived of their old sources of income.

Their chief reasons for making war were either revenge or plunder, pure and simple. On the Asaba side all available property was looted, and any captives taken were condemned to slavery and all that this fate entailed, including human sacrifice; but there is no record of cannibalism being practised in that district. Knowing the danger to property from marauding bands, the people usually stored their yams in some hidden retreat in the forest, in the hope that they might remain undiscovered by the robbers. With the Abams on the eastern side the heads of victims were in great demand as trophies, and the man-slayer was saluted publicly as "obu madu" (he kills men). Living captives were disposed of as slaves, offered as human sacrifices and also killed for food, cannibalism being general in the eastern districts.

In a great number of Ibo towns may be seen towers rising some thirty feet above ground-level. They are circular or square according to fancy, the former being exceptionally well-turned structures. The walls are of clay built up in very thick courses to withstand wind and the wash from the torrential rains. An upper floor is provided which is reached by a ladder placed inside the building. Outside the walls are decorated with rows of empty gin bottles; the tower rises well above the compound, but being very deficient in window openings or loopholes it does not command a view of the situation. In the upper chamber the owner stores his treasures; he frequently sleeps therein, drawing up the ladder after him should he have the slightest suspicion that thieves are in the neighbourhood. Ordinarily the room is just a storehouse, but in troublous times the owner defends his castle as the last refuge for himself and his goods.

A very favourite method of bringing destruction and confusion upon an attacking force was by the use of concealed pitfalls (awbu). Surrounding each town was a belt of dense bush, and all paths leading through this were tortuous and intricate. Alongside these paths pits were dug and upright spikes embedded in the bottom, on which any unfortunate who fell into the hole was impaled. Entering a strange town one day, I noticed my guide carefully picking his way. I found it expedient to follow his example, the path being herring-boned on either side with pitfalls.

Outside the towns, clear of the thick bush, earthworks (ekpe) were constructed. These were thrown up in the form of embankments, with a trench on the defensive side.

The base was from six to eight feet thick, tapering up to a conical ridge, and they were just high enough to afford comfortable cover from bullets, but not so high that a man could not easily peep over the top to observe the enemy. The earthworks were often laid out in parallel lines, thus enabling the defenders to fall back from one line of defence to another, without unduly exposing themselves.

Some towns were surrounded by moats—dry for the greater part of the year. Usually they were from eight to ten feet deep and about the same in width. Single planks made from split palm trees were thrown over to serve as bridges where paths crossed the moat, it being an easy task to remove these quickly. Normally the obstacle was not a serious affair to tackle and could be crossed without much effort, bridge or no bridge, but with sturdy, determined fighters in possession of the moat, the forcing of a passage across it was a formidable task.

The crossing of the moat by so slender a bridge had its dangers in times of peace, the plank of split palm tree sometimes breaking under the weight of a man. One evening I was called upon to stitch up a very nasty wound on a man's arm. He was a big burly fellow and when crossing the moat the plank broke; one part fell with him, the other remained embedded in the bank. As he fell his arm caught on the jagged end and the sharp edges pierced the upper part of his arm to the bone, whilst the drag of his fall rolled the flesh up to the top of his shoulder. Happily we were able to make quite a respectable job of patching up the lacerated flesh.

CHAPTER XX

SOME ASPECTS OF RELIGION

In the study of a primitive people there is probably no more debatable subject than that of their religious beliefs. To what extent a knowledge of the Science of Comparative Religion will help the investigator in prosecuting his researches, or whether such preparation may, contrariwise, be rather a hindrance in ascertaining facts, depends upon the inquirer himself. It is certain, however, that unless unlimited time and patience can be devoted to the subject, together with much cross-questioning, backed up by continual observation, no European can ever fathom the depths of the native mind. A knowledge of other religions will lead to confusion should there be any attempt to hurry matters, and any sort of antecedent opinion revealed by the inquirer will assuredly result in his being led astray in his conclusions.

The constitution of the native mind is such that a West African—at any rate, an Ibo—will supply an answer "yes" or "no" exactly in accordance with what he imagines the question expects. I have known cases where utterly false answers have been given simply in order to bring to an end a tiresome catechism. Statements have been accepted as truth which were the very antithesis of the actual facts. I have on occasion remonstrated with interpreters for giving inaccurate information. I have known such to answer a question in the negative, and then upon being further pressed, "But do not the people do this or that?" the original reply has been completely reversed. Whenever the interpreter was rebuked for leading the inquirer to a false conclusion the excuse invariably was, "But that was what he wanted; his opinion was already formed, and who am I that I should contradict the white man ? "

It is no uncommon practice to charge missionaries with a lack of respect for native religions ; especially is this done by travellers who have the pen of a ready writer but who cannot wait to investigate. It stands to reason that it is part of the missionary's business to understand the mind of the native, just as much as it is the soldier's aim to reconnoitre the enemy's position. The missionary cannot be the indiscriminating, unsympathetic person. Were he such he could never endure the long years of service ; nor, indeed, would he be tolerated by the natives for a week if he put himself in open and wanton antagonism to their beliefs. Mr. E. D. Morel in his book, *Nigeria : its People and its Problems*[1] is at considerable pains to point out the alleged contempt of a missionary towards a native ju-ju. For one thing he does not inform his readers whether that particular ju-ju was inhabited by the " spirit " at the time or not ? This is a point which has great significance. It is similar to a church in England which is in daily use as compared with a cluster of ruined walls. The latter may, perchance, be restored and become a real church once more, but for the nonce they are ruins, the abode of bats and owls. In the instance quoted it is worth noting that the missionary charged was one who had spent some twenty years in the country, and whose

[1] It is difficult to reconcile the allegations against missionaries with the actual state of affairs. Sixty years ago, the foremost West African of his time, versed in the deep things of the native mind, rebutted the charges with such compelling logic that ignorance alone could resurrect them. Surely the following words must commend themselves to all fair-minded students :—" Had we been obstinate in the public exposure of their national superstitions, Christian Missionaries would long ago have been turned out of the country, the converts put to death, and the country would have been long barred against the messengers of salvation. But what is the result of the caution and prudence exercised ? The whole country is opened to us, stations are occupied in different directions, churches are built, congregations are collected, and converts are numbered by hundreds (now thousands, 1917) ; and yet we do not make the least compromise with their superstitions ; but, on the contrary, we are weakening its power, though without open violence, and, in generations to come, it will die a natural death."—Rev. S. Crowther writing of the Yoruba Mission, 1857.

name is a household word amongst the natives of the district. At least, those chiefly concerned do not accuse him of sacrilege or disrespect in regard to the local beliefs.

But if one is really desirous of tracing the sources of so-called disrespect he must look for them amongst the natives themselves. They are the people who manifest the most utter neglect of and even contempt for many of their gods. On every side one sees ruins of shrines either simply left to decay or from which the "spirit" has been driven out. On one occasion a deputation of men from a neighbouring village waited upon me with the request that I would come and cast out their god Ngenne, on the ground that too many people had died in the village in spite of the many sacrifices offered. The people had come to the conclusion that their Ngenne was too much of a knave. Either he had no power to avert disaster, or he was of such a sour disposition that nothing would satisfy him, although they had almost beggared themselves in providing sacrifices.

I inquired of them why, if this was their firm conviction, they did not destroy such a spiteful god? They were anxious to do so, they replied, but declared that the task was beyond their powers; the prospect made them shudder. When I rounded upon them for begging me to do what they were afraid to attempt, and told them that I had no wish to be eaten by the "spirit," or be overwhelmed with disaster, they were emphatic in their declaration that Ngenne could not exercise power over one who prayed to Chukwu (the Supreme Being). These people were pure heathen, wholly untouched by Christian teaching or influence. For the time being I refused to accede to their request, and at a later date I again put them off; I thought that they might be acting upon impulse owing to excitement, and might afterwards repent of their hasty deed. Three months passed and then they came again, a stronger deputation than the preceding ones. I decided to carry out their wishes. The Ngenne figure was installed at one end of a hut set apart for the purpose, and his "spirit" dwelt in a sacred tree just outside. The Ngenne was a wooden block, two feet high, roughly carved to represent a man; this was draped with streamers of filthy cloth, and was thickly coated with a black shiny mass of congealed blood. Near by was a basket and a bowl containing sticks of chalk, and there was a large wicker arrangement into which hundreds of wing feathers of fowls had been stuck. In a prominent place was Ngenne's spear and the two iron bells which are the special symbols of this god. My boys and I removed the whole collection as requested, in open daylight, with all the folk gathered round, and as we moved away the men cheered with delight. They challenged the god; threw dust in the air to express their contempt, and defied him to do his worst, and then they took their matchets and made such an onslaught on the sacred tree that within a few minutes it was hacked into firewood.

Everything else was preserved intact and deposited on the front verandah of my house, where it remained for some nine months visible to all. Should the people regret what they had done, they could reinstate their Ngenne; but they have never repented, and eventually a native destroyed by fire all that the white ants had left. It may be that at some future time a medicine-man will be commissioned to consecrate another Ngenne; but for the old abandoned one there is not one iota of respect. When the spirit withdraws, or is driven out of a ju-ju, the material and visible parts are no more valuable, or worthy of honour, than the shell of a nut after the kernel has been extracted.

Amongst the Ibo people there is a distinct recognition of a Supreme Being—beneficent in character—who is above every other spirit, good or evil. He is believed to control all things in heaven and earth, and dispenses rewards and punishments according to merit. Anything that occurs, for which no visible explanation is forthcoming, is attributed either to Him or His eternal enemy Ekwensu, i.e. the Devil. But Chukwu (as He is called) is supreme, and at His service are many ministering spirits whose sole business it is to fulfil His commands. It is interesting to note that Death is spoken of as as one of the servants of God.

This Supreme Being is designated by different rites, the

chief of which are Chukwu (=Chi-ukwu) i.e. the Great God ; Olisa bulu uwa, usually shortened to Osebulu uwa ; or Olisa simply. The underlying idea of the name is, " God who fashions the world." In the southern districts Chineke (God the Creator) is the prevailing name.

The knowledge of the Supreme Being is practically confined to the name and the interpretation thereof. Besides the recognition of a Beneficent Being, there is a profound belief in an Evil Spirit. The two are eternally opposed to each other, each striving to influence mankind for good or evil, but Chukwu is always classed as superior to Ekwensu.

Certain actions such as murder, theft, and adultery, are esteemed offences against God, as well as against man. The natives hold that in committing such offences, a man is acting contrary to the will of God and the appropriate punishment will assuredly follow. Should the actual sinner escape, his descendants must bear the burden. The fear of retribution, however, is not profound ; it certainly does not act as a deterrent to evil. Though such deeds are reckoned as ajaw-awlu (bad works) there is no actual " sting " in the committal of them. The greatest of all sins is " to be found out," and any man who works so clumsily that his misdeeds are discovered deserves all the punishment that comes to him.

In spite of this theoretical knowledge of good and evil, there is little compunction in committing theft, murder and other misdemeanours. The lure of a title leads a man to steal in order to raise the necessary funds to acquire it. The same motive leads to murder, human heads being emblems of a man's prowess. Human nature is much the same all the world over, and amongst the Ibos, as elsewhere, evil deeds are mostly the outcome of selfish desires.

Some sins stand before others in magnitude. The recognised punishment for murder, the stealing of seed-yams after they have been planted, and adultery with the wife of a chief, was death. In the case of the last the man is held responsible ; they might both be put to death, or the woman may be forgiven—the man never. After these, in importance, come other kinds of theft, and the usual catalogue of offences either against the individual or society, and in each case the punishment is made to fit the crime. All are accounted as bad work or ulu-ani (the defiling of the land). There are many other things which are regarded as sinful, e.g. the breaking or removal of a man's god and treachery, whereas, on the other hand, cannibalism, human sacrifices, infanticide, deceit, lying and such-like are matters of indifference; they certainly are not of the nature of sin.

In dealing with "Objects of Worship," especially those which are more or less public property, some limitation must be put upon the word "worship" since it is very seldom that any object is actually "worshipped," whilst there are a vast variety and number of objects—animate and inanimate—which are held as "sacred." These are reverenced from fear of unexpected consequences should they be injured or destroyed rather than from any desire to worship them. Hence one sees in every town and village these sacred objects, cows, sheep, monkeys, fish, snakes, tortoises and human beings, together with rocks, trees and streams. The animals are fearless of man, wandering where they please without molestation. In a few instances only are gifts presented to these objects, consisting of a kola nut, a few cowrie shells, a small piece of salt, chalk, an egg or a young chick, and these are mostly offered to trees and streams.

The custom of holding certain waters to be sacred appears to be common throughout the Ibo country. It has been thought that the practice has arisen on account of the water itself, without which there would be death and desolation; but this is probably a mistake, for there is little doubt but that it is the fish which are reverenced rather than the water. These fish (and sometimes crocodiles) are commonly spoken of as "our mother" (nne-ayi), the idea being, that they are the protectors of the people. This appears to savour somewhat of ancestor worship. No such fish may be taken from the stream; should one by chance find its way into a water-pot it must be restored as quickly as possible to its native haunts. If a woman inadvertently takes one home in her pot, she must return with it to the stream without delay, and make an offering, seeking forgiveness on the plea that the fish was taken unwittingly. The result is that the fish are quite tame and I have seen a shoal of twenty or thirty together, varying in length up to fifteen or sixteen inches, swimming quite unconcernedly between the legs of the women filling their pots.

Over the greater part, if not over the whole, of the Ibo country the python is sacred, more especially the smaller species called ekke-ntu. These likewise are referred to as "our mother," and to injure one is a very serious offence. If a man has the misfortune to kill one accidentally be will mourn for a year and abstain from shaving his head. Monkeys, birds and various animals are treated similarly in the different districts where they are held sacred.

If a person be injured by any sacred animal or reptile, or by the fall of a sacred tree or stone, it is inferred that some grievous offence has been committed, and that nne-ayi is meting out an appropriate punishment to the transgressor. Favour can be regained only by resort to the medicine-man, who will advise as to the sacrifice to be offered in the circumstances. If the injury should be fatal, as it may be when a tree falls upon a person, then the assumption is that the offence was such as could only be atoned for by the god thus exercising his powers of vengeance. The unfortunate person is left to his or her fate, a crowd of spectators probably looking on with callous indifference, in the belief that the sufferer is but getting his just deserts, and that to attempt a rescue, or to interfere in any way would be but to bring retribution upon themselves.

We turn now to the private and family gods—those which are kept within the house and compound and which have a much closer connection with the individual than those which are public and general. It must be again emphasised that no object in itself is worshipped by the Ibos; it is sacred only as the habitation of a spirit. It has only that relative sanctity to which it is entitled as the shrine or home of a certain spirit. Very seldom are the objects themselves called upon by name; the petitions are invariably addressed to the igaw-maw, i.e. the spirits. Occasionally the god Ikenga is invoked under the title of Ikenga Oweawfa, i.e. " he who splits the shield (of the enemy), hence the strongest one: the bravest one." Under certain conditions this spirit-worship exercises a tremendous influence over the lives of the natives.

Each house contains many sacred objects, but they have not all equal significance, for among the " gods many and lords many " there are higher and lower degrees of importance. The most universal of these household gods, and that which is given first rank, is the Ikenga, and no house may be without one. It is the first god sought by a young man at the beginning of his career, and it is the one to which he looks for good luck in all his enterprises.

The Ikenga is always carved from a solid block of uroko-wood. The height varies from one foot upwards. It represents a man seated upon a stool; two long horns, curling backwards, are the symbol of strength and power. Many examples have a long-stemmed pipe in the mouth, the bowl of the pipe resting on the knees. The right hand of the larger Ikengas grasps a sword, point upwards, whilst the left holds the head of the conquered enemy—this again denoting strength. Occasionally the horns project from a headless trunk and no limbs are provided. Such are simply of cheaper design. For religious purposes all figures of Ikenga stand equal. As a rule only the head of the household may offer sacrifice to them; should he be prevented for any reason the awkpala (next of kin, male) officiates in his stead.

A place is set apart for the alusi (gods) which are memorials to departed relatives. The number of these is fixed by the rank and family of the householder. If he can claim relationship to a deceased chief, then he must consecrate an alusi to represent that chief. But every man must have some alusi to commemorate certain relatives. These consist merely of a piece of wood from ten to twelve inches long cut from a sacred ebwo tree and merely stripped of its bark. A man will never put one of these to represent a woman; on the other hand a woman may dedicate one such alusi in order to show due reverence to her mother's spirit. The memorial set up by a man for a female relative is in the form of a cone of clay, upon the top of which is placed the neck of a water-pot. One of these is made and dedicated upon the death of a mother, wife or daughter.

One alusi is consecrated to Chi the Supreme Being, and this is the only one to which direct sacrifice is occasionally offered.

In addition to the above there are many objects which are held sacred, and others commonly spoken of as fetishes. They consist of anything which appeals to the spiritual imagination of the native, but all have their measure of reverence due to them.

Near the kitchen will be found the ekwu, little cones of clay rubbed with chalk, set up by the women to counteract any designs to poison the food during the process of cooking. At another spot is the agwu, a pot fixed in the ground and encircled with sticks. The pot contains a few feathers from a young chick and some chalk. The special function of the agwu is to protect the owner in every way, either when working, playing or fighting. There are many more fetishes; numbers of them are peculiar to the house only, and are set up for special reasons on the advice of the dibia (priest). Each profession has its patron gods, as farming, hunting and blacksmithing, and the richer women have theirs also to assist them in their trading ventures.

It is interesting to note whence the alusi are obtained, and by what process they are made into gods or rather the habitation of spirits. It will be observed that the spiritual perception of the native is very pronounced, and this is a trait which the average European finds exceedingly difficult to comprehend and appreciate. With the exception of Ikenga the majority of the fetishes are fashioned by their owners; the Ikenga is carved, and the services of a craftsman are needed, otherwise it likewise would be home-made. It may be purchased in the ordinary way in the open market or by private treaty, the latter method being followed when extra or special features are required. Up to this point it remains a piece of merchandise, no ceremony whatever having been performed to consecrate it to a religious use. The buyer, himself, sets it up in his house, pours out a libation of palm wine or gin before it, and offers kola ; and from henceforth it has the sanctity of, and is reverenced as an alusi (ju-ju).

There are no alusi to represent specific forms of disease, such as small-pox, but certain ceremonies are observed for driving away or staving off sickness generally. At Onitsha, for instance, on a day appointed, the inhabitants of a village gather together, each person carrying a firebrand. To the strains of continuous chanting the firebrands are borne away and deposited in a prescribed place. When this ceremony has been performed by each of the villages the king is called upon to conduct the final observances. On this occasion the rallying place is the king's courtyard, and his attendants are the most prominent officials. Again firebrands are used, the torch-bearers form up in procession and, with incessant beating of tom-toms and chanting, march to the riverside where the firebrands are solemnly cast into the water. This ceremony is observed annually to ward off all manner of sicknesses, and is known by the name Awsaw Ekwulo.

There does not appear to be any actual Devil Worship among the Ibos. Two terms are used to indicate the authors of evil, Ekwensu and Obunike. Ekwensu means the Evil One in a general way, the father of all wickedness, anywhere and everywhere. There is *no* idol to represent him, nor is sacrifice offered directly to him. Obunike refers to a deceased companion who is able to work mischief upon those left behind, but of more general significance appears to be "the demon of ill-fortune." There *is* an idol to represent this spirit, and sacrifices are offered regularly to him. In offering sacrifice to Obunike the worshipper hopes to propitiate Ekwensu also.

In most of the towns on the western side of the river, three days in the year are set apart as Ekwensu's Days. for the express purpose of extolling the devil and all his works.[1] During the festival the people indulge freely in

[1] The custom was practised at Onitsha a generation or two ago certainly. The Rev. J. Taylor refers to it in his Journal, September 29th, 1858.

all kinds of excess without the imposition of any restraint. In the old days this unrestricted licence usually led to serious feuds followed by bloodshed. The advent of the Missionary and the Government has, at least, put an end to bloodshed, but the people (heathen) still give themselves up to excessive indulgence during the times appointed to do honour to Ekwensu.

CHAPTER XXI

SACRIFICE AND SACRIFICES

THE idea of sacrifice amongst the Ibo people is very similar to that of many other primitive peoples, i.e. sacrifices are offered, not from any desire to give, but because of the fear that, unless they are offered their lives and interests will be blighted. Every man must contribute his share in public festivals, and all join in the subsequent carousals, but no man offers sacrifice privately until he feels compelled to do so by adverse circumstances ; it is never a voluntary offering. Sacrifice is offered solely to appease a malignant god whose imperative demands are indicated by the god's executive, i.e. the medicine-man (dibia).

The natives are very clear in discriminating between what are " proper " sacrifices and what are not, a distinction which the foreigner does not easily perceive. In the native's estimation some specific gifts will be acknowledged as sacrificial offerings, whilst in other cases of dedicated objects the idea of sacrifice is absent, whereas to the English mind both forms appear to be governed by the same underlying principle. Food offered to certain spirits in the prescribed manner becomes *ex opere operato* a real and proper sacrifice. On the other hand, birds, beasts and even human beings, when presented to the ilaw maw (familiar spirits) have no other significance than merely " making a feast " in honour of those " spirits" in whose existence the people have such a profound belief. There is a further distinguishing feature which immediately declares the nature of the sacrifice. In " proper " acrifices the food offered is *never* consumed by any person, whereas that which is presented to the ilaw maw is always subsequently eaten by those present at the festival.

According to the Ibo, sacrifice is imperative in the case of "strange" spirits only, i.e. other than those he has been accustomed to acknowledge; spirits shrouded in mystery whom he cannot manage, and whom he holds responsible for his present sickness or other trouble. He cannot locate the spirits; he has no conception how or why they persecute him, yet he is convinced that they are the authors of all the evils that overtake him. In his distress he consults the dibia (medicine-man) and, acting on his advice, endeavours to appease the spirits by performing íchú-àjà, lit. to drive evil.

For this observance of íchú-àjà no idol (alusi) is ever used. The only semblance to one is the Awfaw, so named merely because it is a stick from the awfaw tree. This stick is held in the hand and has a double significance: first, Awfaw is considered to possess the functions of a mediator between the spirits and the man, and secondly, on it the man swears that he is innocent of wrongdoing against others. The offering always consists of a selection from the following: food, strips of cloth, a gin bottle, a lizard, a chicken or a kid, and many other things, the choice being made according to the instructions of the dibia.

Íchú-àjà is performed on a few other special occasions. It is prescribed when a person has succumbed to a malignant disease, such as leprosy or smallpox, in the case of suicides, or when a man dies during the period of mourning for his wife. As noted in Chapter X the corpses of such people are borne outside the town for disposal in the ajaw-awfia (bad bush). The method adopted for sacrifice in these cases is as follows: no particular preparations are made, the offering is simply placed in a piece of banana (tree) stem cut roughly to form a dish; sometimes a wooden platter serves the purpose or a small calabash. This is carried beyond the boundaries of the village and deposited by the side of one of the paths leading to the place of burial, usually at the point where two paths meet, and designated by the native as "abu-itaw." The person who

THE "MAW" (SPIRIT) OF A GIRL

The two attendants announce her coming, and generally look after her interests.

conveys the sacrifice must maintain strict silence—he may not even salute another—until the offering has been laid somewhere near what is supposed to be the dwelling-place of the troublesome spirit. Íchû-àjà is also observed before crossing water, in order to ensure a safe passage. When sacrifice is necessary in consequence of alu (abomination), the ceremonies connected therewith are, wherever possible, fulfilled by a priest from Nri. In all other circumstances the person himself assumes the rôle of priest and makes the offering, but always in strict accordance with the injunctions of the dibia, who first diagnoses the source of the trouble and then prescribes the offering. It will be observed that, in what is considered "proper" sacrifice, the shedding of blood is somewhat rare. It is well to emphasise the fact that the Ibo never offers sacrifice until forced to do so by adversity; except at such times there is an utter neglect of sacrifice. This is a point which writers unversed in native ways should bear in mind before making rash statements concerning the attitude of missionaries and others towards the religion of the people.

We next examine the much more prevalent practice of offering gifts before the ilaw-maw. This is akin to what is commonly termed a "peace offering." It is really a feast of good fellowship, a feast of fat things wherewith to make glad the hearts of men in this world, and the spirits dwelling in the underworld also, e.g. in the case of sickness such a festival may be kept in order to promote kindly feelings towards the sufferer, all those partaking of the feast signifying by their action that they are free from any evil intention towards him. The spirits of dead relatives are also coaxed into a genial mood by offerings of meat and drink, and their aid invoked to restore the sick one to health and strength.

In such a case the following is the mode of procedure: a member of the family seeks a consultation with the dibia. Here we must not forget that, for the most part, the natives do not attribute sickness to natural causes, but are convinced that it arises from the spiteful attentions of an evil spirit, or through the agency of witchcraft, or from poison. The dibia puts his visitor through a catechism and, having ascertained all he can as to the nature of the malady, he next proceeds to consult his charms. He is now able to announce what he considers to be the cause of the sickness. In the majority of cases the source of the evil is traced to a woman ! This woman will be forthwith accused of witchcraft, and in past days such an one was forced to undergo a trial by ordeal ; she must drink the cup of poison (awrachi, sass-wood). Practically all condemned to this test died quickly, for it was an exceedingly rare thing for a woman to be in a position to bribe the one appointed to administer the cup lavishly enough to induce him either to omit the poison altogether, or to smuggle in the antidote.

Having found out the cause of the sickness, the dibia states what the offering is to be and whether the ceremony shall be íchú-àjà, i.e. a " proper " sacrifice, or a feast to the ilaw-maw.

Assuming that it is the latter, the necessary arrangements will be made without delay. At the time appointed the alusi (idols) are brought out of the house, and placed in order of rank. In the central and most prominent position is the Ikenga, and he is flanked on the one side by the piece of ebwo wood representing the deceased father of the man, and on the other by the stick representing Chi (his own guardian spirit). Around these three the minor alusi are grouped ; all being in due order water is poured over the alusi that they may " wash their hands " before eating. Kola nut is then formally presented, followed by pounded yam dipped in soup, a portion being placed upon the head of each alusi. For such ceremonies each wife supplies her share of the food required. The food having been duly offered, and the essence thereof consumed by the spirits, a child comes forward and takes the food from the head of one of the alusi and eats it. Any other children present follow the example of the first ; they may eat it immediately or take it away and re-divide it amongst themselves at their leisure. The hunger of the spirits having thus been appeased, they are refreshed with palm wine or gin. A small quantity is poured over the alusi, and the company present drink the remainder. Finally, water is again poured over them to enable the spirits to "wash their hands" after eating.

The ceremony, as an institution, is observed on the five fixed festivals of the year. All other occasions, as noted above, are the forced result of sickness, witchcraft and other untoward circumstances. The five fixed festivals are:

1. Aja-Chi.—The sacrifice to one's chief guardian spirit, commonly spoken of as "God." Chi is, however, not to be confused with Chukwu, the Great, Supreme God.

2. Iwa-ji.—The feast of new yam: lit. the breaking of the yam—Harvest Thanksgiving.

3. Ikelli-be-ji.—A feast in which the yam must not be pounded, but cut into chunks.

4. Osisi-ibe.—A sort of cook's festival; a feast to the spirits who mount guard over the cooking utensils and the food to prevent poison from being put into them.

5. Ife-ji-awku.—A Harvest Festival connected with the farm. An offering to the spirits of the farm, with special reference to the presiding deity of the yam crop. The fowls to be offered must all be taken to the farm and slain there, the blood being sprinkled on a few choice yams. When the ceremony is completed everything is taken home; the yams are laid up before the alusi, together with all farming implements, hoes, and matchets; the carcases of the fowls are used up in a big bout of feasting. The whole town or village joins in this feast on the day appointed.

There is a further clear and definite line of demarcation between sacrifice proper and the "peace offering." In the case of the former (íchú-àjà) it is open to every man to offer the sacrifice, rich and poor alike, as its observance costs little or nothing, but offering to the ilaw-maw is arbitrarily restricted to men of means who have the wherewithal to provide the necessary feast ; the richer the man, of course, the more elaborate the programme, the finer the feast, and the more ingratiating to both the quick and the dead.

Some ten years back I was the guest of a prominent chief at a town seventy miles east of Onitsha, and whilst residing in his compound I had the good fortune to be a spectator all through the observance of an offering to the ilaw-maw. I was left quite undisturbed and was able to watch and note events closely.

The chief was old, wrinkled, and troubled with rheumatics ; he was seeking the cause of this complaint and the means for its removal. Many sacrifices had been offered, but all to no purpose, and now, as a last resort, the dibia had fixed upon one of the younger wives as the author of his pains. With this pronouncement were also directions for the sacrifice necessary to secure relief.

On the day appointed a space was swept at the base of a small sacred tree growing in the compound immediately before the chief's own hut. In this space the alusi (idols) were ranged in due order. The next item on the programme was an exciting chase after a hen which, when caught, was tied by the leg to another tree with a cord long enough for the fowl to be waved freely over the alusi.

The preparations were now complete, and the sick man's elder brother (the awkpala—the family priest) came forward and took up his position, sitting on a low stool before the alusi. Amongst the assembled spectators conversation was general until the awkpala began his oration to the spirits (ilaw-maw), when there was complete silence, all being intent on hearing every word he uttered. It was a wonderful oration, full of eloquence, and gradually working up to intense emotion ; nobody could have been unmoved by the whole-souled earnestness of his appeal to the spirits. Starting in a low key, his voice increased in passionate entreaty until he was crying out at the top of his voice, his words all the time being punctuated by gestures, swaying of the body, and swinging of his arms. In the course of his oration he called upon the spirits to exercise their saving powers ; to send relief to the afflicted one, and to execute justice upon the wicked author of the sickness.

At this point the duties of the elder brother were concluded, and he made preparations to withdraw, transferring his office to a younger brother. The old man took the right hand of the younger and placed it on the central alusi, and in this manner delegated the priestly functions. He then withdrew with great dignity amidst a profound stillness.

As soon as he had departed the wives of the sick chief came to the front, they all being directly concerned in the business. Each, in turn, took the captive fowl in her hands, and, standing before the alusi and turning towards the assembly, made a solemn declaration of innocence; then she waved the fowl over the alusi and called upon the spirits to bear witness of her non-complicity in bringing sickness upon her husband. Were she not speaking the truth let the gods do so unto her, and more also, according to her deserts. All the wives acted in this manner with the execption of the one accused of causing the sickness. This particular one, in her turn, stepped to the front of the alusi and made a statement somewhat similar to the others, but refrained from touching the fowl. In the case of the first women it was a question of "let my life be as this fowl's life if I be guilty of this offence." The veracity of the last wife being in doubt, she was not in a position to swear positive innocence ; all she could affirm was that were she guilty she had trespassed unwittingly.

Confession is not infrequently made by women of being the primal cause of a husband's sickness. This is done, the woman fully believing herself guilty, when the sickness is pronounced to be the result of ifi (adultery).

After the last wife had made her statement, the priest presented the fowl to the alusi with invocations and prayers that the avenging spirits would accept the sacrifice now being offered. He, thereupon, took the bird by the wings and, with his knife, sawed across its throat so that the blood might trickle slowly. Each alusi was sprinkled in order of precedence, and then tufts of the smaller feathers were plucked from the fowl and stuck to the alusi by means of the blood, the wretched bird still alive and struggling, until this part of the ceremony was completed. The life-blood having ceased to flow, the priest threw the carcase several yards from him as a thing of nought, and the service ended.

The dead fowl had scarcely fallen to the ground when it was seized by a young man of the crowd who hastily began to pluck off the remaining feathers, another, meanwhile, kindling a fire of grass and twigs. As soon as the fire burned freely, the remaining feathers were singed off, and then the fowl was hacked to pieces in a most revolting manner and the bits held over the fire on skewers to cook. This was an affair of but a few minutes, for as soon as the flesh was charred with fire and smoke it was pounced upon, and after further hacking was consumed by the men present; the women stayed as spectators; they did not partake of the flesh.

We note that íchú-àjà is offered to evil spirits only; there is no form of direct sacrifice to the Supreme Being. Annually—in July—when food is more scarce than at any other time of the year, a feast is held in honour of Chi, and this is known as Ajà-Chi; but though the word for sacrifice is used it is simply a loose way of using it. The procedure is exactly on the lines of any other feast to the ilaw-maw. It is not a "proper" sacrifice, but a festival in honour of the man's own guardian spirit—the one which is present with him at all times and in all places and circumstances. This Chi is not to be confused with Chukwu (lit. Chi-Ukwu, the Great God, the Supreme Being).

HUMAN SACRIFICES

Probably there is no part of West Africa in which the offering of human sacrifices has not been customary at some period. Only by the advance of Christianity and civilisation and the power of good government is the practice being stamped out. Amongst the Ibos the custom was widespread; life was accounted of little value, especially that of the slave and the poor, and the belief in the efficacy of human sacrifice was (and amongst the old still is) very deep and tenacious.

The victims were offered either as sacrifices proper or at funerals. As the latter have already been dealt with in Chapter X we need only discuss the former. In principle these sacrifices were the same as the ordinary íchú-àjà, the difference being rather of degree and value; they were more often communal than private and personal. Should political affairs become unusually complicated, or the town be threatened by a powerful enemy, or laid under a devastating epidemic, or afflicted by any catastrophe whatever, the king or chief consulted with the dibias (medicine-men). That certain malignant spirits were in league against the town was evident, and recourse must be had to such measures as would lead to the removal of their antagonism. These spirits of the lower regions might be manifesting their wrath against the whole town for its sins, or simply for those of one man, possibly even of the king himself. The dibias alone could discern the root cause of the calamity and indicate the remedy. In the majority of cases resort was first had to the sacrifice of animals; the whole business being forced upon the people by dire necessity they sought relief on the cheapest terms. It was only when all other forms of sacrifice failed that they were finally driven back upon human beings as their last hope. When this extreme form of sacrifice was needed the victim was never a fellow-townsman—he was always a slave purchased especially for the purpose, or a captive of war. He must be a young man for choice, strong and vigorous, well able to bear the sins of those in whose behalf he was to die. He was known as ónyé-ùmà. It is difficult to render into English the word ùmà, but the underlying idea is exactly that of Deuteronomy xxi, **23**: "He that is hanged is accursed of God." The man was to die an ignominious death—he himself becoming an abomination—a cursed thing. Indeed the ceremony itself is termed ikpu-alu (to carry away abomination). He was the sin-bearer, whether for the one or the many.

The victim was conducted to an ebwo tree to which he was bound after his arms and legs had been tied; the king stepped forward and solemnly transferred first his own sins, then the sins of his household, and finally the sins of the community to the head of the sacrifice. The trespass-transfer being thus fulfilled the man was loosed from the tree (his legs and arms remaining bound) and a rope was attached to his ankle and forthwith he was dragged round the town by two slaves appointed to the task. The whole populace treated the wretched creature as an accursed thing; he was reviled, spat upon, kicked, stoned; dust was thrown upon him, and in every form imaginable he was despitefully treated and denounced as an abomination. The slaves continued to drag him through the streets until life was extinct, and then the corpse was taken back to the king's quarters and cast away in the spot reserved for the bodies of human sacrifices. The victims were not buried; they would have been left to rot but for the fact that the corpses were stolen during the succeeding night by the friends of the official executioners who were not members of that community. The bodies were taken away to the native town of these officials and were there eaten. In towns adjacent to the river the corpses were sometimes cast into the water.[1]

Occasionally instead of dragging the man through the streets, after the ceremony at the ebwo tree, he was put upright in a hole and buried alive, his head being left

[1] Under the date February 27th, 1858, the Rev. J. Taylor, the first missionary settled amongst the Ibos at Onitsha, records a case of human sacrifice witnessed by himself and an agent of the factory. The victim was a "poor young woman. Her hands were tied behind her back, and her legs fastened together with a rope, decorated with young palm-leaves. In this position she was drawn, with her face to the earth, from the king's house to the river, a distance of two miles. . . . The young woman was dying, through the suffocation of dust and sand in the streets. The motley groups who attended her premature funeral cried, as they drew along the unfortunate creature, victimised for the sins of their land, 'Alo-o! alo! alo!' i.e. Abomination, or that which defiles. This alarm is given to notify to the passers by to screen themselves from witnessing the scene. The sacrifice was to take away the iniquities of the land. The woman was dragged along in a merciless manner and finally cast into the river. A man was killed too, as a sacrifice for the sins of the king."—*Niger Expedition*, 1857–1859, by Crowther and Taylor, pp. 343–5.

above the ground. Here he was subject to all manner of abuse and ill-treatment, the sufferings of the unhappy creature evoking gross ridicule, but never a thought of pity. The corpse was left in this state, the memorial of an accursed thing to every one that passed by.

Again the form of death might be changed. After the initial ceremonies, the man, bound hand and foot as above, was placed on the ground and covered with grass and wood and burned to death.

But what was considered, and undoubtedly was, the most terrible fate of all, was when, after the transfer of the sins to him, the victim was simply left bound to the tree. The tortures were not so painful at the beginning as any of the above described forms of death, but they were prolonged to a maddening length. The degrading insults of the mob continued longer and sometimes death was long delayed. A young man in the prime of life might live days before being released by death; meantime he had to endure unspeakable and unmitigated agonies from heat, hunger, thirst, the galling attacks of ants and every form of horror conceivable. Knowing West Africa and the capabilities of the native for inflicting torture, the thought of such a death makes one shudder. Is this an effective reply to those who object to foreign missions, who argue that the native's religion is the best for him, that he ought not to be disturbed and denationalised? Such, surely, can have no real conception of the dark side of the native religion with its many horrors; and surely, too, their belief in the Gospel of the Son of God, who is also Son of Man, must be a doubtful quantity.

The whole of the above information has been obtained from personal experience, and from reliable native sources. In the matter of human sacrifices my chief informant was one who had himself actually been chosen as a victim. He had been bound to the sacred tree and all preparations made for observing the last rites. The ceremony of transferring the sins to his head was about to be performed when, through the unceasing exertions of a friend, he was released and another suffered the penalty in his stead, he himself being witness of the tortures and sufferings of his substitute. I knew the old man well; we were acquainted for several years, and none could listen to his simple narrative without a thrill. To him, at any rate, there was never any difficulty in accepting the fact of the substitutionary sacrifice of Christ on his behalf; his actual experiences were too real and vivid to allow of doubt on that point.

CHAPTER XXII

SECRET SOCIETIES

WITH the exception of the Eku-meku society noticed in Chapter XIX, amongst the Ibos we do not find any of those distinctive secret societies, such as the Human Leopard society of Sierra Leone or the Ogboni of the Yorubas. I am not acquainted with any society, other than the Eku-meku, in which absolute secrecy is enjoined upon its members, and where, for the revealing of its plans and practices the penalty is death. At the same time if a man openly and wantonly proclaimed the methods of making "maw," i.e. spirit, he would be liable to suffer a peculiarly painful death.

There is a great deal of alleged intercourse with the spirit-world, and the custom of making maw (ju-ju) is an almost daily affair. In a general way it is extremely common, with a few special forms for particular times and occasions. This making ju-ju has no religious significance; it is held to be a visitation of the spirits of the dead to their late familiar haunts, and especially during festivals when the spirits manifest a lively desire to participate in the general rejoicings.

The custom is confined entirely to men; women are not only prohibited from making ju-ju but are debarred from being in the presence of a maw on pain of severe punishment. Any man at any time may arrange for a visitation. Usually the inspiration comes to a young man, and he forthwith enters into negotiations with other young men of leisure who happen to be suffering from an attack of ennui. The originator of the play enters a house and blows signals on an igwe (*vide* p. 236) and thus attracts followers to his train. The number of spirits who shall manifest themselves is chiefly dependent on the quantity of making-up material available. Those chosen to represent the spirits of the dead are completely concealed in the weirdest costumes, anything but artistic in the majority of cases, and, as the dresses vary so much, a general description must suffice. The figure must be entirely hidden, no part whatever of the body being visible. Trousers of cloth, dyed with stain from yellow clay, encase the legs and feet, and the dress is continued until arms and head are covered. Two small peep-holes in the cloth allow the maw to see his way about, and a tiny slit is cut through which to breathe. Some maws don voluminous kilts composed of ufelli (agwaw), the stems of the leaves of the ngwaw palm. These kilts are called egwuwu, a name which suggests fear; others, such as the ejelle-egwu, have the head and shoulders enveloped in these cane flounces. Certain maws are intended to represent the spirits of departed virgins (abaw-maw) and the dress is always one which distinguishes a girl at the time she is passing through the nkpu ceremony preparatory to marriage. The headgear may be part of the dress itself or it may be a mask. The masks are carved from blocks of wood, and are usually made to slip over the head, but in certain instances they are simply face masks. They are often of great weight, the pressure of which comes directly on the crown of the head. Some are given regular features very much like Egyptian patterns; the face is always painted white, to enhance the idea of the supernatural; it must be something quite different from the ordinary mortal. Others again are the most hideous examples of pantomimic imagination. A man must be physically strong to endure the heat, semi-suffocation and strain demanded of him when so disguised. He is indeed far from being a disembodied spirit; there is nothing ethereal about him.

An igwe is inserted in the mouth which serves to disguise the voice. It is an instrument cut from a small reed, with a mouthpiece, made from spider's web, stuck on with liquid rubber; it is reserved solely for the custom of making ju-ju. The sound produced is very like that made by blowing through a comb enveloped in thin paper.

In passing, one might remark that it is bad manners to perform on the paper-covered comb in the presence of Ibos; such music will be awarded a reception quite different from that expected; it will probably be taken as an insult rather than a joke.

As soon as the making-up process is completed, the remaining preliminaries are got through quickly, and the maw sallies forth accompanied by his satellites. These latter have no particular costume but remain as they were, and merely arm themselves with a switch each with which to clear the way for the spirit. The maw enters the village walking, dancing, rushing hither aud thither and altogether acting as the spirit moves him. At the sound of the igwe, women and children flee helter-skelter in abject fear of a thrashing, for they have reason to expect that they will meet with no mercy if haply they fall into the clutches of the maw. He is a highly privileged being, enters any house he chooses, and wherever he condescends to visit he must be mollified with gifts by the owner of the house. During certain seasons of the year dozens of these maws will parade the town, and are in their way somewhat of a nuisance. Nowadays they dance and pirouette in the presence of a white man, but I remember the time when they quite expected him to collapse in fear. Many maws then believed that, in some mysterious manner, they were supernaturally endowed, and they were astonished that the European did not seem to recognise the fact. Moreover, by virtue of the unassailable status of a spirit, a maw was "onye-nwe-obodo," an equivalent title to our "lord of creation." In the old days we should have had to describe them as cheeky, at times little short of insolent, but perhaps they might retort that we did not play the game; our unmoved attitude was contrary to the rules. But the real thing, as is the case with so many other practices, is rapidly decaying, and in many places it is becoming more or less a Saturday and Sunday pastime, and the serious side has vanished.

It is difficult to gauge the extent of the Ibo man's belief that these maws are re-embodied spirits. They undoubtedly think that they are not men, and that the ceremony of making maw has somehow transformed the man and endowed him with extraordinary supernatural qualities. Amongst the women and children the belief is complete, and so tenacious is the idea with them, that even when it is disproved they cannot abandon it ; it is much too deeply ingrained. Nor is one greatly surprised at their attitude, for some of the maws, in a country where fetishism is universal, are of such an uncanny appearance that anyone might experience a creepy sensation. At the Christmas festivities held at a large girls' school I was invited to impersonate Father Christmas. The early part of the entertainment passed off excellently, until the advent of the venerable father became due. Full of excitement the girls waited for the promised visitor, but when he did appear, dressed in the conventional garb, with the traditional white hair and flowing beard, the whole crowd of girls cried out in fear, arose and fled ! It was some time before they could be induced to return, in spite of the old man's benevolent aspect ; and when they did come back they could scarcely be persuaded to accept presents from his hand ; they quite believed that the spirit of an ancient crony was actually present before them. A similar experience invariably follows when a common Guy Fawkes mask is placed over the face.

Making ju-ju is divided into two sections, differentiated as "day" and "night" maws. The former are those already described. The night maws are much more serious affairs, and far surpass any of the day ones both in importance and in the stringency of the laws which regulate them. For the night maws there is no peculiar dress or personal preparation whatever ; the chief and most widespread society is that known as the Ayakka, the members of which require absolute darkness for their operations and are active for a portion of the year only, viz. from January to March. It is during this period that the bush-fires rage, and the belief is that the fires exert a quickening effect upon the spirits of the dead ; the Ayakka is the roaming abroad of these spirits disturbed in their rest.

Towards midnight, suddenly, out of the dense darkness, a clear ringing "cooee" falls upon the ear. This is repeated at intervals and it is not long before answering cooees come from all sides of the bush. The members spread themselves over a large area of the country around the village, creeping stealthily through the jungle. Presently the blood-curdling moanings of the ōdègillìgillì reverberate and these sounds fill the women and children with terror and they quickly hide themselves. The ōdegillìgillì is a thin strip of wood, twelve inches long by two or three inches in width, notched at the edges and attached to a cord by which it is whirled round in the air, the volume of sound and the variation of the note changing according to the speed and power of the revolutions. The scattered members gradually collect at the spot to which they have been attracted by the cooees of the leader and his calls upon the ōdègillìgillì. They then form up in procession and march to the town, chanting as they go in their peculiar but pleasant falsetto tones. Fresh members are continually attaching themselves to the company, until eventually there is a large crowd, sometimes numbering several hundreds.

Should they meet a man who is not a member of the Ayakka they lay violent hands upon him, he is soundly beaten, carried away and thrown into the bush.

No fire or other light must be visible in any house or compound ; failure to observe this rule leads to the house being surrounded by the men, who hasten to destroy it.

No man of the company may laugh during the procession ; severe penalties are prescribed for any infringement of this regulation. Even should a member cough he is soundly cursed, and he is accused of doing something which is liable to expose the whole business ; spirits must not be so human as to laugh or cough !

During the earlier part of the Ayakka season, each section (or ward) of a town observes its own ceremonies. Should companies from two different villages select the same night for their enterprise, and should they happen to meet, fierce fighting ensues ; neither side will give way to the other until forced to do so. At the end of the season the villages may combine for a big final demonstration.

On entering the town the members of the Ayakka may call at any house they please, and when they do so they clamour for gifts. Whatever is presented, however, must come directly from the hands of the head of the household. They state that they are visitors from a far-distant country and that what is darkness to living folk is daylight to the spirits. The headman never refuses to propitiate them with gifts; were he to do anything to give umbrage to the party, certain of the members would be told off to act as ju-ju men, and these, at a convenient opportunity, would wreak vengeance on the offender. Hence for the sake of his property the headman hurries to present his offerings. The members of the band do not expose themselves in his presence, but a hand comes round the corner of the door and seizes the gift. As the headman pleads with the Ayakka to accept his offering and to return to the place whence they came, the hand snatches the present and instantly disappears.

The round of calls being accomplished, the members retire as they came to the original rallying place, thence they scatter into the bush, making their way homewards quietly, and as far as possible secretly. Every man must be back in his own quarters by the break of day. Often they arrive home very much exhausted after the excitement, the running about and the long bouts of chanting.

Boys pass through the initiatory rites of the Ayakka society on attaining what is considered an understanding age, i.e. about ten years. The ceremony is known as "Iba na maw" or the "entering into the domain of spirit." The preliminary stages are carried through by, and at the instigation of, the elder men of the family. Should the father be alive, he begins by offering palm wine to the Umunna, i.e. the male relatives (of the lad) who are already full members of the society, and on the night fixed for his son to enter ju-ju he brings presents of soup and yams. It is usually so arranged that several lads may be initiated at the same time; this saves trouble and expense. The novices sit in the appointed place and are left to themselves; here they remain until all preparations are completed for the ceremony. They are then

BRIDES-ELECT
Girls passing through "Nkpu" ceremonies.

led into the courtyard of the house where the ju-ju is waiting for them to appear. They are ordered to lie prone on their stomachs with their eyes to the ground; the maw or ju-ju proceeds to step over each candidate in turn, after which they are bidden to roll over and over (instead of walking) and finally retire once more into their room. Here a piece of bone—preferably the tooth of a goat—is handed to each lad and he is bidden to chew it, the instructors stating that these are the teeth of the ju-ju. This is known as the ceremony of Awlupulu Maw (lit. "eating dirt off the teeth of the spirit!"

By this time the youths have been worked up into a more or less frightened condition, and are huddled together in a corner. As the night advances—the performance having begun about nine o'clock—the maw enters the room and makes a great pretence of removing certain parts of the bodies of the lads, because these are demanded by the ju-ju, as his special prerogative, for food. Meantime the members of the society who are present are urging the candidates to produce their gifts, promising to intercede with the spirits if it be made worth their while. It is the only way for a lad to secure merciful treatment, and moreover the threat is held out that unless the present is forthcoming the friends will not work for the boy's release from the power of the maw, which means that, having been drawn down into the spirit-world, the niggardly candidate will have to stay there. The candidates are told that they will be made to pass through the hole of an abwissi (a tiny insect) and thence be obliged to cross a very wide river on a thread. For this perilous journey one needs friendly assistance, and this may be assured by means of an acceptable present to the masters of the ceremonies. Neglect the gift and you must walk the miniature tight-rope unaided.

Food is now brought forth and the lads are asked to partake thereof, but they are much too frightened to eat. The members, however, make short work of it and soon clear the dishes. Absolute silence succeeds the meal and in due course everybody drops off to sleep. On waking from their slumbers the candidates are informed that their presents were very acceptable and that, in consequence, their friends had begged so fervently for them that they had prevailed upon the maw to conduct them to and from the spirit-world whilst they were asleep and unconscious of fear. They had had a merciful escape and were very fortunate to have made the adventurous journey with so little inconvenience.

By this time day begins to break, and the fathers of the youths, and other old men, come to release the initiated novices, bearing in their hands certain leaves. Water is brought and with the leaves the lads sponge their bodies and they are thus cleansed of the earth stains resulting from their journey to the nether regions. The maw conducts each lad home separately and receives a gratuity from the thankful mother in token of her joy at the safe return of her boy.

But although from henceforth the youth will be included in the ranks of the Ayakka society, yet he has actually learned nothing about the secrets of ju-juism: there still remains the rite of "ikpu-ani." The candidate himself is responsible for all the business connected with this part of his education. A beginning is made by presenting gifts to each man of the Umunna. When, at length, their demands have been satisfied, they arrange for the rite to be performed. On the day fixed the youth is called into the okwule—a dark inner room, the secret place of the ju-ju—where are kept all the awawlaw, i.e. all the paraphernalia required for the making up of a complete ju-ju. The word relates to the mask and dress of the maw and in meaning is almost equivalent to the action of a snake in casting its skin. In this room the novice is told to lie down and wait. Before long the ju-ju appears and immediately administers a few lively strokes with a stick upon the back of the stranger. His wrath being appeased, one of two things happens; either the maw loosens his dress and casts it from him, or one of the young men present puts into his own mouth an igwe and demonstrates how the voice of the ju-ju is produced; either one or both these things may be done. In any case the secret is out; the novice at once sees clearly that the apparition was no sort of resurrected spirit, but simply one of his neighbours, and probably a relative, who had been masquerading as a spirit. The youth is sworn to secrecy and is held thereto by the threat that the revealing of any of the ceremonies will be punished by torture and death. It is questionable whether this threat was ever carried out, chiefly because a really wholesome fear was created and partly because, having been deceived themselves, the novices wished to enjoy the sport of deceiving others in their turn.

Should a woman or a man who is not a member of the society, enter unwittingly into the apartment containing the awawlaw, severe punishment can be escaped only by payment of heavy damages. The same rule applies should an outsider place an igwe in his mouth, even when acting in ignorance of the laws of the Ayakka society.

CHAPTER XXIII

IN THE SHADOW OF DEATH

Akin in several respects, yet quite different from and additional to the religious rites and ceremonies of the Ibo people, is the veneration accorded to certain local deities accredited with supernatural powers of divination. These deities inspire great awe and they are consulted on various pretexts, and in case of serious dispute they are the final courts of appeal, and no one dare question their verdicts.

Of all the frauds practised in Africa there can be none greater than those connected with these municipal deities; a steady source of income to their guardians. They are deceptions of a most impudent and specious nature, and yet they are tolerated with guileless simplicity by those who submit to their verdicts, but who cannot fathom their mysteries. They play an important part in the settlement of accusations of witchcraft and similar offences, and litigants resort to them in lieu of trial by ordeal. In the majority of cases an appeal to the deity was as fatal as the poison cup; moreover, the suspense was more prolonged and the expense entailed drained the resources of both the disputing parties.

The ceremonies employed are strictly religious rites, nor do they come under the category of the proceedings of secret societies; they partake of the nature of both. The approaches to the sacred grove are jealously guarded, and the observances and ritual are governed by laws enjoining absolute secrecy on the part of those holding proprietary rights in the oracle. It is this rigid maintenance of the oath of secrecy which has for generations veiled the proceedings in mystery, and has led to an unquestioned belief in the powers of the deity on the part of the community at large. No one but a townsman dare approach the sacred precincts on his own initiative; Instant reprisals, in the form of death by violence, would follow such indiscretion. Applicants for the judiciary pronouncements of the oracle are primed with stories concerning the ferocious attributes of the god and reduced to a state of abject fear, so much so that they are led to believe every fable uttered by the intermediaries. The credulity manifested beggars description; it is a fact to be realised only by those who have lived in its atmosphere. I count myself fortunate in having lived in close proximity to one of these deities, and having had the opportunity of investigating on the spot some of the facts connected with it, and of meeting actual participators in these nefarious practices.

One of the chief oracles, indeed probably the one which exercised the most wide-reaching influence of all the divining deities in the the Ibo country, is located at Awka, some twenty-five miles east of Onitsha on the right bank of the Niger. The town is large and straggling, typical of the district. From time immemorial it has been famous, partly because of its clever blacksmiths (who travel throughout the length and breadth of the land plying their trade), and perhaps even more so on account of the prestige accruing to it as the home of a notable deity, reputed to be endowed with marvellous gifts of divination. Strangers were conducted thither from all parts of the country in order that they might hold consultations with the deity. The Awka blacksmiths made it as much their business to advertise their oracle as to carry on their normal trade. Both honour and profit are to be gained in this way, and the Awka man is always ready to conduct the case of an applicant.

Locally the deity is known as the Abwala. The name is somewhat difficult to explain. It may merely mean a "woman"; such a one as is mentioned in Acts xvi. 16 as endowed with a "spirit of divination." A more convenient term perhaps is oracle. How this Abwala came into existence no one can tell; her origin is unknown to any living person and tradition does not offer much assistance. She is, however, declared to be the daughter of the great oracle, commonly known as the "Long Ju-Ju" of Aro-Chuku, the destruction of which was one of the objectives of the military expedition of 1902. One peculiarity is that though the Abwala is feminine and is the daughter of "Igwe-ka-Ani," yet in the ceremonies she is always addressed as "Father," and the masculine pronoun is used.

According to local tradition there are three great deities. (1) Igwe-ka-Ani; (2) Abwala; and (3) Eblu-okpa-bia. The first name indicates a "King who is higher (greater) than the land," and Abwala is his daughter. Eblu-okpa-bia may be interpreted as the "One who receives you graciously and fills your basket;" in other words, "a kind and generous benefactor."

Of these three Abwala takes first rank throughout the Ibo country. She is proclaimed as The God, the creator of all things, a discerner of the secrets of men, the judge of poisoners, the revealer of witchcraft, the omnipotent one, the forgiver of sins, and the dispenser of blessings of every kind, including the gift of children.

The shrine of the Abwala is situated at Ezi-Awka, and to the people of this village is entrusted the guardianship of the deity. Their huts are built right up to the edge of the sacred precincts on the two sides that give access to the shrine, and strict watch is maintained against trespassers. The path leading to the oracle is narrow and tortuous; suddenly it opens out into a spacious square, in the centre of which are the remains of a rude hut sheltering a huge but somewhat dilapidated tom-tom. There are ruins of small ju-ju houses in other parts of the square and, at times, there are folk in residence who have been devoted to the deity.

The ancient tom-tom is some nine feet in length and about seven in circumference. One end is shouldered off and shaped to represent the head and neck of a man, the other end is similarly worked, but with a woman's head. On one side the drum is ornamented with six faces, three at each end, carved in high relief. On the far side of the square an opening in the dense bush gives access to a narrow defile. The track through this glade is rough, and overhanging trees cast deep shadows, shrouding the path in semi-darkness. The path descends for some seventy yards and then further progress is barred by a wall erected to protect the shrine from strangers. Entrance is gained through a narrow aperture, but only the chief actors in the drama may pass through this opening. Beyond the wall the light is still more subdued; the bush is denser; it is altogether more gloomy and uncanny until, at the end of another twenty-five yards, the path broadens out into a leafy bower. In the centre stood the two sacred trees, but one only remains at the present time, the second having fallen and decayed away. Turning sharply to the right, and passing on a few paces, we discern a narrow opening between high banks; this is the entrance to an artificial winding alley ending after a few yards in a cul-de-sac, where, at the foot of the bank, a log is stretched across the track. We are now in the sanctuary—the actual abode of the deity.

The above is a brief description of the shrine and its approaches, as noted by the stranger. There is, however, a secret entrance by means of which communications can be maintained between those impersonating the Abwala and her attendants, and those who are conducting affairs in the square above or in the lane leading to the barrier.

We now turn our attention to the mode of operations for prosecuting a trial. As previously observed no stranger is permitted to enter the sacred precincts, except under the leadership of a duly authorised guide, and when effectively prevented from making observations through being closely blindfolded. We must also bear in mind that every Awka man, whilst practising his ordinary profession in any part of the country is prepared to conduct parties to consult the Abwala. This leader is bound to collect, at the actual place of dispute, all possible information concerning the case, prior to starting for Awka. He must leave no stone unturned in eliciting facts about the parties themselves, the grounds of the accusations, the circumstances and the resources of those involved and so forth. He thus returns to Awka well posted with details whereby the Abwala will have little difficulty in pronouncing a verdict which will be quite startling to the litigants, inasmuch as it shows an intimate and accurate knowledge of the facts.

Fees, directly and in the shape of presents, together with the killing of goats and fowls in honour of the leader, must be forthcoming from the very beginning of the transaction. When matters are ripe the interested parties make the journey to Awka, some coming very long distances. On arrival they are billeted in the houses of the conductor and his personal friends, and from this time the victims are gradually but surely drained of their money. The wife of the conductor has the right to shave the hair of strangers and in payment receives a piece of cloth from each. Each must purchase a fowl and many yams; these are offered as the first sacrifice, and are afterwards consumed as a sort of family feast. A present and about ten pounds are demanded as first fees on behalf of the Abwala, but really are quietly pocketed by the leader. Whilst waiting the last details of the case are gleaned, and the prospects fluctuate *pro rata*, according to the presents distributed. Considerable delay, sometimes extending months, may ensue in this manner before the favourable day arrives for presenting themselves before the Abwala. This, with sublime coincidence invariably happens when funds show signs of giving out. The formal arrangements are now made and an appointment fixed. The parties are led along the winding tracks into the large square where the preliminary formalities are observed, and the first sacrifices offered. Having complied with the regulations, preparations are made for the settlement of the case. The plaintiffs and defendants are securely blindfolded and led to the opening in the glade leading down to the shrine; here they are turned round and forced to walk backwards until the barrier is reached, the gateway of which has been covered with a hanging cloth. The parties wait at this spot; no stranger may enter the "kamanu," the secret dwelling-place of the Abwala, under any pretext.

Making Palm-leaf Mats for Thatching Purposes

The Wonderful Tom-Tom of Umu-nze

Presently the leader commences to cry out, "Oh, Abwala-Awka, hear us! Oh, Igwe-Ani, hear us! Prove by thy power which of these people is guilty (who is a poisoner or an extortioner or guilty of the sin of witchcraft). Thou that revealest all secrets, hear us! Thou that killest and rewardest with life, hear us! Oh, Igwe-Ani, hear us!"

After a brief interval the voice of the "Son of Abwala" is heard begging that the god will take heed to the appeal of the strangers. "Oh, my father, awake! Awake and listen to the petitions of those who come from afar to prove thee. Arise and show that thou art the discerner of all hearts."

Suddenly, and apparently from the very bowels of the earth, a thunderous voice peals forth, causing utter consternation and terror to the strangers present. It is the voice of Abwala replying to the request: "E-e-e-e-dum-e-nwam e-nwam." "Oh yes, my son. I have the power of life and death. He who often proves me sees with eyes. I am the beginning and the end."

As this oration concludes there is a great commotion and Osu-Abwala, the servant of the oracle bursts forth from the bush. His person is liberally adorned with eagle feathers and in his hands are short sticks, with which he lays about him vigorously, beating the petitioners until they make it worth his while to desist! He declares that Abwala is angry at being awakened and must be appeased with money and honourable gifts. The demand is backed up by the oracle himself, who forthwith commands the strangers "to advance no further lest they be swallowed up in the great water" (which does not exist).

The deity having been conciliated with gifts, the parties are ordered to state their case. They strive earnestly, each endeavouring to vindicate himself by declaring his innocence of all crime from the day of his birth. May the god do so to him and more also if he has been the cause of any man's death, whether by the sword or by poison; may he suffer if he be guilty of the sin of witchcraft or of extortion. He has been accused falsely and now appeals to Abwala for righteous judgment.

It is at this stage that the impersonator of the deity needs to have his wits about him. He must be on the alert to detect the signals which will enable him to declare, without mistake, which are guilty and which are innocent; any error in this respect would be fatal. In reality the verdict has long been a settled question, but care must be exercised lest the reputation of the god be jeopardised. The first man selected for judgment is practically certain to be proclaimed innocent. He is bidden to rise from the ground where he has been crouching behind the barrier wall, and to listen as Abwala pronounces a verdict which declares that he is innocent of crime. His honour is vindicated and blessings are heaped upon his head. Before, however, these can operate in his favour he must give thankofferings to the righteous god in the shape of three or four cows or a couple of slaves. An eagle's feather is presented to him as a badge of his innocence, together with "medicine" which he is enjoined to store carefully in his own house on arrival there. It is a preparation absolutely to be relied on as a safeguard against every form of evil, natural and spiritual. The happy man is led back to the open square above, and immediately the bandage is removed from his eyes he rushes around dancing and shouting, "Abwala neylum ugo-ugo-ugu (Abwala has given me the eagle feather)." Such a one has abundant cause for rejoicing. On his return to his own town he is fêted and honoured as one who has triumphantly emerged from the greatest of all ordeals. He gladly pays all amounts demanded; these are handed to the man who has managed his case so successfully, and who gives a solemn assurance to use them for the benefit of the deity!

There may be others likewise declared innocent, and the programme is repeated; but eventually a guilty man must take his turn. The preliminaries are similar to those followed in the case of the innocent. The man on hearing his name announced is inspired by hope, he having heard the happy verdict to his predecessors. He humbly offers his salutations to the diety, but the answer immediately and unmistakably disillusions him. With vehemence and angry tones the Abwala taunts him as an evildoer, or it may be accuses him directly of being a poisoner or extortioner, or of being guilty of witchcraft. Every protestation of innocence is contemptuously ignored and the poor wretch has no alternative but to grovel on the ground, pleading for mercy and a way of escape. The god retorts that there is no escape from the trap in which he is now caught except by the payment of three cows as a fine, and he urges the condemned man to hurry and bring these. The man eagerly consents and rises to obey the injunction, but as he stands up a noose is cleverly thrown round his neck and he is violently jerked and hauled over the wall thus falling into the fatal clutches of the god. If, after this ordeal, he is not already dead, he may be resuscitated in order to be sold as a slave, or if the Abwala signifies that blood only will satisfy him the victim is hacked to death with cutlasses.

The executioner is the only regularly appointed official attached to the deity. His sole occupation is the slaying of those appointed to die. He may not travel nor can he plant a farm; he must let nothing distract him from his business, and he must be ready at any time for his ghastly work. All corpses are hurled into the valley sloping away from the lower edge of the shrine; they are afterwards collected and disposed of in accordance with the usual custom prevailing in a cannibal country.

There are cases in which the Abwala is consulted for the purpose of obtaining some personal benefit, entirely distinct from criminal trials. The blessing of the god may be sought in order that sons may be born to the suppliant —of course on receipt of adequate compensation. A not uncommon practice is for a man to beseech the Abwala to deliver him from the hands of his enemies by bringing death and destruction upon them. One of the attributes of the deity is the faculty of exercising his deadly powers over persons at any distance, hence the appeal to him. This can be done privately, the unsuspecting enemy being in total ignorance of the designs upon his life. The unfortunate one is mentioned by name and, at the conclusion of sacrifices and payments, the Abwala orders a piece of iron to be driven into the tree as if the man in question were actually executed on the spot. Some of these irons are roughly shaped staples, some have chisel edges, others are spear heads. Green leaves are sometimes rolled up containing "medicine," and the spike driven through the bundle. On one occasion I happened to stray into the grove within a few hours (at the most) of a ceremonial function. There was a bundle of fresh leaves held in position by the usual piece of iron which, on being extracted and the bundle unrolled, was found to contain the head of a small snake spitted through the throat with a sharp stick.

No one man is consecrated to the priesthood of the deity. It is entirely a matter of mutual arrangement, and any Awka man can impersonate the god and fulfil all the functions connected with the observance of the ceremonies. The conductor of the suppliants undertakes the management of the business from beginning to end, and he appoints his acquaintances to act as the Abwala, Osu-Abwala, the servant of the god, and other officials. These together constitute themselves into a limited company for dispensing divinations—a concern which pays a handsome dividend to its shareholders; the chairman, i.e. the conductor of the party, naturally absorbing the lion's share of the proceeds.

Apart from the fact that all strangers are blindfolded before entering the sacred precincts, the profoundest source of deception is the peculiar voice of the Abwala and his votaries. This is disguised to represent the noise of rolling thunder rising from the nether regions; moreover, the note is taken up on all sides so that the location of the deity cannot be fixed. The voices come first from in front, then from behind, and finally all round until the strangers are hopelessly bewildered. There are three sets of voices—that of the Abwala himself, that of his special attendant, Osu-Abwala, and those of the chorus raised by the Umu-Chuku, i.e. the children of god.

The change from the natural voice is wrought by means of small clay pots specially manufactured for the purpose, called "mbaw." They are four inches in diameter, with wide necks, and a little hole is punched through the bottom of each. One of these pots is fixed over the mouth of each man assisting in the ceremony. The effect of shouting into the pot may be better grasped by the reader if he will try the experiment of speaking loudly with a large tumbler or jam jar over his mouth.

Of how many lives have been "eaten" (lit.) by the Abwala-Awka, it would be folly to offer an estimate. One of the facts proved by experience is that no reliable figures are ever given by natives living in primitive conditions; concrete numbers are unlucky, and "many, many" is all that they will state; but one of the free men of Awka informed me that the lives so sacrificed were incalculable; and there is reliable authority for believing that more than thirty persons have perished in a single day. The policy of frequent executions was zealously upheld lest the idea should grow that the power of the Abwala was dwindling. It was a sure method of instilling abject fear into strangers, and, at the same time maintaining the dignity of the oracle. If the pieces of iron embedded in the sacred trees may be taken as any indication, then there can be no question but that many hundreds of people lost their lives as a result of appeal to the Abwala. When I first saw the trees they were, from ground level to eight feet above, thickly studded with spikes. The trunks are black with the marks of the irons driven into them. One of the trees has since fallen, as stated above, and the trunk has rotted away.

The Abwala was a source of huge profit to the town, and the people of Awka suffered heavy pecuniary loss when, in 1905, a military expedition gave the oracle its death-blow. The prestige of the deity, however, was not entirely broken and recourse continues to be had to his oracular powers, but many of the ancient practices are no longer retained. The rendezvous of the god has been changed, and further, it is clearly recognised that he cannot any longer demand the life of any who may be brought before him for judgment, nor condemn them to slavery. The old-time ceremonies are followed as closely as possible, but fines have been substituted for the former sentences of capital punishment and slavery. Fear of the British

Government has also been fairly generally inculcated in the native mind, and the number of those prepared to risk the consequences of perpetuating the profitable deception has been greatly reduced. With the further spread of British influence, and the inevitable opening up of the country, and in no small measure owing to the influence of Christian missions in Awka and the neighbourhood, there is not the slightest doubt that the fate of the Abwala has been sealed. His reputation and his very existence are doomed, and ere long—if affairs proceed along the present progressive lines—the deity and all that appertains to him will cease to be. On the other hand, should the Government relax its vigilance or, worse still, withdraw from the country, the prestige of the Abwala would be immediately and completely restored. Matters are in a state of transition; a very large majority of the people are in favour of the deity, and would revive their proprietary rights in him, gladly, had they reason to think they could do so with impunity.

CHAPTER XXIV

CHIEFS AND THEIR ORDERS

THE desire for rank and honour is not confined to the Ibo people, nor is the essential element in the transaction peculiar to them; money is always the controlling factor in the business.

Kings, as such, can hardly be said to exist in these days, though amongst the people on the western side of the Niger there still linger, here and there, marks of the autocratic state of former days. The fall of Benin led to a general disruption in all this part of the country, and with it went the position and power of the tributary kings. The influence of Benin was paramount, and the chiefs of the surrounding districts settled all important business under its inspiration. The title of "king" is still in use and to some extent the holder receives the homage and service of his subjects, but in actual fact it is now little more than a courtesy title. There has been a marked decline of the kingly prestige even in the last few years. In 1900, when I visited Isele-Ukwu and Agbor, a call on the king involved considerable time and display of ceremonial etiquette, but all this has dwindled down to a mere shadow of its former greatness.

On the left bank of the river, the only town which boasts a king is undoubtedly due to the former influence of Benin. This royal family claims to be of Bini descent, and all the circumstances are unique on this side of the Niger.

The most popular and widespread form of native government has been through the administration of chiefs, the position of each one being determined by his rank plus his seniority in the order. It is the ambition of every free-born youth to rise to chieftainship, and in this democratic country the highest honours are open to every freeman equally. At the same time but few were able to enter the most exalted orders in the old days. In modern times the dignity of the chieftainship has been degraded and the tendency is to bring the whole system into disrepute, owing to the wholesale and indiscriminate sale of titles to any youth who can produce the stipulated fees. This is another example of the inevitable results of the opening of the country.

It would be a tedious task to describe all the grades, the installation fees and modes of initiation whereby a man attains to the position of a leading chief in the country. As a matter of fact each town has its own recognised titles and regulations governing them. In some there are as many as ten progressive degrees ; in others there are no more than three. Likewise the fees in one town may be greatly in excess of those in another ; it all depends on ancient custom, local circumstances, and the ability of candidates to pay—the last being the most essential qualification.

In the central districts of the Ibo country probably the most honourable title is that of Obu Madu, i.e. the one who has killed (his) man. It was no unusual thing for a captured stranger to be brought home alive for the express purpose of "making title." The victim was securely bound to a tree and a young lad, armed with a matchet, hacked off the man's head. The time taken to accomplish the deed depended, of course, on the lad's size and strength, but throughout the task he was urged on by the cheers of the assembled company. By fulfilling this gruesome piece of work, usually specially arranged by a father for his son, the lad earned the coveted title "man-slayer."

The general procedure is for a man to begin with the lowest degree, and ascend as funds permit. He may hand over the fees in a lump sum, or he can pay on the instalment system, but in the latter case the whole amount must be completed before he can assume the title or partake of its privileges.

Some titles descend to an eldest son by inheritance and thence he can proceed to the higher orders, for the most advanced are not hereditary; on the other hand a title may be conferred by proxy. A father, providing he himself be a titular chief, can pay the fees and arrange all ceremonial details on behalf of an absent son. The son, thereupon, is empowered to carry the insignia of his order and to receive the courtesy salutation attached to it.

Similarly a wealthy son may procure a title for his father; but in this case, as well as in the former, the father must remain at least one degree in advance of his son; the child must never take precedence of the parent; an attempt to do so would be dishonourable, and moreover his application to the Council of Chiefs would be instantly vetoed.

A slave, whether acquired or born in that state, is ineligible as a candidate for a title, but he may be called upon to contribute towards the sum required to enable his master to enter a higher degree.

There are practically no essential qualifications other than birth and money. A man desirous of the honour and dignity of a chief casts about in his mind to see whether he can raise the necessary fees. It is extremely improbable that any enquiries will be made as to their origin, nor is his candidature likely to be affected by questions as to character. He may have stolen every penny of the money he tenders. Some councils prohibit the applicant stealing from fellow tribesmen, i.e. men of the same town, but allow full liberty to rob outside natives or foreigners for the purpose of taking title. Even murder may be no bar; indeed in certain circumstances it is more likely to enhance the reputation of the candidate. It is not regarded as quite correct etiquette to engage in direct stealing; it is preferable to practise deception and fraud upon the stranger in order to raise the funds. In other words theft and other serious offences are not accounted crime when committed outside the limits of one's own town.

As a typical example of the regulations and principles for the granting of titular regulations and principles, the following sets forth those in force in the town of Awka, one of the most advanced and, withal, one of the most expensive in which to assume the rank of a chief.

GENERAL RULES GOVERNING THE CONFERRING OF TITULAR HONOURS

1. The orders are open to any free-born man, even an alien, provided he be a resident in the town at the time of his election. Should he migrate later he can appoint an official receiver to collect his share of the entrance fees paid by later candidates.

2. All fees received are divided amongst the members of the particular order concerned. Sometimes the senior members receive a small sum extra.

3. A wife can pay for a title on behalf of her husband, but she herself, in common with all other women, is ineligible for election. A wife, however, is granted special rights and privileges. She takes a new name corresponding to the one assumed by her husband on taking up a title, and she is allowed to wear certain distinctive insignia equivalent to those worn by him.

4. All Awzaw titles die with the holder. Other titles may be inherited.

At Awka the order of precedence in the degrees or titles is as follows :—

1. AMANWULU.
2. CHI.
3. AJA-AMA.
IFE-II-AWKU
AMAWANLI — These three are usually taken together.
4. AJALIJA.
5. EKWU.
6. AWZAW subdivided into AWZAW-UNAW and NUKWU AWZÀW.
7. FU or AJA-CHI. Sometimes spoken of as PU, F and P being interchangeable in this locality.

The following notes treat of these in closer detail.

1. AMANWULU.

To obtain this title fees to the amount of about £10 must be paid in cash and kind, goats forming part of the latter.

The insignia of the order consists of one corded string specially made for the purpose, fastened around the waist, and others round the ankles, the former being discarded on the fulfilment of all the ceremonies. The staff is merely a whittled stick of osaga or okeakpa wood.

The benefits accruing to a member of this order are a share in the entrance fees of future candidates; the right to wear a loincloth or other forms of clothing. Until this title has been taken it was formerly not permissible for a male to wear any garment; he must, perforce, be satisfied with a piece of cord and a tiny fragment of cloth. This old rule is now superseded, save in unopened districts; men wear what they like irrespective of any regulations whatsoever.

Usually this title is taken up in quite early youth.

2. Chi.

To proceed to this degree means an outlay of at least £20. It is a distinct advance upon Amanwulu. The recipient is authorised to carry an iron staff, about five feet in length, and ornamented with a three-inch brass binding at the top. He also carries one of the smaller ivory horns whereby he may proclaim his presence and rank to all and sundry. He is entitled to choose a new name for himself, and to receive his share of all fees.

3. (i) Aja-Ama.
   (ii) Ife-Ii-Awku.
   (iii) Amawanlu.

These three minor orders are not considered of any real importance beyond the fact that they are stepping-stones to the higher degrees. They are taken simultaneously, the three involving an expenditure of about £10 to £12. There is no special insignia and the only benefit is the usual share of the profits.

4. Ajalija.

At this stage the titles become more select, owing to the greatly increased cost. The entrance fees for this order work out between £50 and £90. The amount depends to some extent on the past actions of the candidate. Should he have roused in some way the ill-will of one or more of the existing members he must seek reconciliation, and this will not be valid unless a payment of £10 is offered to each member of the Ajalija who considers that he has cause for complaint.

The members are divided into ten sections, each section receiving one-tenth of the entrance fees for redistribution amongst them individually. The candidate will also supply sufficient cows to allow one for each party, and on account of this a member of the order is occasionally saluted as "Obu-Efi" (i.e. he who has killed a cow, for making title), though he is not formally entitled to this salutation. Sometimes more cows are provided than are wanted for the purposes of sacrifice and feasting; in such case they are turned loose and henceforth are free to roam and are no man's property. They often become semi-wild and frequently become a great nuisance, especially when they stray amongst the young corn. On several occasions requests have been made to us to shoot them as they had become too wild for the natives to control.

The insignia of the order are an iron staff nine feet long, forked at the top end, spear-pointed at the bottom, with brass bindings at top, bottom and centre, and copper anklets from three to four inches wide. The holder is privileged to carry a full-sized ivory horn and a goat-skin bag; he has the right to be buried in a coffin within the precincts of his house and to have a cow sacrificed at his funeral. He is entitled to use a chief's carved stool, and to carry a goat-skin for spreading on the floor to sit upon.

In this order a son is granted a share of the profits on account of a deceased father, providing, of course, that the father had himself been a member of the order, hence it follows that many men bearing the Ajalija title are empowered to take two slaves when profits are being distributed, viz. his own and his late father's. On taking up this title a man may add three new names to those he already possesses.

In the great majority of cases men are content when they have reached this grade, and but few make any serious attempt to advance further. They have reached quite an honourable position in the community and are influential citizens.

5. Ekwu.

The fee for this title figures out at about £15. This sum includes the expense of providing goats and a liberal supply of palm-wine. It has no special benefits other than the usual share in the profits. It is really the preliminary order leading to the most important of all, and is never taken except by men proceeding to the Awzaw orders.

6. Awzaw.

This is subdivided into Awzaw-Unaw and Nukwu Awzaw, the idea being that the candidate is recognised as an Awzaw chief by those of his own family first (hence the addition of the word "Unaw" house), and then passes on to the complete title, i.e. Nukwu (great).

This is the most expensive of all titles and it is extremely difficult to state precisely the sum required. The lowest estimate is £120, of which some two-thirds must be in cash, and the remainder in cows, goats, gin, palm wine, etc. The first £25 must be paid to the members of the candidate's own umunna, i.e. to those who can claim any sort of kinship with him. The next payment—perhaps £40 in cash and £20 in kind—is handed to the Awzaw chiefs of the particular quarter in which the would-be-chief resides. Other payments to the remaining chiefs of the whole town follow. In addition there are many expenses in connection with drummers, dancers and all the paraphernalia associated with the conferring of this title. Whenever possible a horse must be slain as part of the ceremony. The condition of the poor brute matters not, so long as it is not actually dead. The recipient of the title must let out its lifeblood. Sometimes the animals are in such a decrepit condition that they have to be carried to the place of sacrifice. The killing of the horse confers the courtesy title of Otibwu-Anyinya on the chief, and henceforth he is saluted by that name, "the one who has killed a horse." Horses, of course, are difficult to procure and more difficult to keep alive owing to the devastating effects of the tsetse fly, and this accounts for the special honour attached to the killing of a horse.

The first part of the concluding ceremonies is performed at night, and then ensues a rather protracted series of purifications. The newly made Awzaw must not venture forth in public for two months. He may not sleep in his own compound; indeed, his feet must not come under the roof of a house. Usually he is accommodated in a friend's compound, where a small booth is specially erected for his benefit. Should it rain heavily he may sit under the eave of his friend's house with the stipulation that he keeps his feet outside. During these months he is smeared with chalk from head to foot. He must see none but his own immediate relatives and keep to his first wife, i.e. "anassi" only.

After all these preliminaries are fulfilled he makes ready to parade the town. It is a time of great rejoicing. A new bell called the "ogenne" is carried before him and solemnly beaten to announce the approach of the new chief. This bell is made of beaten iron and is fully three feet in length; it is oval in shape with flattened edges and the note is a deep-sounding one. On reaching the market place, or other recognised open space, the Awzaw publicly embraces his wife and eldest son.

The insignia of the order are, first an iron spear with a crownlike head of twisted iron. In the centre there is a series of six or eight pieces of iron similarly twisted, bellying out on the shank of the spear; at intervals the shaft is bound with brass. Around the ankles of an Awzaw chief are bound cords red with ufie (camwood) stain. A huge ivory horn forms part of the regalia, also a special stool of a pattern jealously restricted to the use of members of the Awzaw order.

The peculiar benefits that accrue to members of the order are: absolute exemption from all forms of manual labour; immunity from bodily assault from any native whether from his own town or another. He has the right to inflict punishment on any man who tampers with his wives. He sits upon the council which exercises jurisdiction in civil and criminal cases in the town, and which regulates customs, promulgates laws, etc.

He is publicly saluted with the title of Obwu-Efi (cow-killer) or Otibwu-Anyinya (horse-killer) according to whether his great sacrifice has been a cow or a horse. And last, but far from least, he receives his share of entrance and other fees paid into the treasury of the order.

There are certain general rules controlling the affairs of the order of which the more important only need be mentioned.

1. The Awzaw title can be assumed by no man prior to the decease of his father. (This rule has been quite discarded at Onitsha—another sign of the disintegrating forces of the times.)

2. On assuming the title the holder takes four additional names.

3. An Awzaw chief committing a theft is liable to be expelled from being an active member of the council.

4. It is not permissible for an Awzaw chief to sit upon the bare ground ; he must either use a stool or an untanned skin.

5. He is forbidden to cross water. (This rule has also been abolished under the new conditions of life in Iboland.)

6. Should necessity arise for the arrest of an Awzaw chief it is contrary to all etiquette that he should be handcuffed or tied in any manner.

7. A wife can pay the costs necessary to enable her husband to enter the Awzaw order. She herself receives no actual title but is recognised as the wife of such a chief, and wears cards round her ankles, and puts on other marks to indicate corresponding rank to that of her husband.

8. The title is not hereditary.

There is one other point in connection with the Awzaw order which, incidentally, sheds an interesting light upon the priesthood. It becomes apparent in the order when deciding the question of precedence amongst the members. This is controlled chiefly by the chief who is technically known as the "okpala." The okpala is the recognised head of the family who, in virtue of his position, is also the priest of the clan. There are three grades actually.

1. The okpala of the family or household simply.
2. The okpala of the clan. This is confined to the descendants of one family.
3. The okpala of the town generally. This is held by the head of each clan in turn.

Now an okpala by birth, who is also a member of the Awzaw order, always takes precedence of an Awzaw who has not that distinction. A true okpala can only be one by birth, but an Awzaw chief who does not possess that qualification may act either as deputy for a proper (minor) okpala or he may act in his own right in certain special circumstances, as the confession of adultery and other offences.

7. Fu or Pu.

This is the last of the orders in vogue in the town of Awka. It is taken up on very rare occasions. The costs amount to about £30. No one but an Awzaw can enter the order, and from a material point of view there is no gain but a participation in the entrance fees. In this instance the share is a small one, inasmuch as the relatives of deceased holders of the title receive the share that the Ndi Fu would receive were they still alive, the number being, consequently, greatly in excess of those actually holding the title.

The distinctive salutation is "obuzulu," conveying the idea that all the killings have been completed.

Of all these titles the only one that really counts is the Awzaw. In past days this order was undoubtedly a great power in the land. The members exercised a widespread influence and they administered all the affairs of the town. They were treated with the utmost respect on the one hand and they were feared on the other. They had the power of life and death, and were the fully accredited rulers of the town.

Unfortunately the order has degenerated of recent years into little more than a money-making concern. In many

Playing Okwe

A Native Orchestra

cases the holders of the title are mere youths who inspire no feelings of respect and who detract from its dignity rather than add to it. Young men acting as clerks, interpreters, carpenters and so forth, have seized the opportunity of making money which presented itself simultaneously with the opening up of the country by the Government, and earning (or otherwise collecting) money quickly, have immediately offered themselves as candidates for the Awzaw order. The old chiefs, always willing to accept fees, have done so in the cases of these young men ; they have reaped a monetary benefit ; their original investment has turned out more profitable than ever they anticipated, but this greedy procedure led to the degradation of the whole system ; with such a collection of irresponsible young men as members of the order, all right to exercise any real control over the affairs of the community has been forfeited. The old men, for the sake of temporary gain, have sacrificed the dignity and the privileges of the Awzaw order and are chiefs in the proper meaning of the term no longer.

CHAPTER XXV

SOME POINTS OF ETIQUETTE

THE fact is sometimes overlooked that amongst uncivilised races there are, as a rule, clearly defined standards of etiquette. It is so with the Ibo people. They have rules for the regulation of conduct applicable to almost every detail of life. Habits are naturally engendered and developed; they are a subconscious part of the native's being and, amongst the older generation, it is a rare thing to find one failing to observe the traditional rules of conduct. The code of etiquette had a definite place in the social life of the people, but the disintegrating forces of a transition period are plainly visible, and the old system of conduct and etiquette is rapidly losing its significance and its hold upon them. A generation is springing up with a disposition to cast off the manners and traditions of its ancestors. This is a source of no little concern to the old people and for many obvious reasons it is much to be regretted.

There are many things which it is an advantage to bear in mind when holding intercourse with the people. The one which perhaps impresses the average foreigner more than any other is the ancient custom of sharing the kola nut. When about to call upon a chief it is not necessary to notify him of one's intention. The visitor walks into the compound and is either led to the reception-room, or, if none of the household be visible, he shouts, or by other means makes his presence known. An attendant soon appears and the visitor is accommodated with a stool, or, it may be, a skin is spread on the clay seat for him. I have had to be content with the outer husk of a coco-nut split in half with the flat side to the ground. This is not an ideal seat, it is not too comfortable, and it needs considerable care to preserve one's dignity.

A chief seldom exhibits signs of haste in his formal reception of the ordinary visitor; but the announcement of the arrival of a Government official speeds up the chief's movements wonderfully! The delay is deliberate in order to impress on the caller the dignity of the chief and to signify that it is a matter of condescension on his part to receive a stranger at all. And the greater the chief the longer he keeps his visitors waiting, particularly if they are strangers. When he does appear he is attired in state dress and at once takes his seat upon the ukpo (throne, seat of honour), and then settles himself to receive the salutations of the strangers. These are somewhat protracted, consisting of expressions of welcome and pleasure and inquiries concerning the health of himself and his people. If it be a first call it is incumbent to explain whence one has come and why. When visiting a strange town it was our invariable practice to inquire for the leading chief, and at once claim his friendship and, if necessary, his good services on our behalf. Native etiquette demanded that the stranger should, in such circumstances, be received hospitably, and we were always treated well, although occasionally, the welcome was not exactly cordial.

The preliminary salutations having petered out, a slave boy advanced bearing a wooden bowl, or other receptacle, containing one or more kola nuts.[1] The dish was handed to the chief, who, in turn, passed it on to the visitor.

[1] Kola (Cola, or *Sterculia acuminata* and *macrocarpa*). Tree twenty to thirty feet in height, both indigenous and cultivated in most parts of West Africa between 5° S. and 10° N. Lat. It thrives on all soils, and is found at all heights, from sea-level to three thousand feet and more. The nuts, which are bitter in taste, are highly esteemed by the natives. In England they are worked up with cocoa and other food products. To the Mohammedan of West Africa the kola nut supplies the place of coffee. For satisfying the cravings of hunger and for sustaining properties it is deemed equal to the dried dates of the Bedouins. The roots are favoured as "chew-sticks" for cleaning the teeth and sweetening the breath. The nuts grow in pods, and vary in size from one to two inches in diameter. Each nut has three or four natural divisions enabling it to be split easily. In colour it ranges from white to red. Kola nuts enter into the daily life of all West African Mohammedans and constitute almost a language.

In the case of a perfect stranger the chief would probably put the nuts to his own mouth before presenting them, to indicate that they were offered in all good faith and were free from poison and ju-ju influence. It is the visitor's privilege to divide the kola nut, an easy operation if the nut be held bottom end upwards and the thumb nails pressed firmly into the natural lines of division. These portions are usually broken into still smaller fragments and then the pieces are placed in the dish. The proper etiquette is to offer the nut to the chief first and he, in turn, hands the dish back to the visitor. The two leading personages having thus partaken, the remainder of the nut is passed to the other men in attendance, in order of rank and seniority. The ceremony is not confined to men, but they take precedence of any women present.

The right hand must always be used ; to offer or receive a gift with the left hand, or to present it for any purpose, is equivalent to a direct insult. The joint partaking of kola nut is supposed to be the ceremony which seals an unbreakable friendship, but it would be injudicious to rely implicitly upon this outward expression of good will. A native would pay little respect to its binding claims should circumstances arise to lead him to change his attitude towards the stranger. The ceremony is brought to a conclusion by an interchange of presents, either whilst still sitting in the reception-chamber or after the parties have departed to their respective quarters.

The presents offered by the chiefs are sometimes more interesting than attractive. So long as they consist of live meat, yams, and such-like, they are as agreeable as

Offers of marriage, refusals and acceptances, declarations of war, and countless other transactions are arranged by means of the number and colour of kola nuts strung together (or otherwise) and sent by one party to another. The first act of friendship and hospitality is a present of white nuts, and before commencing any discussion on any subject the sharing of the kola nut as an act of friendship is a necessity.

The export of kola nuts is a very flourishing trade, and they are in great demand throughout all the countries of the Soudan as far as Khartoum. The value increases according to the distance they have to be carried until they cost from sixty to one hundred times their original value.—Modified extract from *British Nigeria*, Mockler-Ferryman, p. 317.

they are acceptable. When dead meat is offered, one cannot but feel disgust, however strongly one may try to repress it.

On one occasion a worthy and venerable old cannibal chief smilingly presented me with a large dish of meat. There were several joints, all black with smoke and their origin a matter for speculation; but the climax was reached when the old gentleman suddenly bent down and vigoro-ously licked the surface of the meat as a preliminary to presenting it; this, of course, being done to remove any possible suspicion of poison.

Where a chief is privileged to hold the courtesy title of "king" the native salutation is accompanied by the sincerest form of obeisance, the visitor prostrating himself and placing his forehead on the ground. He repeats this act several times, and each time he raises his head he utters the kingly salutation "Igwe" or "Obi," instead of one of the customary words used in greeting commoners. In theory no visitor may depart from any house without partaking of kola nut or some equivalent. In practice the custom is frequently omitted, the omission being atoned for by the words "Enwerom ojji (I have no kola), the underlying idea being an apology for the fact that no kola nut has been offered; not that there was any intention of slight, or want of respect, but the host had nothing to offer.

All persons, irrespective of age, sex, or rank, salute each other as they meet. None but an ill-mannered person, lacking in common courtesy, would fail to return the customary greeting, unless, indeed, he were mourning for the dead or in the act of bearing an offering to the spirits of the dead.

As a matter of fact, at times there are so many people to greet and the salutation is such a parrot-like utterance, that it is apt to jar on the foreigner's nerves and exhaust his patience. The underlying thought of the salutation is practically the same all over the country, bearing a general idea of "welcome," more or less equivalent to the English "glad to see you." The word may be repeated any number of times—often with monotonous and wearisome precision. Curiously enough, in most districts, there is a total absence of variable salutations. All who meet in the morning greet one another with the words "Have you come out from sleep?" and this salutation is pressed into service throughout the day—and night too if need be! There is nothing which corresponds to "good afternoon" or "good evening." To the foreigner it sounds rather ludicrous to be asked at 6 p.m. "Have you come out from sleep?" There is one exception which comes into use when one meets a person at work; the right thing then is to salute the labourer with the words "Thank you for working," the words to be repeated as often and as vigorously as the work appears to warrant.

Should one wish to beckon to another the right hand must be used with the palm turned downwards, i.e. with a sort of drawing motion. On the other hand, to close the fist, with thumb turned upward, and shake it in the face of a person, is equivalent to hurling the most deadly threats and curses upon him.

A person drawing near whilst a meal is in progress is immediately greeted with an invitation "to come and eat." The invitation is always given, but the answer is almost invariably to the effect that the visitor has already eaten; it is a rare thing for one to accept food in these circumstances. The invitation is an act of courtesy which, though always expressed, expects the answer "No!"

In every sphere of life man takes precedence over woman; he is lord and master, but not necessarily in an overbearing manner. The sexes recognize clearly each other's rights and privileges, and they do not spoil matters by attempting to interfere with each other's affairs and vocations. In assemblies where both sexes are present, the men sit on one side and the women on the other. When travelling by road no regular order is followed, but more often than not the husband brings up the rear—his women-folk bearing the loads before him; the man seldom carries a load himself.[1] When canoeing, a woman usually

[1] This custom, no doubt, is a survival of the ancient law of necessity whereby the man, fully armed, and unhampered by any burden, brought up the rear. His business was to shepherd his women folk and be ready to

steers and women also do the greater part of the paddling. Natives invariably walk in single file whatever the condition of the road may be, whether a good open highway or a bush track. A woman may not wear an article of male attire nor in any way act as a man; severe penalties follow the infringement of this rule. European ladies sometimes rouse the very strong indignation and prejudice of the natives when they least suspect it, and I have known them to be in considerable danger of molestation all because of some garment, which may be eminently suitable to the country, but which, in the biassed mind of the native, savours of masculine tendencies, and is therefore subject to grave disapproval.

When meeting a person, after the customary salutation, one enquires as to his health and that of his relatives (whether they are acquaintances or not). Likewise when saying "good-bye" one sends salutations to the household to which the man is proceeding. These are not referred to by name but merely as "Ndi-bei," i.e. those of your house. But it is not etiquette to make inquiries regarding the number of those who constitute the household. It is even worse manners to ask how many wives a man has or the number of his children. No one of experience would ever expect to get a direct answer to such questions, and if a definite number were to be mentioned it would be safe to assume that it was false. One would have to be satisfied by "some" or a "few" or "many" at the best. It is a question full of ill-omen; to announce the number would be a direct challenge to the malignant spirits and they would speedily get to work and play havoc with the family.

Anyone leaving the compound on an errand from which, in the ordinary course of things, he must sooner or later return is saluted with the words "Nabo," really an expression of the wish that the person may go forth and return in safety. Distance and probable lapse of time have no bearing on the situation. Even when one is leaving the

act on the defensive. In days gone by his rôle was a most important and frequently a dangerous one. Foreigners are apt to accuse him of laziness, whereas really he is only observing the practice of his forefathers.

country altogether—say for furlough in England—the salutation is the same; frequently the native refuses to use the word which indicates a final good-bye.

With men the common form of greeting is effected with the first two fingers of the right hand. The fingers are pressed firmly together and then pulled backwards, producing, if done properly, a sharp clicking sound similar to that resulting from the familiar snap of the thumb and bare finger. The women are much more demonstrative and embrace each other (but without kissing) or, as they say, "Ti-obi," i.e. to clasp each other to the heart.

Making Water and Cooking Pots

Women Clearing Farm of Weeds

CHAPTER XXVI

FABLES—FOLKLORE—PROVERBS

THE following are a few examples of folklore and fables in common use amongst the Ibo people. The stories narrated by the old folk are of absorbing interest to the children and a large volume could easily be filled with them. Proverbs, fables and stories enter very largely into the ordinary conversation of the people, and some acquaintance with them is absolutely necessary in order to take an intelligent interest in any subject of discussion. Some hundreds of proverbs are in constant use, and answers to questions are frequently given in this form. The meaning of some of the proverbs and fables is clearly obvious, but others are quite enigmatical. The usual practice in narrating fables and tales is to refer to animals and birds as persons, as will be observed by a perusal of the few examples here given.

A pig and a deer started on a journey together. After a time they reached a spot where the path forked. They began to dispute as to which of the roads they should follow. The pig proposed the longer route but the deer urged the claims of the shorter. The quarrel became so heated that it led to a separation, and each chose the path he preferred. The pig travelled by the longer way and arrived at his destination; the deer proceeded by the nearer road but had only gone a short distance when he was shot and killed.

Moral: The easiest is not always the best. cf. All is not gold that glitters.

One day a rat saw some fish and, being of a covetous

disposition, he immediately planned to steal them. In his eagerness he did not observe that the fish were in a trap and, consequently, he himself was caught. He cried out to the trap, "Why are you treating me in this manner? I know of no cause of quarrel between us." "Oh," replied the trap, "it is because you came to steal what was in my possession and so I caught you also."

Moral: To steal other people's goods leads to the punishment of the thief.

A frog challenged a deer to a race. Before the day appointed for the contest, the frog entered into a league with all his companions and arranged that they should station themselves at regular intervals along the course, and that each should wait in readiness to answer the calls of the deer as he raced along towards the goal. The race started. The deer thought to outstrip the frog with ease, and soon called back in mocking tones to ask where the frog was. To his surprise the answer "Here I am" came from the opposite direction to what he expected. He raced along once more and repeated the challenge. Again a voice answered from in front of him, and once more he was deceived and thought he was being left behind in the race. The strategy was repeated all along the course until the deer fell down exhausted and died.

One fine afternoon a tortoise met a fowl and inquired of him whither he was going? The fowl replied that he was on his way to call upon the tortoise. The tortoise answered, "I am sorry, but I have nothing nice in my house wherewith to entertain you this afternoon. If, however, you will accompany me I will lead you to a beautiful udala[1] tree laden with ripe juicy fruit." When they arrived at the spot the tortoise besought his friend, the udala tree, to give them some fruit, but the proposal did not commend itself to the tree. Thereupon

[1] The Udala tree bears a fruit the size of a small apple. The rind is russet coloured, thin and brittle. It contains a milk-white sticky juice which the natives, especially children, are fond of "licking."

the tortoise suggested that the tree should drop one of its fruits on his back. The tree did so, and the udala split on the shell of the tortoise and he and the fowl licked up the juice.

The tortoise said it was now the fowl's turn to stand so that an udala might fall upon his head. The idea frightened the fowl. He declared that if the hard fruit fell upon his head the blow would kill him. He was willing for it to fall upon his back but not upon his head. The tortoise was annoyed at this display of caution and taunted the fowl with it, which led to a sharp quarrel between them. Meantime neither of them could enjoy the fruit and, realizing this, the fowl at length consented to the proposal. He called upon the tree to drop another fruit. When it fell on the fowl's head it killed him. The tortoise, regardless of his friend's fate, licked up the juice of the udala and then carried the dead fowl to his home and cooked and ate him.

From one of the legs of the fowl he manufactured a flute and he used to sit outside his house and play "tilo ntiloo tiloo, egwu nara n'obodo ayi," i.e. "music and dancing are taking place (being played) in our town." One day a hawk flew down and said, "Oh! tortoise, what price did you pay for the flute? Let me examine it; it appears to be a very nice one, please let me try it." "Oh! no!" replied the tortoise. "I know your cunning craftiness. Were I to place it in your hands (claws) you would immediately fly off with it." The hawk declared he would not be guilty of such a naughty trick, and that if the tortoise did not trust him let him cling to his feathers and thus prevent him from flying off with the flute. The suspicions of the tortoise were allayed; he caught hold of a feather and allowed the hawk to take the flute. Suddenly the hawk soared up into the air leaving the tortoise nothing but the feather. He was extremely vexed with the hawk and at once began to plan how he might recover his instrument. He kept a close watch on the movements of the hawk and one day saw him set forth on an important mission. The tortoise made his way to the hawk's nest in the guise of a messenger. He met the hawk's mother and informed her that her son had forgotten to take his flute when starting on his journey, and that he had been commissioned to bring it. Unsuspectingly the mother handed over the flute to the tortoise, who quickly made his way again to his own home.

On his return, the hawk heard the sounds of music and recognised whence they came. At once he inquired of his mother who had restored the flute to the tortoise? She replied that she had done so under the impression that she was fulfilling his command, whereupon the hawk was so enraged that he seized her and threw her on the fire. Afterwards he repented of his hasty action and went to try and rescue his parent, but he was too late.

This is the reason why the hawks hover over bush fires! They are seeking their old, old grandmother!

Once upon a time a man had a daughter named Manu (oil). She was very tall and beautiful. Many suitors sought her in marriage, but they withdrew when the parents informed them that, though their daughter possessed many attractive qualities, yet she could neither cook food nor work in the sun. Such limitations were fatal; no man in his senses would marry a girl who could not cook! Later on, however, a rich farmer came along and agreed to marry her for her beauty. He led her to his home and gave strict instructions to all his servants on no account to allow fire to come near her, and to prevent her venturing out into the sun.

Some time afterwards the farmer departed to his farm taking all his servants with him, with the exception of one who feigned sickness. This one was ordered to cook for the lady, but he deliberately neglected this duty. Presently Manu grew hungry and, no food being forthcoming, she went to the kitchen in order to prepare a meal for herself. The heat overcame her; she collapsed and melted! The parrot was taking note of all these things but knew no way of informing the farmer. Whilst in this state of perplexity he had an inspiration. He dipped his tail in the now liquid Manu (which is of a reddish colour) and flew to where the farmer was at work and, perching on a tree near by, began to sing :—

> " O ! merry farmer, look at me,
> And if you look at me you'll see
> That what you left at home is lost.
> Look at my tail and you will guess."

The farmer looked at the parrot and perceived that his tail, which was formerly grey, was now red and, immediately he realized that his wife Manu had met with an accident and had melted.

This is the reason why the tail of the West African grey parrot is red !

One day a tortoise challenged a buffalo to a tug-of-war. The buffalo poked fun at him and said, " Who will give you strength to pull against me ? " The tortoise replied, " Never mind; wait and see." So they appointed a day and drew up rules for the contest, deciding particularly upon the signal for starting. The tortoise straightway went and challenged an elephant, and concluded arrangements for a contest on the same terms.

When the day arrived the tortoise fastened one end of the rope round the neck of the buffalo and then acted as if he were proceeding to take hold of the other end. But the rope was of such a length that, when stretched, one competitor was out of sight of the other. The tortoise called the elephant and tied the rope to his neck, and went through a similar manœuvre to that practised with the buffalo. At the agreed signal the two began to pull and strain, and the struggle became so furious that it ended in the death of both.

The tortoise congratulated himself on the strategy whereby he had obtained so much meat for so little trouble. As he was cutting it up, he heard the wind singing in the trees, and he thought some people were approaching who might rob him of the spoil. He became angry and in his excitement fell upon his knife and killed himself.

Moral : The cunning deceiver is apt to meet with a fate quite as miserable as that of the deceived.

One day Apia (a bird impersonated in several Ibo fables) gave his wife some yams to cook. When she had prepared them he told her she could eat them herself, as he intended to dine at the house of his mother-in-law. He flew off, only to find that he had arrived too late for the meal. Full of chagrin he hastened back home and called for supper. In his absence his wife had consumed the food and he had, perforce, to go without! This is the reason why the Apia is so lean and flat-chested!

Moral: "Be content with such things as ye have," or its equivalent, "A bird in the hand is worth two in the bush."

There was a great famine at Idu (Benin Districts). At that time the big market was held on the king's ground "Ojisaw." Suffering from shortness of supplies, the tortoise hired a rabbit to burrow a tunnel from his hole to the market-place. When all the people were assembled with their wares, the tortoise and the rabbit, remaining hidden in the burrow, began to sing "Ubwaw ojisaw tijin tintiji tiji." When the people heard the unfamiliar sounds, and could not perceive whence they came, they were frightened and ran away, believing that the market had been invaded by the pixies. The tortoise and the rabbit thereupon ran out and replenished their larders from the goods left in the market. They practised this manœuvre from time to time as need arose.

One day they invited a lizard called Akatampwo (male lizard) to join them in their raiding expedition. As on previous occasions the people fled when they heard the sound of underground singing, whereat the three thieves ran out to steal. Akatampwo was eager to secure fish, and greedily seized a piece. The result was that a bone stuck in his mouth and he could neither eject nor swallow it! He stood still, vainly bobbing his head up and down in his efforts to rid himself of the bone, and, as he did so, he accidentally dipped his head into a vessel containing palm oil. Hence the head of Akatampwo is red to this day!

Finally, he returned to the hole, and the tortoise and the rabbit inquired why he had come home empty-handed? But Akatampwo could no longer speak; he could do nothing but bob his head. So it is to this day. This lizard is continually raising himself on his fore legs and bobbing his head up and down in his struggles to rid himself of that fishbone!

Later on the suspicions of the market people were aroused and they accused the tortoise of trickery. He stoutly denied the charge and declared his readiness to submit the case for trial. A day was fixed for swearing on the ju-ju. During the interval the tortoise made a compact with the birds called Asha. He put a large number of them into a pot and instructed them to utter cries in accordance with a code of signals. The tortoise concealed the pot under a weird collection of fetish accessories, and he contrived to render its appearance so awe-inspiring that it was, in itself, sufficient to startle the people. When the birds began to sing it was too much for the assembled crowd, and they refused to proceed with the uncanny business. Thus the tortoise escaped by means of his skilful trickery.

The tortoise returned triumphantly to his quarters, carrying the pot containing the little birds with him. They had served him loyally, but he returned evil for good. He placed the pot upon the fire and when the birds cried for mercy he mocked them. "Never before," said he, "had birds been used as ju-ju in such a manner."

Presently he removed the pot from the fire expecting to find all the birds ready for eating. As he lifted the cover, however, one bird flew out, the only survivor, and alighted on the head of the tortoise's son. The tortoise cried out to his son to stand quite still, seized a cutlass and struck viciously, but the bird hopped to one side and the blow fell upon the head of the tortoise's son, killing him on the spot. When the tortoise recovered a little from the shock he turned and saw the bird perched on the back of his daughter. Striking blindly in his fury he was again deceived by the bird's quickness and, consequently, slew his daughter also. The bird flew to the top of a tree and, watching his opportunity, alighted swiftly on the back of the tortoise himself who, utterly perplexed with this action, pondered how he might overthrow his little enemy.

CHAPTER XXVII

THE DAY OF BETTER THINGS

It would not be fitting to close the foregoing sketch of the life and customs of the Ibo people without giving a brief account of missionary enterprise amongst them. The advent of Christianity has had a powerful and stimulating effect and great numbers of these sturdy folk have been led " out of darkness into light, and from the power of Satan unto God." Many are rejoicing to-day in the " liberty wherewith Christ has made us free." Among the annals of Missions there are few which can show such a noteworthy record as that of the Niger. The early and subsequent history is a subject of absorbing interest, rivalling and, in many ways, corresponding with, the chequered course of the exploration of the river. The task of tracing the Niger from its source to the Delta furnishes a narrative in which unbounded enthusiasm and blighted hopes are in sharp and unusual contrast. The record of the establishment of missions in these regions is very similar in character.

Failure and success, disappointment and encouragement, grief and joy, are interwoven in a manner unparalleled in the conquests of the Cross. But as, out of death and disaster, there finally emerged British Nigeria, so likewise from feeble and uncertain beginnings Christianity is steadily progressing, gathering force, and extending its influence daily. For many years the tide ebbed and flowed, hope and despair alternated, but for the last fifteen years especially, expansion has been the key-note of all things Nigerian, including missions. Simultaneously with the general opening up of the country and increase of prosperity on the Niger, the frontiers of the kingdom of God have been enlarged more and more.

Certain names stand out pre-eminently in the early history of the Niger Mission. In the Expedition of 1841 room was found for two uncommonly able men, the Rev. J. Schön, a distinguished linguist, at that time a missionary in Sierra Leone, and Samuel Adjai Crowther. The life of the latter is inextricably bound up with the establishment of Christianity amongst the Ibos and other tribes of Southern Nigeria. For fifty years the whole history of the Mission centres round this extraordinary man. He was instrumental in laying the foundations of the work, and if his associates had proved as zealous and faithful as he was himself, there would have been a truly marvellous story to relate. His career was absolutely unique; there is nothing to equal it in the records of West Africa. "A kidnapped slave in 1821, rescued in 1822, a Mission school-boy in 1823, a baptized Christian in 1825, a college student in 1826, a teacher in 1828, a clergyman in 1843, a missionary to the country whence he had been stolen in 1845, the founder of a new Mission (the Niger) in 1857, the first negro bishop in 1864—where is the parallel to such a life? Ten times in seventy years he came to England. He accomplished much in Africa. Amid circumstances of almost unexampled difficulty he went steadily on his way; and if the Upper Niger in his lifetime bore little fruit, the Delta to-day, with its cannibalism and infanticide and horrible superstitions practically at an end—though not its Sin, and who could expect *that?*—is a monument to Bishop Crowther's indomitable perseverance in a holy cause. He lived in an atmosphere of suspicion and scandal, yet no tongue, however malicious, ventured to whisper reproach against his personal character. Some might criticise his administration; no one ever questioned his sincerity and simplicity." Such is the testimony as written by Dr. Stock, the historian of the C.M.S. in the Preface contributed by him to Jesse Page's valuable life of the Black Bishop.

Schön recorded it as his opinion that on the Niger there was a wide field open to the Gospel, but that not were addressed each in its own language. At the same time he advised that, in whatever part of the country a mission was established, English should be introduced. He was greatly impressed with the necessity for the employment of natives as evangelists and teachers, in a country, the unhealthiness of which rendered it impossible, as he thought, for Europeans to carry on the work. He urged the adoption of measures whereby the natives of Africa should become missionaries to their own people.

The first two proposals were, and still are, in strict accordance with the general policy adopted in all missions of the Church Missionary Society, i.e. the insistence on the use of the vernacular in all primary work, followed at the proper stage by the introduction of English. Translations of the Scriptures and other books have been made, and this branch of work continues to occupy a prominent position in our missionary policy.

The employment of natives in this unhealthy sphere, sound enough in its conception, proved disastrous in practice. Its adoption led to bitter disappointment, and the incubus of failure was only removed when the original plan was modified and European missionaries were sent out to support and direct the labours of their African brethren.

The advantages of Native Agency were never more obvious than they are at the present moment, but experience proves, beyond all doubt, that the most effective work is that accomplished by the united efforts of Europeans and Africans. Native workers are absolutely essential to the cause of Missions, and Schön's main principle remains substantially as he laid it down. It is modified only by the introduction of a European element whose paramount work is to train and direct the native teachers. Working on these lines signs are not wanting to prove that the forces of the Gospel are steadily making their influence felt over a great part of Southern Nigeria, and even to the regions beyond.

Aboh was the first place suggested as a possible Mission Station on the Niger. In early days it appears to have been an important centre. The king (obi) was greatly impressed by the fact that a former slave, well known in the district, had been taught to read and write. Indeed it was chiefly owing to this ex-slave's valuable assistance that Dr. Baikie and his companions in the expedition of 1854 were given a peaceable reception instead of the hostile one which they feared. The king expressed himself as perfectly willing to allow teachers to reside amongst his people, and a parcel of land was selected for a mission centre. Little, however, was ever done at this town, and as the years have passed, its importance has gradually declined. Further up the river, Osumali was thought to offer favourable prospects, more particularly because great numbers of people from the interior were accustomed to visit it for trading purposes. For some years it had a resident evangelist, but the station was abandoned before my time (1900) and it has not since been re-occupied. Onitsha was finally chosen as the base of operations, and later, Asaba, these two places seeming the most promising for commencing missionary work amongst the Ibos. It was to the former place that the Rev. S. Crowther (to whom was entrusted the task of founding the Niger Mission) appointed the Rev. J. Taylor, with instructions to begin work at once. They arrived on July 27th, 1857. Taylor was a native clergyman, born in Sierra Leone, whose parents had been deported from the Ibo country as slaves.[1]

Dr. Baikie (in command of the expedition) and Captain Grant, visited the King of Onitsha. The former explained the objects of their visit, and Taylor was introduced as the religious teacher who was to reside amongst them. King and people expressed their agreement with the proposals set forth. The site then selected for the Mission Church was taken over by the Government about ten years ago and converted into a cemetery. The original land granted to the Mission on which to build dwelling houses is still in the occupation of the C.M.S., and in July, 1907, the jubilee of the establishment of the

[1] Judging from Taylor's translational work his parents were natives of the Bonny District.

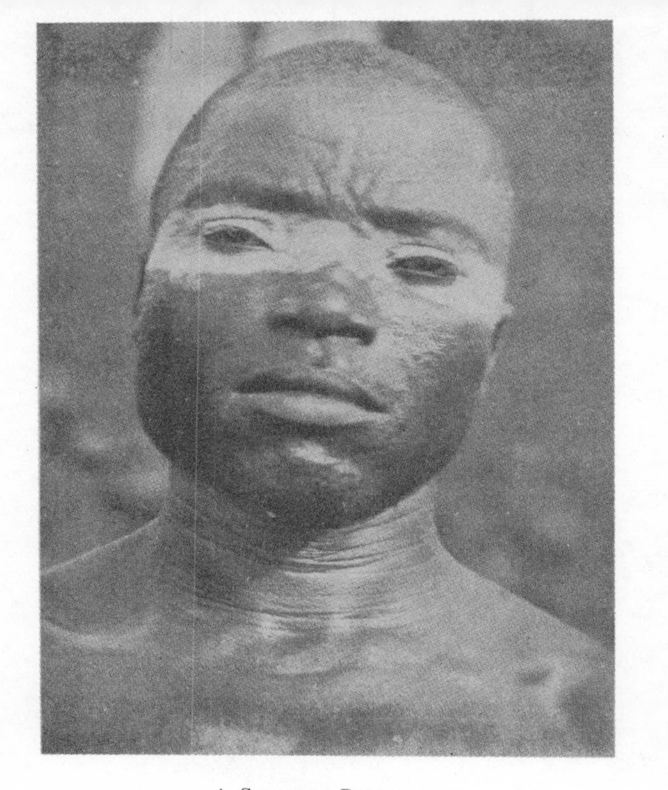

A STRANGE PASSPORT

The white lines serve as a passport after a visit to a strange town. host provides the chalk, and is responsible for the safety of his guest.

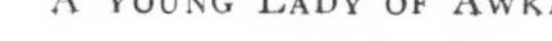

A YOUNG LADY OF AWKA

Mission was celebrated beneath the tamarisk tree which Crowther had planted fifty years previously.[1] Before proceeding up river Dr. Baikie, Lieut. Grover and the Rev. S. Crowther again visited the king, and he, with his councillors, "promised to abolish human sacrifices, and to exclude strangers from the white man's country from the law which allows no mat, or any kind of seat except the bare ground, to strangers visiting the Court."

Crowther issued for Taylor's guidance written instructions, remarkable for their perception and sound judgment. He enjoins him to remember that "the first and most important place to which your attention should be chiefly directed is Onitsha, which appears to be the high road to the heart of the Ibo nation." On August 27th, Divine service was conducted for the first time in Ibo-land. Missionaries and traders combined in this prophetic effort, which was attended by from 200 to 400 natives. On the afternoon of the same day a much larger audience was present in the compound of King Akazua. On Sept. 13th, use was made for the first time of Taylor's revised Ibo translation of the Lord's Prayer; ten days later a visit was paid to Obusi, to the S.S.E. of Onitsha. In November, a canoe journey up the Anambala Creek gave the missionary party an opportunity of inaugurating work at Nsubwe, where they received a cordial welcome. On December 11th, the foundation of the first Mission House was laid, and three months later it was ready for occupation. Taylor paid visits to Oko and Asaba, and during the fifteen months he lived at Onitsha he succeeded in gathering around him a devoted little congregation. He busied himself in translational work and collected information concerning the country and the customs of the people. To those acquainted with Onitsha at the present time the journal compiled by Taylor is of the greatest interest. To this son of rescued Ibo slaves belongs the honour of introducing Christianity into the Ibo country.

[1] Boxes of plants selected by Mr. Barter, the botanist of the expedition, were brought from Sierra Leone and Fernando Po. These were planted at Onitsha and Lokoja, hence the oranges, guavas, mangoes, limes and other fruits now abounding in the compounds of all the old mission stations.

On Oct. 27th, 1858, Crowther and Taylor left Onitsha on the *Rainbow*.[1] As the vessel was navigating the waters of the Delta, she was fired upon by the natives and two men were killed. The Government failed to provide the gunboat which they had promised should accompany the next trading steamer, and Crowther and Taylor, who had proceeded to the Nun entrance of the river to await it, were forced to return to Lagos disappointed. The death of Macgregor Laird followed soon after, and this event led to the withdrawal of his steamers and the closing of his trading factories on the Niger.

Crowther then gathered together a missionary party of thirty-three persons and journeyed with them to Akassa, with a view to the permanent occupation of missionary stations on the Niger. It was confidently expected that passages would be available on H.M.S. *Investigator*, but when she appeared, to the chagrin of Crowther, the commander announced that he had received no instructions to carry passengers, but so great was the sympathy of the ship's company, that room was made for twenty-seven of the party.

Te strengthen the Mission, five Europeans were appointed, but only two of them reached even the mouth of the Niger. One of these quickly fell a victim to malaria and died; the other was invalided to England.

It seemed hopeless to expect Europeans to live on the Niger, hence the idea was conceived of forming a mission to be staffed entirely by Africans. Necessity seemed to demand this course and with the necessity came the man for the task.

In March, 1864, Crowther came to England, reported on his experiences, and laid his proposals before the authorities. Negotiations were opened with a view to his consecration as Bishop of the Niger, Archbishop Longley warmly pressing the scheme on the Government. Lord John Russell, then Foreign Secretary, cordially assented, and the Queen's licence was issued to the Primate, empowering him to consecrate "Our trusty and well-beloved

[1] The *Dayspring*, the vessel which had taken out the expedition, was wrecked at Rabba on October 27th, the previous year.

Samuel Adjai Crowther, Clerk in Holy Orders, to be a Bishop of the Church of England in the West African territories beyond the British Dominions."

His linguistic and other talents were recognised and the University of Oxford conferred upon him an honorary D.D. degree, Convocation conferring it almost unanimously. On St. Peter's Day (June 29th), 1864, in Canterbury Cathedral, he was consecrated Bishop of the Niger.

On his return to West Africa, the "black Bishop" was treated with the utmost respect by the Governors of Sierra Leone, the Gold Coast and Lagos. He proceeded to the Niger on *H.M.S. Investigator*, which was taking stores for Dr. Baikie, who was now established as Consul at Lokoja. Crowther visited the Mission Stations, ordained deacon one of the catechists, confirmed some converts, and returned to Lagos, his permanent head-quarters. He paid visits of some months' duration to the Niger as opportunity offered. For these journeys he was entirely dependent upon the occasional visits of Government vessels, until traders, already active in the Delta, began to settle up the river. Gradually he was able to increase his mission staff, obtaining negro catechists and schoolmasters from Sierra Leone, appointing them to different stations, and ordaining those who seemed fit. By 1871, he had ordained eight such men, in addition to his own son Daudeson.[1] The principal work continued to be up the river, especially at Onitsha, and at Lokoja. Crowther never asked a favour to be allowed to send a teacher to a town; he always insisted that he came for the good of the people, and that they must provide the necessary dwelling and other buildings, or give him the money to build them.

In 1861, King William Pepple,[2] of Bonny, wrote to the Bishop of London requesting that a Christian Mission should be established in his country. The appeal was passed on to Crowther, and in 1864 a schoolmaster began

[1] Since 1878, Archdeacon of the Delta Pastorate Church. He took charge of the Mission at Bonny in 1871.

[2] This man was of titular rank and also a trader. Whilst on a visit to England he had received this name in baptism.

work in a small way; in 1866 a proper building was opened for services. The history of the early years of the Bonny mission is full of thrilling incidents, such as the jealous counter-moves of the ju-ju priests, the destruction of the sacred iguanas through the influence of King William Pepple, and, in 1873, the outbreak of persecutions, which extended for several years, and resulted in the martyrdom of some of the converts. The leading persecutor was "Captain Hart," a native chief, who had assumed an English name. For five years he troubled the Church and then, in 1878, softened by the death of his wife, he "sent for Mr. Crowther, listened to his words, went to the other chiefs, and then, with them, granted religious liberty." In the following year he died, having on his death-bed renounced idolatry, and given orders for the destruction of all his idols. From this time huge congregations attended St. Stephen's Church, and great progress was made.

Three important steps were taken in 1878, viz. the fitting out of a steamer to facilitate travelling on the Niger, the sending out of an English layman to take charge of the boat, to keep the accounts and to do other secular duties of the Mission, and the appointing of two African clergymen to be Archdeacons.

The native evangelists had been much isolated and did not receive the guidance and superintendence that were necessary. However upright their lives, they were liable to suspicion and false accusations (the bane of West African Society). They were, indeed, beset by manifold temptations, and some fell grievously. In their lonely Stations they lacked the stimulating influence of Christian fellowship. Some succumbed to the peculiarly besetting sins of West Africa—drink and immorality, whilst others, overcome by avarice, were tempted to forsake their high calling in order to become traders. Reports of these irregularities gave rise to great anxiety amongst the mission authorities in London, which was increased when communications came to hand giving details of a serious offence committed at Onitsha. The case was made the subject of a great debate in the House of Lords; bitter attacks were made upon the C.M.S., and the Niger Mission was particularly denounced. These scathing criticisms were, however, valiantly met and vanquished by Earl Cairns and Archbishop Benson, both of whom paid high tributes to the work of the Society.

Out of this fiery sifting, from the debris of what appeared to be a ruined cause, there sprang forth a new order of things. That was the darkest hour, which ushered in the dawn of brighter hopes ; a dawn which has continued to shine forth more and whose light must grow brighter and clearer until the Sun of Righteousness shall illumine the whole of Ibo-land. Even in those dark days there were evidences of the power of the Gospel. At Onitsha, for instance, there was a marked movement towards Christianity. In the Delta, snake and lizard worship was disappearing, and Mr. (now Sir) H. H. Johnston, lecturing before the Royal Geographical Society (Nov. 12th, 1888) declared that : "For its effectual abolishment, which has been of the greatest benefit to the well-being of Europeans and natives alike, we owe our thanks, not to the intervention of Naval or Consular officials, nor to the bluff remonstrances of traders, but to the quiet, increasing labours of the agents of the Church Missionary Society."

In 1887, the Rev. John Alfred Robinson, the Cambridge Scholar, went to live on the Niger as English Secretary. He was not satisfied with the native teachers nor with the plans and policy of the Mission in some respects, nor with the results achieved. He was later on joined by Graham Wilmot Brooke,[1] and these two became joint leaders of a new Mission to the Mohammedans in the Northern Provinces. The adoption of their proposals led to a change

[1] Son of Colonel Brooke ; a young man of extraordinary capacity and great fervour who had been educated for the Army. He had been trying to reach the heart of Mohammedan Africa, as a result of his intercourse with General Gordon in 1881. In 1884, he essayed to cross the Sahara from Algiers, but failed. In 1885, he went up the Senegal but could not get far enough. In 1887–8, he was on the Congo and ascended the Mobangi lat. 2° N. but was driven back by cannibal tribes. Then he visited the Niger and at once concluded that it was the true way to the Central Soudan.

in organisation. From this time the Lower Niger and the Delta formed a separate Mission.

On Dec. 31st, 1891, came the news of the death of that unique product of modern missions, Bishop Samuel Crowther, after seventy years of ceaseless activity in the service of God in West Africa. "His works do follow him." No man could wish for a grander and more fitting memorial than the striking expansion of the Missions which he was privileged to found on the banks of the Niger.

Soon after the death of Bishop Crowther, the work in the Delta was consolidated into a Native Pastorate. It speaks well for the initiative and ability of West African Christians that from that day to this they have staffed and maintained the Churches in the Delta districts, and have perseveringly developed the various organisations in connection therewith, without financial assistance from the parent society. It was a bold adventure, demanding great faith on the part of the originators of the scheme. That they have not attained all they desire or deserve, and that their work has not advanced with the rapidity and vigour that they hoped is, perhaps, natural; but the fact cannot be gainsaid that a truly marvellous work has been accomplished in circumstances that have frequently been the reverse of easy. There are many evidences of self-sacrifice and painstaking energy on behalf of the Kingdom of God in these swampy and pestilential districts.

The formation of the Niger Delta Pastorate enabled the C.M.S. to concentrate their forces more particularly on the central parts of the Ibo country, with Onitsha as the base of missionaries' operations. The advent of lady-missionaries, in the early nineties, led to further developments. At a later stage, Medical Mission work was started, an agency of inestimable blessing and value to Europeans and natives alike. Its salutary effects are manifest on all sides, and its influence on every other department of missionary organisation is of the greatest benefit. It removes prejudice, creates opportunities for evangelistic effort and alleviates an immense amount of suffering. By it natives from unknown parts are brought into direct contact with Christianity in a particularly attractive and appealing form, and this leads to the evangelisation of hitherto unoccupied towns and villages.

The decade 1890–1900 was a peculiarly trying and difficult one for various reasons. The Mission was sadly crippled from time to time owing to the death or compulsory withdrawals of European helpers. The climatic conditions taxed the health of the English missionaries greatly, the traditional evil reputation of the Niger being fully maintained in this respect. Nevertheless there was no looking back. A much-needed work of purification and consolidation was accomplished and the foundations of the Mission more firmly established.

On the eastern side of the river the hostility of the natives was an effective bar to the extension of operations into new territory. This, to a certain extent, was providential, inasmuch as it resulted in the labours of the missionaries being focussed on the old stations of Onitsha, Obusi, and Asaba, and it was from these places that native teachers were drawn when the opportunity to advance presented itself. On the western side of the river this advance became feasible several years earlier than on the eastern, and vigorous steps were taken which led to new and successful work in the hinterland of Asaba.

An adequate review of this period in the history of the Mission would require a volume to itself. Space fails us to tell of the selfless devotion and burning zeal of Robinson and Brooke, cut short by death as they crossed the threshold of the great sphere of work upon which they had set their hearts; of the band of consecrated men and women who rallied to the side of Bishop Hill, as he set forth intent on the great work committed to his charge; of the utter breakdown of the plans for advance, and the crushing blow which their fair prospects sustained within a few weeks, owing to the terrible disasters which befell the party (only one of Bishop Hill's party reached Onitsha, and within eighteen months he too laid down his life, leaving but one survivor of the fourteen who had set forth fired with the bold enthusiasm of their leader) and of the steadfast and patient labours of Henry Hughes Dobinson, who by his self-sacrificing life and magnanimous spirit won the affection of the Ibo people as perhaps no other European has been privileged to do. To these simple folk he was the embodiment of the mind and character of Christ, and to this day his memory is fragrant amongst them. His grave at Onitsha serves to remind us of his well-spent life, and his name is perpetuated by the substantial building which has been erected to form the Out-patient Department of the Medical Mission—a fitting tribute to one who poured out his life in the service of others. Repton and Oxford never trained a man who was more loved, and whose powers were more deeply consecrated to his God. He could ill be spared, yet God took him, and the splendid cause for which he laid down his life calls more insistently than ever for others to follow in his steps.

Others there were whose names are less widely known but who counted not their lives dear unto themselves, and whose faithful ministry has left an indelible impression upon the hearts of the people. They laboured to build up the Church of God in this part of Ibo-land, adding their quota of living stones, whether few or many, to the sacred edifice, until, their work accomplished, they entered into rest, or were transferred to other spheres of service. Lack of space forbids that a record be made here of their deeds of faith, but this at least must be said, that their labour of love has not been in vain. The names of many are as "precious ointment" and "their works do follow them." The blood of the martyrs, the seed of the Church, has been sown, and was, and is, in the unfailing Providence of God, destined to bring forth an abundant harvest in this great field.

CHAPTER XXVIII

CHRISTIANITY AND ISLAM

Of late years it has become fashionable to write freely and not always with due regard to accuracy, concerning the apparent success of Mohammedanism in Nigeria, and the alleged failure of Christianity. It is asserted that the ethics of the former are eminently suited to the Nigerian. " Everything," it is stated, " is in favour of Islam." It does not " insist upon exacting demands with regard to sex-relationships, contrary to the promptings of nature." In other words, it stands for the flesh which " lusteth against the Spirit." It is the expression of the doctrine to " do-as-you-please," to follow the " promptings of nature," as against the crucifixion of the " flesh with the affections and lusts " ; in short, it is the very antithesis of the teaching of Jesus Christ. " Conversion to Islam does not mean for the converted a break with his interests (there is neither demand for repentance nor need of forgiveness), his family, his social life, his respect for the authority of his rulers. He is not left stranded as the Christian Church, having once converted, leaves him, a pitiful, rudderless barque upon a troubled sea. He does not become, through conversion, an alien in thought, in custom, and in outlook ; a foreigner in his own land, a citizen of none." [1]

Contrast the above with the words of H. E. Sir Frederick Lugard, who has spent the best part of his life in Africa, as against the former writer's three months' tour. Whilst admitting that " Mohammedanism has done much to check the cruelty consequent on the superstitions of

[1] *Nigeria : Its Peoples and its Problems*," E. D. Morel, p. 217.

pagan people," yet, "in our view it does not, either as an ethical code or as a spiritual force, approach to the Gospel."

Or again, compare the statements of another student of many years' experience in Northern Nigeria, who says,[1] in his notes upon the Nupe kingdom, and the effects of its adoption of Islam:

"Mohammedanism has introduced no new manufactures, has drenched the country with blood, has destroyed numberless towns and villages, and has, as far as one can learn, distinctly lowered the morals of the people. True it has introduced a better idea of justice by creating the office of judge as distinct from that of a king, and we must also place to the credit of Islam the beginnings of the idea of education. It is also a distinct gain to the people that they have been taught the idea of a life beyond the grave, and of rewards and punishments after this life is over.

"On the other side must be placed the degradation of womanhood that has followed the introduction of Islam. The average pagan negro has his own ideas as to the subordination of women, but there is nothing to prevent a woman from rising, by her industry or ability, to high positions. But Mohammedanism changes all this, and woman has a distinctly lower position in a Mohammedan community than she occupies among pagans.

"Closely connected with this, and with the organised system of divorce that Mohammedanism introduces, is the prevalence of immorality in the Mohammedan areas of the country. The Mohammedan towns are terrible hotbeds of disease, while the pagan tribes are comparatively free from this scourge. Last of all, Mohammedanism cannot escape the onus of having added vastly to the sum of human misery in Nigeria by its relentless and systematic slave-raiding. The selling of captives taken in warfare, and the kidnapping of stray people along the roads used to go on everywhere, but it was the Moslems who, as it were, reduced it to a fine art, and practically made it their great business in life. A favourite saying among the Moham-

[1] *Moslem World*, Vol. II, No. 2.

medan Nupes is, 'God has given us the heathen for bread,' and slave-raiding was practically their means of living until the British Government came and put it down with a strong hand. A living tribute of men and women was demanded from the surrounding pagan tribes every year, and if they refused to give it their country was raided and hundreds were captured. Whole districts have been depopulated, not only by these raids, but by the systematic draining away of all the young and able-bodied people as tribute, year after year, till only the old and infirm were left. An impartial examination of what Mohammedanism has done for the Nupes would show conclusively that the evil far outweighs the good."

And this is the religious system which, we are asked to believe, is the one above all others most suited to the Nigerian. It seems incredible that any English writer could be found to advocate it. It is not only non-Christian, but essentially non-British in its conceptions, its ideals, its ethics, and its principles. Mr. Morel's assertions would be ludicrous were they not so ingeniously stated, and thus calculated to mislead many who depend upon and form their opinions on what they gather from books.

Moreover, it is affirmed that Christianity is injurious to family life and affection ; it introduces elements of discord ; it leads to disloyalty to rulers and want of respect to elders. Further, that it has a " hurtful and disintegrating influence." It sets up a system of social inequality ; it destroys racial identity, and it has one very serious handicap, viz. it separates and distinguishes between politics and religion. It is somewhat difficult to consider this last as a handicap to Christianity. Most religiously-minded people would probably be inclined to regard the inseparability of religion and politics as a reason for opposing Islam ! Apparently, then, Christianity is hopelessly outmatched. Such a clever prima facie case is made out for Mohammedanism that to continue Christian Missions would appear to be culpable stupidity. The Christian religion obviously has no chance against Islam. We marvel at the flow of rhetorical invective ; yet, in spite of it all, not one single missionary, white or black, male or female, Anglican or Free Church, Protestant or Catholic, has been induced to abandon the task or deviate from the course which he or she has adopted. We are strongly inclined to think that not many in Nigeria have been led astray by Mr. Morel's conclusions, and probably not one of the 4,500 agents of the Protestant missionary societies in Africa would subscribe to his views. The consensus of opinion from workers on the spot, supported by their 2,000,000 converts to Christianity, needs a lot of explaining away.

In Mr. Morel's book, *Nigeria: Its Peoples and its Problems*, a long paragraph is devoted to the question of African dress. He says that it is "picturesque." "The robe of the Moslem is much healthier for him." The author proceeds to say: "Nothing to my mind is more pitiable than to visit school after school in West Africa and to see boys and girls in an alien dress." The writer is quite correct in describing the Mohammedan costume as "picturesque," but it is very evident that he viewed it chiefly from a distance. Had he mingled freely with the Moslems in the markets his olfactory nerve would have convinced him that it was something else besides "picturesque." The combined odour of generous applications of musk, and the effluvia of yards of unwashed cloth, is not particularly choice, nor can trousers with a waistband twelve feet in circumference, with its accumulation of gathers round the body, be honestly commended as specially hygienic in the tropics! Similar comments apply to the unwieldly tobe (outer gown covering the wearer's whole body), so graceful, and as a rule so dirty. Abundance of material is a prominent feature of its make-up, and the long flowing skirts and surplice-like sleeves constantly trail along the ground as the men walk, and when they sit down the voluminous garments act as a germ trap, unrivalled by any other form of dress worn in the tropics. The occupation, in leisure moments, of those who wear this costume, may more suitably be imagined than described! The fact that the native becomes inured to the bites of certain insects, does not make the "picturesque" dress more sanitary. A layman makes an unqualified assertion that such a garb is healthy; the medical profession would probably pronounce a decidedly opposite verdict. It certainly is not clean. The general effect is pleasing to the eye, but of the things not seen the less said the better.[1]

Again, quoting from the writer of the notes on the Nupe nation,[2] we find an allusion to this prejudice against "alien dress."

He says, "Another powerful factor in favour of Islam as opposed to Christianity, is the curious attitude of contempt towards native Christians generally adopted by officials, most of whom seem to think that Christianity should be reserved exclusively for Europeans. The average official sees a 'mission boy' clothed in a washing jacket and trousers, and he says how unnecessary it all is; he sees a native (Moslem) in his voluminous and filthy garments which are never washed, and are quite unsuited for almost any kind of manual work, and he says 'how picturesque.' He is annoyed when he finds that a native, by reason of his being a Christian, can read and write, but he looks with awe and admiration at the native scribe who writes a crabbed Arabic script that can scarcely be read."

One further point calls for notice. Where did Mr. Morel "visit school after school"? During his few days' stay in the Ibo country there is no record of his entering a single C.M.S. school, hence his remarks must apply either to the one Roman Catholic or the one Government school which he might have visited. If he paid no more attention to schools in other parts of the Protectorate than he did to those on the Niger during his rapid tour, then his statements are not based upon personal investigation, and are for all practical purposes worthless.

I will confine my concluding remarks to the effects of

[1] The average European makes a great mistake. Whenever he sees a native dressed in a tobe he is apt, without further inquiry, to conclude that the wearer is a Mohammedan. This is a fruitful source of error, inasmuch as a great many natives adopt this form of dress who are not, and never were, Moslems.

[2] *Moslem World,* Vol. II, No. 2.

Mohammedanism upon the Ibos. We are told that "in the great native markets, such as Onitsha, the tattooed pagan Ibo rubs shoulders with the Mohammedan Hausa, Nupe and Igarra." Does this imply that he is influenced in any other way than in matters of trade? Mr. Morel omits to state that on the very edge of that same market, within a stone's throw of the old Mohammedan slave mart, there stands the largest church in Ibo-land, and one of three built in Onitsha after many years of Moslem immigration. I am not aware of the existence of a single mosque there, or anywhere else in the Ibo country.

At Onitsha the forces of Christianity and Islam are side by side, and what do we find? Islam is still entirely confined to foreigners; not a single Ibo is known to us, so far, who has embraced Mohammedanism. The Moslem population has increased enormously during the last twenty years, but the increase is solely due to the influx of immigrants from the north, and amongst these there is a growing tendency to practise the barest modicum of the outward forms of their religion. By many nominal adherents of Islam, abstinence from such things as spirits and tobacco has been abandoned, together with many of the rules so rigidly observed by strict Moslems, and they make no pretence to anything more than the mechanical performance of their religious duties.

I have made inquiries during the last seventeen years, in many directions, of missionaries, commissioners and traders, and also of intelligent natives, and have yet to hear of the first case of an Ibo forsaking paganism for Mohammedanism. As far as the Ibos are concerned I have not the slightest hesitation in asserting that the chapter dealing with Christianity and Islam, above quoted, is utterly misleading. The arguments advanced are specious and skilfully marshalled, but they are based very largely on antecedent presumptions and not on experience. Such sweeping statements are not borne out by facts and ought not to be offered even to the guileless British public.

Whilst there is no case on record of an Ibo becoming a convert to Islam, yet every Christian missionary is keenly alive to the threatening situation. All are aware of the increased numbers of the emissaries of the Prophet in the country. We are fully prepared to admit that their influence must make itself felt sooner or later. We recognise facts as they are and endeavour to do so in a level-headed and unbiassed manner. Wherever we go we meet with the ubiquitous representatives of Islam. The pacification of the country by the British has opened up trade to the Mohammedan as effectively as to the European, in fact more so, because the former can carry his goods here, there and everywhere, he can subsist on native food, and is inured to the treacherous climate. He possesses enormous natural advantages over the European. Many large towns now have a Mohammedan quarter or the beginning of one. The Mohammedan invasion, no doubt, is playing its part in the break-up of the ancient pagan systems. The selling of Moslem amulets and charms is a profitable business; the Ibos buy them and regard them as glorified fetishes. They do not in any way connect them with the Moslem faith, in fact, the Mohammedans themselves treat them, generally speaking, as simple fetish charms. We recognise, too, that every follower of Islam is, in a certain sense, a missionary. By this we mean that he is never ashamed of his religion, and is prepared to endure persecution, and possibly loss, rather than forsake or hide it. It is an essential part of him, and has its place in his daily life.

The Ibo is a cute man, however, and naturally endowed with considerable powers of discrimination. He is quite capable of distinguishing between profession and practice. Consequently he is not favourably impressed with the religion of a man who is a past master in lying and deceit. He is disgusted when he discovers that the coin paid to him as a shilling is but a halfpenny washed in silver, and he is angry when his lamp will not burn properly because the kerosene oil he bought has been diluted with water, or when on drinking his gin he finds it weaker than usual, and it dawns upon him that it has been liberally watered. These are only a few of the Moslem tricks which act as deterrents to the propagation of Mohammedanism among the Ibos. Nor does the pagan relish being treated as a "bush man," unworthy of respect or consideration. The arrogance of the average Moslem, and the insolent contempt with which he treats the pagan are notorious. The result is that now that Mohammedanism cannot be spread by its former methods of fire and sword, converts are not readily won. The statement that "where the negro is given the option he will invariably choose Christianity in preference to Mohammedanism" has been amply justified in places where the two forces are at work side by side. Statistics irrefutably support this opinion. On examination of the figures available for the Ibo country we find them wholly in favour of Christianity. The progress of Christianity, and the failure of Islam to make converts can be gauged from the following returns:[1]

	Adherents to Christianity in C.M.S. Niger Mission—Ibo people.	Scholars in Christian Schools, C.M.S. Niger Mission—Ibo children.
1896 . .	584	560
1906 . .	2,452	1,516
1916 . .	20,668	25,000

	Ibo Converts to Islam.	Ibo children in Mohammedan Schools.
1896 . .	Nil	Nil
1906 . .	Nil	Nil
1916 . .	None known	None known

These Christians have built more than three hundred churches, whereas Islam cannot yet boast a single mosque.

The statistics here recorded relate solely to the C.M.S. Niger Mission. To the numbers quoted must be added the Ibo adherents attached to the Anglican churches of the Niger Delta Pastorate, the members of the Scotch Free and the Primitive Methodist Churches, and the large

[1] For more enlightening and convincing statistics see *C.M.S. Review*, December, 1917

body of converts to Roman Catholicism. A comparison of these figures with the nil returns of Islam in the Ibo country during the last twenty years should convince even the most prejudiced critic. However strongly he assail Christianity the facts in its favour are indisputable. The reckless general statements that Mohammedanism is pre-eminently the religion for the pagan Nigerian, and the misleading implications arising from such assertions as "the Islamic wave rolls on all-conquering," will not bear scrutiny. The "wave rolls on," truly, but any increase in volume comes from behind; it has not gathered additional force from its contact with the Ibo people. It is only just that the real state of affairs should be made public, even if only for the enlightenment of those who have been led astray by untrustworthy generalisation as to Christianity and Islam in Nigeria.

At the same time we recognise that the ultimate issue lies with the Christian Church. If she can be induced to abandon the *laissez-faire* attitude of the past and to show a disposition to grapple seriously with the task of evangelising the pagan races of Nigeria, there is overwhelming evidence to prove that they will embrace the Christian religion with alacrity. The ethics of the Gospel, and the Love of God as manifested in Christ, appeal irresistibly to the pagan negro of whatever tribe or language. Mohammedanism deprived of compulsory methods makes little progress when it is compelled to prove itself alongside the persuasive attractiveness of Christianity..

In the southern provinces of Nigeria we are not called upon to engage in a campaign *against* Islam, but to endeavour to forestall it. In the immediate realisation of this fact lies the key to success. Now is the "acceptable time." The situation is dominated by the one great time factor "Now." Victory is assured to the Christian faith, provided its exponents act with the promptness which the occasion demands. The spread of Islam is a challenge which should stimulate the Church of Christ to forsake the nerveless policy which has prevailed hitherto. A still more emphatic challenge comes from the pagans themselves, who, in their thousands, to-day are pleading earnestly and pathetically for Christian teachers. Woe be to us if we miss the golden opportunity, if we turn a deaf ear to their importunate calls for help.

> "The cry of myriads as of one,
>
> . . . .
>
> The soul's exceeding bitter cry,
> 'Come o'er and help us, or we die.'"

BIBLIOGRAPHICAL NOTE TO THE 1966 EDITION

I GENERAL STUDIES

"Akwa: Town of Smiths," *Nigeria,* 61, 1959, pp. 136-156. *Akwa* lies between *Onitsha* and *Enugu.* Many illustrations.

Basden, G. T., *Niger Ibos,* 1938. (New impression in preparation, Frank Cass and Co. Ltd.)

Dike, K. Onwuka, *Trade and Politics in the Niger Delta* 1830–1885, 1956.

Forde, Daryll and Jones, G. I., *The Ibo and Ibibio-Speaking Peoples of South-eastern Nigeria,* 1950. The standard short work on the subject.

Green, Margaret, *Igbo Village Affairs.* (2nd edition, 1964, Frank Cass & Co. Ltd., contains new preface by the author commenting on changes which have occurred since its first publication.) Work is chiefly with reference to the Village of *Umueke Abgaja* in the *Isu-Ama* group of Southern Ibo. See also review by G. I. Jones cited in III *Social Organization and Political Structure.*

Jones, G. I., *The Trading States of the Oil Rivers,* 1963. Subtitled "A Study of Political Development in Eastern Nigeria."

Leith-Ross, S., *African Conversation Piece* (A Picture of Ibo Life), 1944.

Leith-Ross, S., *African Women,* 1939 (reprint, 1965).

Meek, C. K., *Law and Authority in a Nigerian Tribe: A Study in Indirect Rule.* (2nd impression, 1950.) Contains chapters on Ibo history, Environment, Religion, Social and Political Structure, Titles, Kinship, Age-Grades, Law and Administration, Law of Marriage, Birth and Training of Children, Death and Inheritance.

Murdock, George Peter, *Africa Its Peoples and Their Culture History,* 1959. See Chapter 31.

Nzekwu, J. O., "Onitsha," Nigeria, 50, 1956, pp. 200-233. Sketches *Onitsha* history from traditional accounts.

Ottenberg, Simon, "The Development of Local Government in a Nigerian Township," *Anthropologica,* n.s. 4, 1, 1962, pp. 121-161.

Ottenberg, Simon, "The Present State of Ibo Studies," *Journal of the Historical Society of Nigeria,* volume 2, no. 2, December 1961, pp. 211-230. Reviews the major forms of research and the publications on the Ibo since World War II and makes recommendations for types of research projects that would be of value in the future. Bibliography.

Talbot, P. Amaury, *The Peoples of Southern Nigeria,* 4 vols., 1926. Contains mine of information on various tribes of Southern Nigeria, including the Ibo. Volume I History; Volumes II and III Ethnology; and Volume IV Languages and Statistics. Study evolved out of 1921 Census.

Talbot, P. Amaury, *The Tribes of the Niger Delta,* 1932.

Wood, A. H. St. John, " Nigeria: Fifty Years of Political Development Among the Ibos " in *From Tribal Rule to Modern Government.* (13th Conference of the Rhodes-Livingstone Institute for Social Research, 1959, pp. 121-136.)

II HISTORY, LITERATURE, ARTS AND CRAFTS

Achebe, Chinua, *Things Fall Apart,* 1958. A novel about the Ibo.

Azikiwe, Nnamdi, " Fragments of Onitsha History," *The Journal of Negro History,* 15, 1930, pp. 474-97. An early study by the first President of Nigeria, himself an Ibo.

Boston, J. S., " Notes on Contact Between the Igala and the Ibo," *Journal of the Historical Society of Nigeria,* Volume 2, No. 1, December 1960, pp. 52-58. Summarizes evidence from traditional and written historical sources about the relationship of some of the Ibo-speaking peoples with their neighbours, the Igala, who live north of Ibo territory between the left bank of the Niger and the country of the Idoma peoples.

Chadwick, E. R., "An Ibo Village Art Gallery," *Nigerian Field,* 4, 4, October 1935, pp. 175-183.

Ewo, Dixon Ogaranya, *History and Customs of Ogbaland,* 1952.

Field, J. M. O., " Bronze Castings found at Igbo, Southern Nigeria," *Man,* 40, 1, January 1940, pp. 1-6. First report on castings found at Igbo, Awka Division. See recent articles by Shaw (cited below) who followed up Field's study.

Ike, A., *The Origin of the Ibos,* 1951, 44 pp. Attempts to establish Hebrew origins of Ibo by use of historical material from the Bible and cultural data.

Kalu, Eke, " An Ibo Autobiography," *Nigerian Field,* 7, 4, October 1938, pp. 158-170.

Murray, K. C., " Ogbom " (Ibo Carvings), *Nigerian Field,* 10, October 1941, pp. 127-131.

" Nri Traditions," *Nigeria,* 54, 1957, pp. 273-288. Ibo clan which author claims has tended more than other Ibo clans to keep its life based on ancient traditions.

Nzekwu, J. O., " Ofala Festival," *Nigeria,* 61, 1959, pp. 104-122. The *Onitsha* festival of the year, climaxing the New Yam Festival, the traditional annual, thanksgiving celebration.

Nzekwu, Onuora, " Ibo Dancing," *Nigeria Magazine,* 73, June 1962, pp. 35-43. Author claims dancing remains the most developed and most important art form of the Ibo as well as their most important pastime.

Shaw, Thurstan, " Excavations at Igobu-Ukwu, Eastern Nigeria: An Interim Report," *Man,* 60, 210, November 1960, pp. 161-164. Follow up to Field's report in which author estimates dates of castings discovered to be 17th century. Findings seemed to represent sacred vessels and regalia of a former day as kept in storage between ceremonies. Burial uncovered appeared to be that of actual former *Eze Nri* (Priest-king). See also Shaw's articles in *West African Review,* 31, 197, pp. 30-37, and *Journal Historical Society of Nigeria,* Vol. 2, No. 1, pp. 162-165.

III SOCIAL ORGANISATION AND POLITICAL STRUCTURE

Ardener, Edwin W., " Lineage and Locality Among the Mba-Ise Ibo," *Africa,* 29, 2, April 1959, pp. 113-133. Discusses inter-relationships between lineage, territorial organization, and other kinds of groupings of an exceptionally dense population (186,300 people confined to 167 sq. miles), in *Owerri* Division.

Ardener, Edwin W., " The Kinship Terminology of a Group of Southern Ibo," *Africa,* 24, 2, April 1954, pp. 85-99. Evolved out of 2½ year study of administrative unit of *Mba-Ise.*

Brown, Paula, " Patterns of Authority in West Africa," *Africa,* 21, 4, October 1951, pp. 261-278. Concerns eight West African societies, including the Ibo, analyzing authority exercised by persons holding certain positions in kinship groups, associations, and states, as well as total pattern of authority in societies having certain combinations of these groups.

Chinwuba Obi, S. N., *The Ibo Law of Property,* 1963. Study by a Nigerian lawyer of the Ibo customary law relating to property.

Chubb, L. T., *Ibo Land Tenure,* 115 pp., 1961 (first published by Gaskiya Corporation 1947, this second issue is by Ibadan University Press). Result of 1945 recommendation by committee headed by Lord Hailey to investigate land tenure in Africa. Author urged wider participation of experts in fields of anthropology and agriculture in coping with problems of land tenure in six localities.

Esenwa, F. A., " Marriage Customs in Asaba Division," *Nigerian Field,* 13, 2, October 1948, pp. 71-81.

Green, Margaret, *Land Tenure in an Ibo Village* (London School of Economics Monographs on Social Anthropology, No. 6), 1941.

Harris, Jack, " Some Aspects of Slavery in South-eastern Nigeria," *Journal of Negro History,* 27, 1, January 1942, pp. 37-54.

Horton, W. R. G., " The Ohu System of Slavery in a Northern Ibo Village Group," *Africa,* 24, 1954, pp. 311-335. Discusses role of *Nike* (village group to immediate north-east of Enugu, capital of Eastern Provinces of Nigeria) who tradition held to be principal slave-traders in northern Iboland before advent of British administration.

Jeffreys, M. D. W., " Dual Organization in Africa," *African Studies,* 5, 2, June 1946, pp. 82-105.

Jones, G. I., " Dual Organization in Ibo Social Structure," *Africa,* 19, 2, April 1949, pp. 150-156. Review article of Margaret Green's *Igbo Village Affairs.*

Jones, G. I., " Ibo Age Organization with Special Reference to the Cross River and North-eastern Ibo," *Journal of the Royal Anthropological Institute,* 92, 2, July-December 1962, pp. 191-211.

Jones, G. I., " Ibo Land Tenure," *Africa,* 19, 4, October 1949, pp. 309-323. Remarks limited to Northern, Southern, and Cross-River Ibo. Concerns land tenure in relation to social structure and processes of change in population density, soil-types, and other socio-ecological conditions.

Meek, C. K., " Ibo Law " (in Essays to C. G. Seligman), 1934.

Meek, C. K., *Report on Social and Political Organization in the Owerri Division,* 1933.

Correia, R. P. J. Alves, "Le Sens moral chez les Ibos de la Nigéria," *Anthropos,* 18-19, 1923–1924, pp. 880-889. Topics covered are La justice; L'Amour, La Vérité; Tempérance, Pudeur nigérienne; and Obéissance a la loi du pays et discipline.

Correia, R. P. J. Alves, "Vocables religieux et philosophiques des peuples Ibos," *Bibliothecha Africana,* 1, 1925, pp. 104-113.

Horton, W. R. G., "God, Man, and the Land in a Northern Ibo Village-group," *Africa,* 26, 1, January 1956, pp. 17-28. Explains Ibo conceptions of the deity. Study conducted among the *Nike.*

Jeffreys, M. D. W., "Ikenga: the Ibo Ram-headed God," *African Studies,* 13, 1, March 1954, pp. 25-40. Discusses religious cult associated with good fortune, success, and the ability and strength of the right arm. Mentions other instances of the Ram-headed god, including the ancient Egyptian rite from whence the author asserts is derived the ram-god cults of the rest of Africa.

Jeffreys, M. D. W., "The Divine Umundri King," *Africa,* 8, 3, July 1935, pp. 346-354. Describes coronation-ceremony of two divine kings who are the spiritual heads of the *Umundri* Ibo of *Onitsha* Province.

Jeffreys, M. D. W., "The Umundri Tradition of Origin," *African Studies,* 15, 3, September 1956, pp. 119-131. Result of survey begun in 1930 under auspices of Nigerian government to uncover magico-religious beliefs of Ibo in the environs of *Awka* Division.

Leith-Ross, S., "Notes on the Osu System Among the Ibo of Owerri Province, Nigeria," *Africa,* 10, 1937, pp. 206-220. The *Osu* group in this province traditionally held task of offering sacrifices on behalf of their masters and of tending the shrines of the *jujus* (i.e., spirit-like deities).

Noon, John A., "A Preliminary Examination of the Death Concepts of the Ibo," *American Anthropologist,* 44, October-December 1944, pp. 638-654. The author used an Ibo informant for his investigations.

O'Donnell, W. E., "Religion and Morality Among the Ibo of Southern Nigeria," *Primitive Man,* 4, 4, 1931, pp. 54-60.

Ottenberg, Simon, "Ibo Oracles and Intergroup Relations," *Southwestern Journal of Anthropology,* 14, 3, Autumn 1958, pp. 295-317. Based on research conducted on *Afikpo* Village Group. Author traces origin and expansion of organizations associated with oracles which he claims derive from the European and American slave trade along Eastern coast of Nigeria between about 1650 and 1850. Study is concerned with how oracles organizations functioned to provide a degree of integration of these Ibo groups.

Thomas, Northcote W., "Some Ibo Burial Customs," *Journal of the Royal Anthropological Institute,* 1917, pp. 160-213.

VI ECONOMY

Ardener, Shirley G., "The Social and Economic Significance of the Contribution Club Among a Section of the Southern Ibo," pp. 128-142. A publication of the *Annual Conference, Sociology Section, March* 1953, University College, Ibadan. (West African Institute of Social and Economic Research, University College, Ibadan.)

Ottenberg, Simon, " Double Descent in an Ibo Village-group." (*Selected Papers of the 5th International Congress of Anthropological & Ethnological Sciences, Philadelphia*, 1-9 September 1956, ed. by A. F. L. Wallace, pp. 473-481.)

Rowling, C. W., *Notes on Land Tenure in Benin, Kuruku, Ishan and Asaba Divisions of Benin Province*, 1948.

Spörndli, J. I., " Marriage Customs Among the Ibos," *Anthropos*, 37-40, 1-3, 1942–1945, pp. 113-121. Explains marriage customs of Ibo in terms of their religious nature, economy, and culture.

Thomas, Northcote W., *Anthropological Report on the Ibo-speaking Peoples*, 6 vols., 1913–1914. For a critique of Part IV: Law and Custom of the Ibo of the Asaba District, Southern Nigeria, see Hartland, E. S., " Ibo-Speaking Peoples of Southern Nigeria," *Journal of the African Society*, 14, 1915, pp. 271-277. Part I of Thomas's Report is Law and Custom of the Ibo of the Awka Neighbourhood, Southern Nigeria.

Wieschhoff, H. A., " Divorce Laws and Practices in Modern Ibo Culture," *Journal of Negro History*, 26, 3, July 1941, pp. 299-324.

Wieschhoff, H. A., " Social Significance of Names Among the Ibo of Nigeria," *American Anthropologist*, 43, April 1941, pp. 212-222. Naming customs and interpretation and social significance of names, European influences.

IV EDUCATION AND COMMUNITY DEVELOPMENT

Chadwick, E. R., " Communal Development in Udi Division," *Oversea Education*, 19, 2, January 1948, pp. 627-644. Discusses problems and political effects of mass education in *Udi*, a Division of *Onitsha* Province.

Chadwick, E. R., " Mass Education in Udi Division," *African Affairs*, 47, 186, January 1948, pp. 31-41. Concerns self-help project among local inhabitants in reading and writing.

Ottenberg, Simon, " Improvement Associations Among the Afikpo Ibo," *Africa*, 25, 1, January 1955, pp. 1-28. *Afikpo* are Eastern Ibo who reside between the headquarters of *Afikpo* Division, *Ogoja* Province, South-eastern Nigeria and the Cross River to the east. Covers economic, educational, political and social improvement activities directly related to changing cultural conditions.

Ottenberg, Simon, " The Development of Village ' Meetings ' among the Afikpo People," pp. 186-205 (a publication of the *Annual Conference Sociology Section*, March 1953, West African Institute of Social and Economic Research, University College, Ibadan). Discusses village ' improvement ' unions among the *Afikpo*.

V RELIGION

Boston, John, "*Alosi* Shrines in Udi Division," *Nigeria*, 61, 1959, pp. 157-165. The *Alosi* are spirits which are said to occupy forests and rivers lying on fringes of cultivated land. " They are regarded as the spiritual owners of tracts which they occupy, and their shrines are prominent landmarks within their territory, such as large trees, stones, or shady pools."

Correia, R. P. J. Alves, " L'animisme Ibo et les divinités de la Nigéria," *Anthropos*, 16-17, 1921–1922, pp. 360-366. Includes sections on L'idée de Dieu. Produit d'importation: Les dieux Divinités universelles; Divinités locales; and Nature des divinités conçues par l'Ibo.

Forde, Daryll, and Scott, Richenda (edited by Margery Perham), *The Native Economies of Nigeria,* 1946. Part II, Chapter 3 deals with the Southern Ibo community of the *Ozuitem* Ibo of Bende. Topics discussed are Land rights; Farm labour and Food Supplies; Oil-Palm and Other Production for Exchange. Other parts of chapter concern Ibo Economy in a Congested Area: Migrant Wage Labour, Accumulation of Currency, and Levies of Consumption.

Hair, P. E. H., "Enugu: an Industrial and Urban Community in East Nigeria, 1914–1953," pp. 143-167. A publication of the *Annual Conference, Sociology Section, March* 1953, University College, Ibadan. (West African Institute of Social and Economic Research, University College, Ibadan.)

Harris, Jack, "Papers on the Economic Aspect of Life among the Ozuitem Ibo," *Africa,* 14, 1, January 1943, pp. 12-23. Mainly concerned with agriculture and the division of labour between the sexes in crop cultivation.

Harris, Jack, "Some Aspects of the Economics of Sixteen Ibo Individuals," *Africa,* 14, 6, April 1944, pp. 302-335. Study of annual monetary incomes and expenditures of sixteen Ibos living in community of *Ozuitem.*

Jones, G. I., "Agriculture and Ibo Village Planning," *Farm and Forest,* 6, 1, 1945, pp. 9-15.

VII ECOLOGY AND SOCIAL CHANGE

Jones, G. I., "Ecology and Social Structure Among the North-eastern Ibo," *Africa,* 31, 2, April 1961, pp. 117-134. Attempt to show how effects of new environment modified features of the social structure of the *Ezza, Ikwo, Izi,* and *Ngbo* tribes.

Ottenberg, Simon, "Ibo Receptivity to Change," in *Continuity and Change in African Cultures* (ed. Bascom, W. R., & Herskovits, M. J., 1958, pp. 130-143). Author asserts "Ibo probably most receptive to culture change and most willing to accept Western ways of any large group in Nigeria."

Ottenberg, Phoebe, "The Changing Economic Position of Women Among the Afikpo Ibo," in *Continuity and Change in African Cultures* (ed. Bascom, W. R., & Herskovits, M. J., 1958, pp. 205-223). One of several studies conducted among Ibo women after the *Aba* riots of December 1929 in which women attacked administrative authorities. Riots are said to have revealed how ill-suited Indirect Rule was for the Ibo.

John Ralph Willis

London, 1965

INDEX